Internet

by Brian Austin

in easy steps and **in easy steps pocket** are imprints of
Computer Step
Southfield Road . Southam . Warwickshire CV47 OFB . England
Website: www.ineasysteps.com
Email: books@ineasysteps.com

Copyright © 2002 by Computer Step. All rights reserved. No part of this book may be reproduced or transmitted in any form or by any means, electronic or mechanical, including photocopying, recording, or by any information storage or retrieval system, without prior written permission from the publisher.

Notice of Liability
Every effort has been made to ensure that this book contains accurate and current information. However, Computer Step and the author shall not be liable for any loss or damage suffered by readers as a result of any information contained herein.

Trademarks
All trademarks are acknowledged as belonging to their respective companies.

Printed and bound in the United Kingdom

ISBN 1-84078-166-1

ReadMe.first

In "Using the Internet", we strive to meet several aims. To:

- **Help** as many people as possible make **effective** use of the Internet through the simple sharing of key knowledge and know-how.

- Provide an incredible, **value-packed** resource that is **affordable** to as many people as possible.

- Invest as much time and effort as is required in order to create an **easy-to-understand** product with **clear and concise plain-English** explanations.

- Include lots of **examples** to help you learn more easily and discover what the Internet really means to you and how you can **benefit** from it.

Researching and writing this book has been a huge task and like any large complex project has had its own special challenges! Although my name is on the cover, like all Computer Step books, "Using the Internet" is the end result of a carefully considered team effort, from researching, writing, editing and finalising to printing and distribution to you our valued reader.

I want to thank my publisher Harshad Kotecha, the ever-helpful staff at Computer Step, distributors/publishers The Random House Group, my wonderful wife Ann for her support and for maintaining a creative environment, and my children for understanding.

Dealing with dead links

We carefully research website addresses and related information. However, the chaotic nature and fast pace of change on the Internet have a way of confounding even the most determined efforts.

If you find that some of the links mentioned no longer work, I promise they were working correctly at the time of our research. Often, you can still find the page you want easily by using the following method. (If you're new to the Internet, don't worry if our explanation below doesn't make much sense to you: all that you need is in the book.)

Imagine you want to find the following (fictional) page: www.ineasysteps.com/updates/latest.html. Now if your web browser were to return a "Page not found..." error message, try modifying your entry to: www.ineasysteps.com/updates/ or simply www.ineasysteps.com. By navigating "backwards", you may find a new link that leads to the page you want. Alternatively, use a search engine or directory to find the relevant website.

Now sit back and enjoy your journey into this new land of amazing colour, vibrancy and opportunity: it's YOUR Internet!

Brian Austin MISTC, Isle of Skye

Contents

1. Introducing the Internet — 1
101 fun things to do on the Net! — 1
What is the Internet? — 16
Essential topics and what they mean — 19
What's the Internet good for? — 21
Who owns the Net? — 27
The drive to bring the Net to everyone — 28
Introducing Netiquette — 29
Copyright: how to become seriously rich or poor — 29
How did the Internet come about? — 31

2. Nethead heaven: how the Internet works — 35
What is TCP/IP and all that jazz? — 35
Internet Protocol (IP): the postman of the Net — 36
Routers – amazing Internet guides — 38
How Internet Backbones speed up the Net — 38

3. Preparing your computer for the Internet — 39

Buying a computer	39
Getting up to speed	45
How's your memory?	45
Hard drive café	46
Choosing a display monitor	47
An ideal Internet-ready PC	49

4. Modems — 53

What is a modem?	53
Why do we need a modem?	56
Modems for networked computers	57
Modem speeds	58
Modems that shake hands	59
Squeezing the lemon and compressing data	61
Zapping those pesky errors	61
A note about Call Waiting services	62
What else do I need to make my modem work?	63
What else can I do with a modem?	64
Sending and receiving faxes	64
Internal modems for desktop computers	65
Modems for portable computers	68
Working with external modems	69

5. Getting online — 71

What do I need to get on the Net?	73
Low-priced and free Internet access	76
Modem roundup	78
Using a printer	78
WebTV: the future here now	79
Internet kiosks and terminals	81
Cybercafés	82
Computer shops	82
Public libraries and the Internet: perfect partners	83
Don't forget trial Internet offers	83
Introducing Internet Service Providers (ISPs)	84
Looking for fast, 24-hour 7-day Internet access?	85
Commercial online services	87
Introducing domain names	88
Finding and choosing an Internet Service Provider	89
Website hosting Internet Service Providers	95
What happens when you connect to the Internet?	97
Connecting for the first time	99
Internet access software: a closer look	102
Checking your Windows 9x (and later) TCP/IP settings	103
Installing Internet software from an Internet Service Provider	105
Some common terms you may come across when establishing your Internet settings	105
Internet dialler software	107
Setting up your email and newsgroup software	108

Setting up other Internet software	110
Dialling the Internet	111
What if I can't connect using a dial-up modem?	113
Introducing Internet software to get things done	117
A simple trick to (sometimes) boost connection speeds	118

6. Exploring the web — 119

Web browsers: windows on the web	120
What happens after I connect?	121
What can I do on the web?	122
How the web works: a quick overview	124
Introducing hyperlinks: the invisible thread that binds the web	125
More on the Home or Index page	126
How do I change my Home/Start page?	127
Introducing the HyperText Markup Language	130
What you need to know about URLs	131
Finding a web page quickly	135
Working with non-web based URLs	136
Web portals: information magnets	137
Streaming multimedia fun on the web	139

7. A closer look at web browsers — 141

What's in Microsoft Internet Explorer?	142
Identifying your Internet Explorer version number	144
Tuning in to your own channel on the web	145

Checking Internet Explorer browser security	146
What's in Netscape Communicator/Navigator?	147
Earlier versions of Netscape Navigator	149
Web browsers: the menu bar	149
Toolbars and buttons	149
Forward and Back buttons	150
The Home button	150
Stop and Refresh/Reload buttons	150
The Address or Go to box	151
The right mouse button short-cuts	151
Bookmarks and Favorites	152
The History list	153
Cleaning out your web browser cache	154
Weaving an easier web with AutoComplete	155
Saving a web page	155
Saving a web page as a desktop shortcut	156
Saving parts of a web page	156
Printing a web page	157
Changing your browser default options	157
Turning images off and on	158
Plug-ins and Helper applications	160
Java, JavaScript and ActiveX	161
Downloading files from the Net	162
Viewing and listening to multimedia content	163
Viewing special effects and animated content	165
Computer cookies	166
Viewing web page source code	168
Viewing web pages offline	169
Key web browser Tips	170

8. Maintaining your security online 173

Dealing with Internet pests	173
Avoiding hoaxes and scams on the Net	175
Computer viruses	177
How to catch a virus	178
Email viruses: a special threat	179
Are HTML emails safe?	182
Antivirus software on the Net	182
Avoiding virus infections	185
Virus infection and remedies	186
Protecting your PC from hackers	189

9. Finding what you want on the Net 191

Types of web search tools	192
How search engines work	197
Searching for what you want in a search engine	199
Making sense of Search results	201
Web directories	202
Finding what you want in a directory	204
Finding a lost web page	204
Email address locators	205
Internet search tips	207

10. Shopping online — 211

Why shop online?	211
Is it safe to shop online?	213
Some things to check before buying online	214
What can I buy?	218
How do I buy online?	218
Internet banking and online trading	220

11. Children and the Internet — 221

Identify the key danger categories	223
What about porn, drugs and other dangers?	225
Getting involved	227
Ideas for creating boundaries & rules	227
Discuss content control and filtering options with your Internet Service Provider	229
Changing your web browser settings	229
The PICS approach	230
RSACi	231
Web filtering and blocking software	231
Using the Internet for homework and adult research projects	233

12. On the road and using the Net — 235

Choosing and using a portable computer	236
Preventing random phone line disconnections	241
Mobile phones	242

Unwired on foreign shores without a computer!	243
Working with fax while on the move	243

13. Speeding up your Internet connection — 245

Free software tools to track your Net connection	246
Using your ISP's proxy server	248
Avoiding Internet traffic jams	249
ISDN & ISDN2	249
ADSL: just what the doctor ordered!	251
Using cable modems	254
Satellite connections	255
Using leased lines	256

14. Getting started with email — 257

Introducing email	257
How do I work with email?	261
Email benefits v. drawbacks	262
What do I need to use email?	273
How does email work?	275
What's an email address?	277
Are there any characters I can't use?	280
Autoresponders: tireless workers on the Net	280
Creating an email address	282
CompuServe and AOL email addresses	283
Getting an email account	283

Storage space for your emails	286
Finding an email provider	286
Free email accounts	287
Working with web email	288
Installing and setting up your email software	289
A word about email security	296
A peek at Microsoft Outlook Express	297

15. Sending and receiving email messages — 301

The email header	302
'You've got mail': receiving an email	304
Reading your email messages	305
Designing reader-friendly email messages	307
1. Developing a compelling email writing style	307
2. Which do I use: plain text- or HTML-based email?	308
3. Keeping order: using left alignment	310
4. Narrow columns = easier reading	310
5. Why short paragraphs make more sense	311
6. Keep it brief and get popular	311
7. Grammar reborn, ouch!	312
8. Watch the file size	312
9. Focusing on your readers: email etiquette	313
Essential email address books	313
Finding an email address	316
Creating a new email message	317
Doubling up with Carbon Copy (Cc) and Blind Carbon Copy (Bcc)	319

The email Subject box	321
Did you really mean to shout?	321
Adding emotion with a Smiley	322
Saving time with abbreviations	323
Sending an email message	324
Marking an email message as urgent	326
Replying to an email	327
Forwarding an email	328
Sending an email to several recipients	330
Re-sending an email message	331
Attaching a file to an email message	332
Compressing an attachment	334
About you: using email signatures	336
Make an impact with a vCard	339
Dealing with email bouncers	339
Sending and receiving HTML email messages	340
Setting up secure email	340
Keep them guessing with PGP encryption	341
Using a digital ID	342
Converting a fax to email	343
Printing your email messages	344

16. Managing your email messages   345

Dealing with the garbage	345
How to keep spammers guessing!	350
Organising your email messages	351
1. Creating new folders	352

2. Grouping and sorting messages	352
3. Changing column widths	354
Rerouting messages automatically	355
Flames, flame wars and email bombs	356
Listen to your email virtually anywhere	357

17. Playing online games — 359

What you need to play online games	359
Getting started	363
Playing in teams	364
Finding online games	366

18. Internet newsgroups — 367

A cautionary note: computer virus warnings	367
Introducing newsgroups	369
Top level newsgroup categories	370
Newsgroup names	372
Newsreader software overview	372
Configuring your newsreader	373
Protecting your email address in newsgroups	375
Moderated and unmoderated newsgroups	377
Discovering what's available in newsgroups	378
Subscribing and unsubscribing to a newsgroup	382
A newsgroup's money-saving strategy	384
The Frequently Asked Questions file	385
Reading newsgroup messages and contributing	385
Posting to a newsgroup	386

Newsgroup spamming	388
Replying to newsgroup messages	389
Downloading and uploading images, programs and audio/video clips	390
Automatically blocking unwanted newsgroup emails	392
Dealing with flames	392

19. Talking and viewing on the Internet — 395

Internet phones	395
Conferencing with Microsoft NetMeeting	397
Internet Chat overview	398
Text-based Chat	399
Chat nicknames and maintaining your privacy	400
Internet Relay Chat (IRC)	401
Chat commands	402
Using web-based Chat	404
One-to-one communication with instant messaging	405
Internet Relay Chat and online games	408

20. Downloading and uploading — 409

Introducing File Transfer Protocol (FTP)	410
What is an FTP site?	412
Private and anonymous FTP	412
What's available from FTP sites	412
Can I use these files free of charge?	417

Working with compressed files	420
Single compressed file archives	421
Configuring your FTP program	422
How do I download something from an FTP site?	424
Busy FTP sites	428
Uploading files with FTP	428
Popular FTP programs	432
Retrieving broken downloads	435
How to find FTP sites	435
Using WSArchie to find files on the Internet	438

21. Creating your own website — 439

Establishing what you need to create web pages	440
Planning and organising on paper	444
More on HTML	444
Web design software	447
Content management using only a web browser: the future today	449
Copyright and legal issues	450
Introducing HTML tags	450
Establishing page size	451
Web page background	451
Working with colours on the web	452
Inserting text onto a page	452
Adding links to a page	453
Things to consider when using images	454
Finding images for your web pages	455
Image formats and preparing images for the web	456

Placing an image on a page	457
Creating a site navigation structure	458
Saving a web page	458
Previewing your web pages	459
Getting web space for individual and personal websites	459
Spell-checking, proofreading, checking & testing	460
Publishing a "local" copy of your website	460
Going live: publishing your website to the web	461
Preferred business web hosting options	462
Creating fancy websites	462
Using cool mouseover effects	462
Getting noticed with animation	464
Dynamic HTML and more about special effects	464
Inserting META tags for maximum exposure	465
Inserting a website search box	465
Including Multimedia content	466
Adding sound to a web page	467
Using frames	469
How about a WebCam on your website?	469

22. Jargon buster   471

Index   483

1

Introducing the Internet

Welcome! If you're new to the Internet, you can jump straight to page 16 to learn the essentials. When you're familiar with a web browser, pages 1–16 contain many interesting websites that cover a range of topics. However, if you can already connect to the Internet and can use a web browser, why not check out the following pages whenever you want?

101 fun things to do on the Net!

Here's a tiny sample of what's available on the Internet many of which relate to the kinds of topics covered in this book:

1. **Ask the Butler!** Put your question to Jeeves and get some answers from: www.askjeeves.com/

2. **Shop till you drop** – without the traffic jams or queues: www.shopguide.co.uk/

3. **Get low-priced or FREE software for your computer** – PC, Apple Mac and others: www.freewareweb.com/

4. **You're counting the days!** Reserve your ticket on that exotic holiday once and for all – and get a great deal: www.pocruises.com/

5. **Escape!** Buy that new book; you know you want to: www.amazon.co.uk/

6. **Wave goodbye to the rat race:** live on a Scottish island: www.hebea.co.uk/ www.skye.co.uk/ and www.skye-properties.co.uk/

7. **Discover what the papers say.** Want to stay informed? Read local or national newspapers from around the world: www.tiscali.co.uk/

8. **In business?** Check out those company accounts: www.companieshouse.com/

9. **Phone anywhere for the cost of a local call** – or less: www.mediaring.com/

10. **Let the train take the strain?** Reserve your ticket online: www.thetrainline.com/

11. **Discover all sorts of key travel information:** www.atuk.co.uk/

12. **Get savvy!** Find cheaper life, home and car insurance: www.screentrade.co.uk/ and www.easycover.com/

13. **Sell your car and buy a Porsche** – or maybe just get a great replacement car: www.carbusters.com/

14. **Beat the blues:** discover the true secret of personal happiness: www.philiphumbert.com/

15. **Perform some financial magic:** visit your bank without queuing or leaving home. Examples: www.natwest.co.uk/ and www.bankofscotland.co.uk/

16. **Discover once and for all if those aliens really are out there:** www.ufomind.com/

17. **Strike gold:** form a new dotcom company: www.GreatDomains.com/

18. **Find your ideal partner and fall in love** – then invite me to the wedding: www.match.com/

19. **Watch your favourite sport online:** www.sports.com/

20. **Complain to your government.** Let 'em know it's just not on. Examples: (USA) www.whitehouse.gov/ (UK) www.pm.gov.uk/

21. **Sell that dusty Picasso lying in the attic** – and retire to Hawaii: www.ebay.co.uk/

22. **Discuss what really matters to you with others around the globe.** Learn how to use Internet Relay Chat: www.irchelp.org/

23. **Create a great website for free using only your web browser.** Discover SiteKit: www.SiteKit.net/ and ShopKit: www.ShopKit.net/

24. **Don't get nervous Carrie:** chill out with Stephen King: www.stephenking.com/

25. **Discover the top 100 most popular websites.** Find the Internet gems: www.web100.com/

26. **Feeling literary and would like some bawdy culture (or not)?** Read Shakespeare for free at: the-tech.mit.edu/Shakespeare/

27. **Play computer games with other users around the world:** www.mpog.com/

28. **Try some retail therapy and relax while you sip a cool Tia Maria.** Find some of the best shops on the Internet: www.shopsonthenet.com/

29. **Seek out the best deal – get impartial financial advice:** www.which.net/

30. **Enough is enough!** Find that dream job – then fire your overbearing boss: www.monster.co.uk/ and www.gisajob.com/

31. **Listen to the radio** on the Net: windowsmedia.com/radiotuner/

32. **Get a great domain name** for your website: www.register.com/ and www.nominet.org.uk/

33. **Discover once and for all how to create a great website that really works.** Check out "Web Page Design in easy steps" at: www.ineasysteps.com/

34. **Learn 50 ways to get rid of blind dates:** www.cog.brown.edu/brochure/people/duchon/humor/blind.dates.html

35. **Find God** at: www.jesussaves.cc/

36. **Invest in the stock market** (get professional advice first): www.etrade.co.uk/

37. **Read "The Daily Telegraph"** newspaper online: www.dailytelegraph.co.uk/

38. **Keep your finger on your money pulse.** Manage your financial investments: www.moneyworld.co.uk/ and news.ft.com/

39. **You've seen it; you've saved for it, now it's time to buy your dream home:** www.homehunter.co.uk/

40. **Zoom down to your home from outer space** (not all locations are yet covered): www.terraserver.com/

41. **Check out what Manchester United Football Club are up to** online: www.manutd.com/

42. **Calm your mind with Tai Chi** at: www.chebucto.ns.ca/Philosophy/Taichi/

43. **Get help from the Samaritans:** www.samaritans.org.uk/

44. **Feel like you know something "they" don't?** Learn how to become a White Witch at: www.maxpages.com/witchesbook2

45. **Carpe Diem** – seize the day! Have a daily motivational message sent to you from: www.inspirelist.com/

46. **Expecting a baby?** Find out more about motherhood – dads too: www.ukmums.co.uk/

47. **Want to cut your gas, electricity, water and mobile phone bills?** Check out: www.buy.co.uk/

48. **Build on the University of life.** Get a degree: www.open.ac.uk/

49. **Wise up. Finish that homework sooner,** then relax: choose from the **free encyclopedias online at:** freeportal.virtualave.net/FreeStuff/FreeBooks/encyclopedia.shtml

50. **Get lots of free business marketing help:** www.marketinguk.co.uk/

51. **Find your true life purpose:** discover your destiny: www.lifeonpurpose.com/

52. **Like trivia? Then get trivial** at: www.funtrivia.com/

53. **Help your plants grow:** play Mozart and other relaxing classical tunes at: www.classicfm.co.uk/

54. **Buy a computer online** and save money at: www.dell.co.uk/

55. **Discover what Harry Potter is up to:** visit the unofficial Harry Potter fan club site at: www.harrypotterfans.net/

56. **Chill out and find the best pubs with The Good Pub Guide:** www.goodguides.com/pubs/search.asp

57. **Learn how to make money on the Internet** from a respected expert with a proven success record: www.marketingtips.com/t.cgi/12939/

58. **Help Amnesty International help someone who can't ask for help:** www.amnesty.org.uk/

59. **Support your favourite charity online:** www.childreninneed.com/

60. **England, 1644. Smell the gunpowder**; Oliver Cromwell's Roundheads meet Prince Rupert's Cavaliers at the Battle of Marston Moor. Visit: www.sealedknot.org/

61. **Want to kick the habit?** Get practical advice and help to quit smoking: www.quitsmoking.com/

62. **Listen in while Police Special Forces catch the guys on the run:** www.policescanner.com/

63. **Let the Internet update and upgrade your Windows software** applications for you at: catchup.cnet.com/

64. **Escape to: "The most beautiful place on Earth":** www.yosemitepark.com/

65. **Enter the time capsule.** Key in a favourite date between 1900 and 1997 in the Time Capsule and discover the popular songs of the time, the big news around that date, birthdays of the famous, and so on: www.dmarie.com/timecap/

66. **Ask George and get some great gardening tips** before you weed the borders at: www.greenfingers.com/

67. **Discover how to pay no tax – legally** at: www.offshoreprofit.com/

68. **Impress your friends: learn the most important useless knowledge** (for example, how fish avoid drowning) at: www.uselessknowledge.com/

69. **Is there more to coincidence?** Learn about The Celestine Prophesy with James Redfield at: www.celestinevision.com/

70. **Feeling clever?** Take an IQ test with MENSA: www.mensa.com/

71. **Listen to what's happening around the world** with the BBC World Service at: www.bbc.co.uk/worldservice/

72. **Are you an aviation enthusiast?** Then check out the Boeing experience at: www.boeing.com/

73. **Visit Number 10 Downing Street** and join me in the Cabinet room: www.number-10.gov.uk/

74. **Pop in and say Hello to the First Lady** at The White House: www.whitehouse.gov/

75. **Get spaced out:** visit NASA and check out the Hubble telescope: spacescience.nasa.gov/

76. **Worship God in the buff with the Christian Naturists:** www.vistapointe.com/~markm/

77. **Get into DIY and finally fix the house at:** www.todayshomeowner.com/ and www.diy.co.uk/

78. **Discover how to cook like my Grandmother:** www.geocities.com/NapaValley/1111/

79. **Fed up with traffic jams? Go vertical:** get a Moller skycar at: www.moller.com/skycar/

80. **Confess your sins online at:** www.ulc.net/confession.html

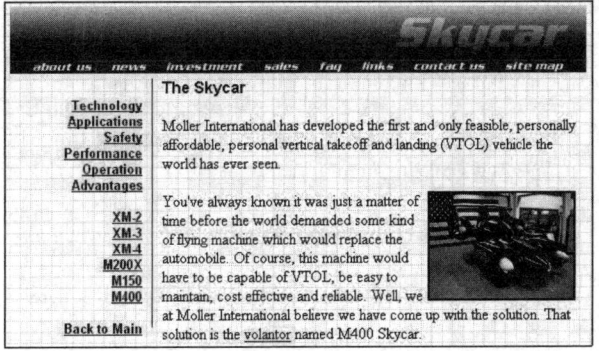

81. **Show that special person how much you love them;** say it with flowers at: www.interflora.co.uk/

82. **Get fit and relaxed: learn yoga:** www.sivananda.org/

83. **Sell your house for nothing** (no commission, no estate agents, no hassle) at: www.easier.co.uk/

84. **Cultivate green fingers.** Brush up on your gardening skills: www.sierra.com/sierrahome/gardening/

85. **Have a warped sense of humour?** Then read what other warpies have to say in this comedy zine at: www.fadetoblack.com/

86. It's a new age in which more doesn't necessarily mean better. **Learn the secrets of how to live simply** at: www.slnet.com/

87. **Get a free tips newsletter on your favourite topic**: www.emazing.com/

88. **Ask an expert or become a guru** at: www.guru.com/

89. **Get cultural!** Visit the Louvre: www.culture.fr/louvre/

90. **For bras and lingerie in a range of styles and sizes,** visit: www.SmartBras.com/

91. **Calm your mind** and visit the wonderful Tyburn Convent in London. Hear the bells toll and take a virtual tour at: www.tyburnconvent.org.uk/

92. **In a hurry and need a gift fast** or looking for a great last minute holiday deal? Visit: www.lastminute.com/

93. **Play safe: choose your condoms at Condomania:** www.condoms4u.com/

94. **Create your own digital films online.** Sit in the Director's chair: www.dfilm.com/

 Although much of the information provided on the Internet is free for anyone to use, you should always check copyright statements associated with the information you want – especially for web-based material: the providers may limit what you can do with their information.

95. **This one's a surprise.** Has serious multimedia eye-candy appeal including some amazing special video and sound effects: www.eye4u.com/

96. **Order delicious Yorkshire cakes from Elizabeth Botham at Whitby,** North Yorkshire, England at: www.botham.co.uk/

97. **Discover how things work**: www.howstuffworks.com/

98. **Visit Shakespeare at the Globe:** shakespeare.eb.com/ and www.reading.ac.uk/globe/

99. **Let your modem take the strain.** Shop at Tesco's online (while relaxing in the garden with a fine wine) at: www.tesco.com/

100. Too much free time? **Learn all about the bizarre art of "phone-bashing":** www.phonebashing.com/

101. OK, ready for a break now? **Want to go Bed & Breakfast?** Check out what's available around the world: www.bedandbreakfast.com/

What is the Internet?

Imagine: millions of computers and other electronic devices around the world that can connect with each other using ordinary telephone lines! On a basic level, that's the Internet, a complex network of different types of electronic devices connected together and essentially "talking" the same language. However, on a deeper level, the Internet is much more than that: it's really millions of people connected together, each having the power to decide with a couple of mouse clicks.

Originally a communications system designed to survive a global nuclear war, the Internet is the first human system that puts power back into the hands of individuals and limits the power of governments – so far. (Debatable, I know). A few individuals have coined other more colourful words and phrases to describe the Internet: "Cyberspace", "The Information Superhighway" or simply the "Net" if you feel like cutting out the excess! The Internet today is really a shorthand way of describing several key technologies, the four most important currently being:

- The **World Wide Web** – or just **the web**: this is the most popular "click-and-go" face of the Internet today (page 119).

- **Email** – or more formally electronic mail (page 257).

- **Newsgroups** – also known as Usenet – providing popular places to discuss topics that interest you (page 367).

- **Chat** – often known as Internet Relay Chat (IRC) – unlike email or newsgroups is "live": you can immediately talk to other Internet users – a little like the futuristic video phones we see in science fiction movies (page 395).

Don't worry if these phrases don't make much sense to you now. These and other essential components that make the Internet function are covered in more depth throughout this book.

So why has the Internet changed our world? In a word: information! Individuals, companies and other organisations, governments, universities and colleges help provide at low cost (or make freely available) a huge range of information. Contributors to the Internet are responsible for ensuring their own connection, yet it's this freedom that is at the heart of why the Internet even works at all: we can only benefit when we connect!

Currently, computers are the most important electronic devices that make up the Internet and cover a wide range of different varieties, ranging from large "old" mainframe computers, to the more familiar desktop and notebook PCs many of us use today. Through the incredible progress of technology and the pace of electronic miniaturisation, many of today's desktop and notebook PCs are many times more powerful than the older, much larger mainframe computers built two decades ago!

However, many people don't have access to a computer or may not want to learn how to use one. As computing and mass communications continues to increase while unit and running costs fall, other popular electronic devices like televisions, mobile phones, even washing machines and microwave ovens are also beginning to get hooked up to the Net!

So why is all this so exciting? Well, if you're fortunate enough to be reading books like this, you are living in what is possibly the most exciting time in the entire history of our world! The framework of the Internet breaks down barriers between countries and empowers ordinary people everywhere to do what they want, to discover what they want and, more often than not, to save money! To get on the Net, essentially, you just need three things:

- An **Internet access device**. Examples include: computers, special mobile phone or WebTV.

- A **connection to the Internet** for most of us, this means an Internet Service Provider and a phone line.

- **Software** that lets you explore and use the Net.

More on these topics later. First, let's explore a few of the basic words and phrases you'll come across when getting involved in and travelling around this exciting new global landscape.

Essential topics and what they mean

Development of the Internet has brought with it many new and strange words and phrases. But never fear: we've also included a full "Jargon buster" on page 473. Don't feel intimidated: you can learn a few new terms at a time while having fun on the Internet. Before you realise it, you'll know more than you might have thought possible. In the following paragraphs, let's examine a few of the most important Internet-related words and phrases.

Computer network: a group of computers and other electronic devices connected together in some way for the purpose of sharing information. That's it: just plug the critters together, add some software to ensure they all talk the same language and there you have a computer network.

A computer network in the same building is often referred to as a Local Area Network or LAN. A network made up of devices in separate buildings or locations is referred to as a Wide Area Network or a WAN. The Internet is actually the largest computer network ever created; the mother of all networks. You'll never see a bigger network until (and if) humans start colonising outer space!

Computer virus: a program designed to affect the normal working of a computer, PC or associated software applications. Some viruses are just plain annoying but nevertheless harmless, while others are highly devastating and can result in all information stored on a computer being lost.

Without doubt, viruses are spread more easily using the Internet. However, there are lots of steps you can take to protect your computer, and applying just a little key knowledge from this book can prevent a lot of heartache for yourself and others. See also page 173.

Downloading and Uploading: when we receive information from another computer on the Internet, we call this downloading. If we send information to another computer on the Net, we're uploading. When using the Internet, downloading and uploading often occur "in the background" automatically especially when using the web. More on page 409.

Online/Offline: online – or on-line – is a shorthand way of saying: "I'm now electronically connected to the Internet." Offline is the opposite: when you're disconnected from the phone line or the Internet. The plugs and connectors between your various electronic devices can remain in place, and you simply use the commands in your software to actually connect and disconnect from the Net.

The web: more formally called the World Wide Web (WWW), this is the largest and most popular "branch" of the Internet. The web is made up of millions of "web pages" or electronic documents stored on tens of thousands of web computers (servers) around the world. You can click on special links in web pages to go to other web pages around the Internet, jumping or "surfing" from page to page within seconds usually. More on pages 119, 141 and 439.

What's the Internet good for?

Wow, what a question! I know I'm probably biased but the Internet is just amazing. You can find out something about almost everything – in fact, practically any piece of information you might ever want to know is probably available somewhere on the Internet! Also, you won't need to know any complicated computer programming languages to use the Internet. If you're happy to cope with any basic computer word processing software, you should have no trouble getting online and having a lot of fun exploring Cyberspace.

If the ultimate guidebook to everything in existence were to exist, it would probably be the Net or stored somewhere on it! From the vast source of information – much of which is often freely available – you can probably solve any problem you're ever likely to come across using the Internet. To perhaps get a clearer picture, let's explore the Net a little more and consider some of the main components that make up the Net and the kinds of things you can do.

Email: you can send and receive email – more formally known as electronic mail – to anyone anywhere who has access to the Internet, using computers, mobile phones, WebTVs and other Internet-ready devices. Get started on page 257.

Shop till you drop: no longer necessary. There are clear benefits to shopping on the Net: no traffic, no queues and if you're careful, little hassle. More and more companies are making their goods and services available for sale online and passing on savings they make to canny Net customers. But you need to know how to get informed and learn a few ground rules. For more about Internet shopping, see page 211.

Go to the movies: before you go and see the latest films, why not go online and view extracts from current popular movies and read the reviews – sometimes even before the films are on show at your local cinema! Find out what's going on behind the scenes and maybe even talk to some popular celebrities.

Computer software: you can obtain most computer software programs and regular updates on the Internet, for the

IBM-compatible PC, Apple Mac, Atari Amiga and possibly others too. Therefore, if you're short on time, instead of visiting your local computer store, often you can choose to visit them on the Internet. This approach can mean less wear and tear on you, your bank balance, your car, the roads and has got to be good for the environment.

However, buying a full software product online may not always offer the best solution. For example, much of today's software is large in file size. If, like most people, you're using a standard computer-type modem to access the Net, you may decide that spending four hours or more downloading a large file is simply not worth the hassle! Nevertheless, technology has a habit of speeding things up while reducing prices, so perhaps when four hours become one hour...

Learn something new: discover key information on a huge range of topics! A variety of easy methods is available to help you find the kind of information you want – once you know how – and this book can help you. For example, you can:

- Find your favourite **food recipe**.

- Read about **current events** in online newspapers or magazines.

- **Visit your government** representatives and find out what they're up to.

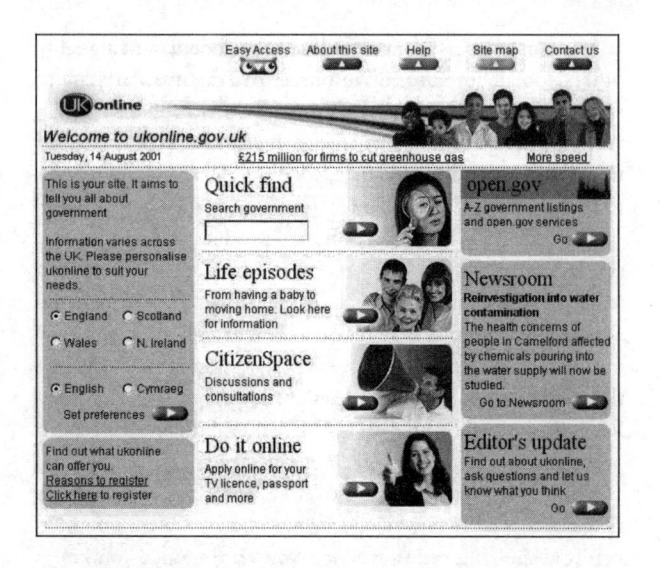

- **Give your brain a workout** browsing a complex academic journal.

- Get help with **school homework**.

- **Enrol on a college course** or take a University degree – the Open University in Britain provides a wide range of courses and the Internet is an ideal way to deliver information.

- **Get answers from an online encyclopedia** – a huge up-to-date information resource. You can use search tools to gain access to all relevant information or you can get quick "snapshot" answers instead of pages and pages of text to wade through. See page 233.

Chill out, relax and play a game: many generous sources on the Internet provide free games like chess, poker and football. Plus you can play many other more animated and interactive games live with opponents living locally or who may live thousands of miles away on another continent! See also page 359.

Newsgroups: known also as discussion groups, newsgroups enable you to discuss topics with other people from around the world. You can solve a problem, get advice, offer a solution, and so on, to freely help others and receive help when you need it. Newsgroups can also be useful for businesses to make a contribution and in return subtly advertise their products and services. See also page 367.

Business: starting any business is a hugely brave step and needs a lot of research and careful consideration. You can learn about what it takes to set up and run a business or start an Internet business! Free and low-cost resources on the Internet can help you get started, avoid expensive mistakes and promote your business to millions around the world for a low cost. You can also learn about Internet marketing, websites and e-commerce and how to provide and carry out safe and secure transactions on the Internet.

New communities: the current growing trend of providing free and low-cost access to the Internet is enabling many individuals from around the globe to communicate using a variety of different and interesting ways. This has led to the formation of new small communities in which people who share the same interests and beliefs can meet and discuss issues even though they may be based thousands of miles apart.

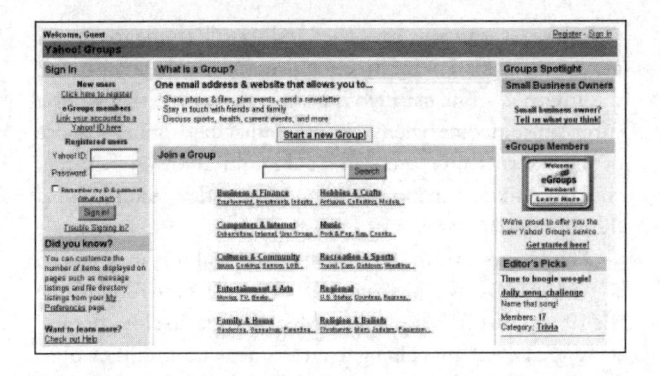

Who owns the Net?

A striking and sometimes confusing fact is that nobody and yet everybody "owns" the Internet! No single government or power has total control of the Internet – an unsettling reality for some authorities – and anyone with a PC/modem or other Internet device, and a phone connection, can gain access to it.

However, a number of large companies and organisations do have the power and influence to "steer" development of the Internet, including Microsoft, CompuServe/America Online (AOL)/Time-Warner and Netscape, plus several others. Other smaller organizations however, play a key role in the nuts and bolts development of the Internet, including: the World Wide Web Consortium (W3C) and domain naming bodies like InterNIC.

Some governments have tried and are still trying to control or censor the kind of information people can gain access to on the Internet – but usually with little success. Perhaps not a surprising outcome when we consider that the original purpose of the Internet was to create a communications system that could continue functioning even after a devastating global thermonuclear war.

The Internet at present is young and still forming, and in some ways it's much like a new "Wild West" or the Klondike of the 19th century. Like the gold fields of that era, the Internet and its "digital gold" are helping to create many multimillionaires. Internet success starts with having the right knowledge and know-how and if you have your eye on mining some Internet gold, books like this one can help you get started quickly. But like those early pioneers, you'll need to tread carefully to avoid unknown dangers!

The drive to bring the Net to everyone

Yesterday, most people had to have a "true" computer to access the Internet. Today, a computer can contain a plug-in TV card and televisions include computer components that provide access to the Internet – WebTV for example. The differences between televisions and computers are slowly becoming hazy – and this trend is only just starting. Also, big changes are on the way with Internet access costs set to fall across the globe. More and more cable television operators and manufacturers around the world are forming alliances to further integrate the Internet into the most popular 21st century communications medium: television.

Most new computers now come with built-in Internet access – which can now also be found in the latest mobile phones, personal organisers (Psion) and a whole host of other emerging Internet access devices.

Introducing Netiquette

When different people with varying outlooks are suddenly brought together, problems and misunderstandings can result. Throughout history, people across the world have developed acceptable methods with which to interact in a polite and positive way, in a spirit of tolerance, understanding and appreciation and acceptance of other views, habits and customs.

This general approach has also been transferred to the Internet to become known a little tongue-in-cheek as "Netiquette" or "Net-etiquette" – which is simply a way of acting with consideration for others.

Copyright: how to become seriously rich or poor

Here's what to some is an obvious statement: every component on the Internet (text, graphics, programs, sound clips and video files) is owned by somebody. Compare this with the popular but dangerously false view among many Internet users that everything on the Internet is free! Although much on the Internet is free of charge to use privately by individuals usually for non-commercial purposes, check the small print or risk being sued. As the Internet is becoming accepted into mainstream business life, sharp copyright and trademark lawyers are quickly learning the rules and can make their clients much richer at the expense of people who decide to "borrow" components from the Internet!

> If in doubt, simple: just ask copyright or trademark owners before using their material and keep copies of all written communications to cover yourself if necessary during any possible future disputes – people may sometimes genuinely forget that they have given permission previously so you need to keep documentary evidence to avoid possible problems and misunderstandings.

Often, an option is provided to download one copy, make a backup copy and print a single copy all for personal, non-commercial use. However, photocopying, re-selling or repeated printing is usually illegal. Arguably, copyright automatically applies to everything that is written, although including a copyright symbol does make ownership more clear. However, usually, even if Internet content is available free of charge, the ownership of that content stays with the copyright or trademark owner.

As a result of copyright and trademark infringements, some organisations have found a highly lucrative addition to their income by setting up systems that regularly scan the Internet (sometimes automatically, 24 hours a day) and suing those parties who violate international copyright laws.

How did the Internet come about?

The "cold war" era of the 20th century was without doubt a tense time. Superpowers rivalled for domination and the entire show was fuelled by mankind's two basic emotions: greed and fear. In the 1960s, key people in the US military were charged with considering the unthinkable: the task of masterminding a communications network that could survive a global nuclear war. Originally, only military computers were linked to form a grid or an "inter-net" of various kinds of computers to form ARPAnet.

During the 1980s, universities and library computer networks were added to the military network to explore new possibilities and the term "Internet" was born. Gradually, others too realised the potential: business and commerce, schools and individuals during the following years "tried out" this new idea until hundreds, thousands, then millions of computers around the world were "connected" to the Internet. The 1990s saw the fastest growth ever of the Internet, arguably fuelled by governmental recognition when American Vice President Al Gore provided special funding to further develop and look more closely into what he referred to as "the Information Superhighway."

Also during the 1990s, the idea of a World Wide Web (WWW) emerged from the amazing and prophetic British researcher Tim Berners-Lee while working at the CERN Laboratory for Particle Physics in Switzerland. The WWW or "web" as it is more popularly known, has developed into the most incredible, most visible and the fastest growing sector of the Internet!

Today, millions of computers have access to the Internet and commercial and individual interests have essentially "taken over" in a big way. This shows no sign of stopping; in fact, my guess is that our use of the Internet is only just beginning!

The Internet is set to become the dominant global communications channel of the 21st century, providing a

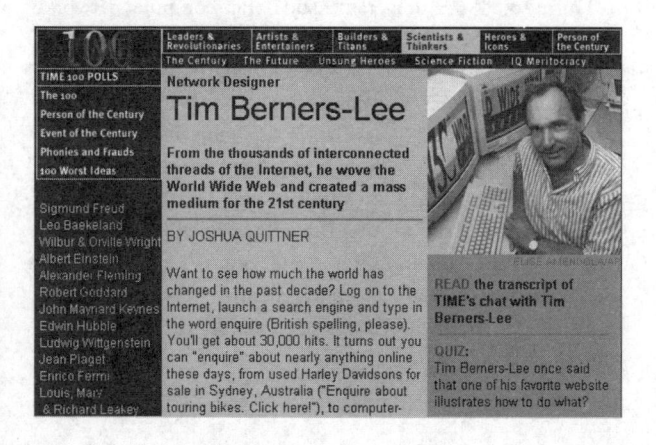

Network Designer

Tim Berners-Lee

From the thousands of interconnected threads of the Internet, he wove the World Wide Web and created a mass medium for the 21st century

BY JOSHUA QUITTNER

Want to see how much the world has changed in the past decade? Log on to the Internet, launch a search engine and type in the word enquire (British spelling, please). You'll get about 30,000 hits. It turns out you can "enquire" about nearly anything online these days, from used Harley Davidsons for sale in Sydney, Australia ("Enquire about touring bikes. Click here!"), to computer-

READ the transcript of TIME's chat with Tim Berners-Lee

QUIZ:
Tim Berners-Lee once said that one of his favorite website illustrates how to do what?

common "melting pot" for television, telecommunications and the sharing of knowledge in all its forms. Since 1998, the Internet population has doubled! This amazing growth rate has astounded and confounded many experts and continues to break records and smash limits while probably changing stock market patterns permanently, even with all the ups and downs that are part of stock market life.

New ways of valuing businesses are emerging based on future growth potential rather than short-term profits. This growth is fuelled by ever-falling communications prices around the world – a trend set to continue. As the price of key technology and Internet access falls, more opportunities for millions of ordinary people in many countries around the world become available – and, just like you, people are curious and keen to discover more.

However, as we have seen with recent computer virus scares, the great strength of the Internet is also its biggest weakness. The more people who use the Internet, the more we as a race come to rely on it, the more interconnected our world becomes, the more precarious our situation: a single continually mutating computer virus can cause widespread chaos.

Perhaps the safest option is to somehow find a balance and understand that the Internet is just another tool for modern living, and not let the ever-increasing drive for self-interest and short-term gains blind us into thinking the Internet is the answer to every problem – it simply isn't!

Create More With
Intel® PC Cameras
Video Phone

Meet Face to Face

Keep in touch with Family
with Intel® Video Phone S

See the Realplayer
G2* Demo (1540K)

If you don't have RealPlayer G2,
<u>download</u> the player for free.

34 > Introducing the Internet

2

Nethead heaven: how the Internet works

When you send or receive information on the Internet, an incredible chain of events occurs. To use the Net, you don't need to know how it works. However, sometimes a little key background knowledge can help clarify explanations provided later in the book. Here's a brief outline of what happens to information as it moves across the Internet.

What is TCP/IP and all that jazz?

Transmission Control Protocol/Internet Protocol – more sensibly referred to as **TCP/IP** – is part of a complex set of rules that computers on the Internet use to communicate. The TCP part first ensures information to be sent is chopped up into smaller chunks known as **packets**.

TCP/IP is responsible for creating the information packets, transmitting the information and then recombining the packets properly to recreate the original information at the receiving end. Your computer first sends the packets to your Internet Service Provider, or equivalent Internet connection service. From your Internet Service Provider, the packets travel across the computer networks and communications links that make up the Internet.

Each packet may travel a different route to the other packets that make up the same piece of information. At the receiving end the packets are recombined and the information re-formed to its original state. If one "connection" to the Internet is broken, information can use "connections" on other routes to ensure that all the information arrives at its destination.

Internet Protocol (IP): the postman of the Net

The Internet Protocol makes sure each packet is sent to the right destination. Each computer connected to the Internet is given a unique number or IP address. A typical **IP address** uses four sets of numbers separated by full stops, for example: 123.456.789.6.

When a computer connects to the Internet, it is assigned an IP address – if using an Internet Service Provider, the numbers that make up the address may change each time you connect. However, thankfully we users don't usually need to be concerned with these numbers, since an automatic system is in

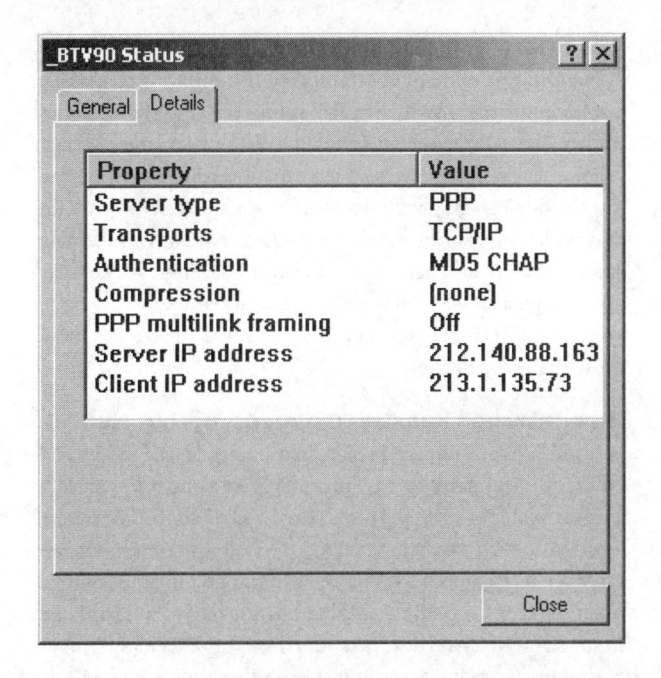

Property	Value
Server type	PPP
Transports	TCP/IP
Authentication	MD5 CHAP
Compression	(none)
PPP multilink framing	Off
Server IP address	212.140.88.163
Client IP address	213.1.135.73

place on the Internet that translates a set of IP numbers to a web address. The **Domain Naming System (DNS)** allows you to enter a more user-friendly name for a website (like www.gardening.com) instead of something like 123.137.456.7 (imaginary **DNS numbers** chosen at random to illustrate the DNS numbering pattern).

Routers – amazing Internet guides

A router is one of many special computers on the Internet that are responsible for controlling the continuous flow of information – often referred to as "traffic" – across the Internet.

When a router receives an information packet as discussed in previous paragraphs, it decides the most efficient route for that packet to take and sends the packet on its way to the next router if necessary. And so on. As a result, a single packet may go through a single router, several routers or many routers to ensure that the packet successfully reaches its final destination. Now isn't that amazing?

How Internet Backbones speed up the Net

Just like some roads are busier than others in our towns and cities, specific parts of the Internet now sometimes have a similar problem too. At "peak" times, say between 3pm and 7pm in the UK (when the USA "wakes up"), parts of the Internet have to move a lot more information in comparison to other parts of the Net, sometimes causing delays and jams. To help combat Internet traffic jams, high-speed "busy" communication lines – or "**Backbones**" as they are popularly known – have been developed and directly interconnect the most important computer networks around the world.

3

Preparing your computer for the Internet

Many different types of computer can be used to access the Internet. Whether you're using an IBM-compatible Personal Computer (PC), Apple Macintosh (iMac), company network terminal, Amiga, or whatever, providing the computer you want to use meets the minimum standards – and most do – then you can get connected.

However, as many websites nowadays do contain a lot of animation and more demanding self-running programs, the most recent, faster computers generally give better results.

Buying a computer
Most computers today are either an IBM-compatible Personal Computer (PC) or an Apple Mac. Apple were the first computer

maker to start using a Graphical User Interface (GUI) – a visual design made up of different types of boxes or "windows", icons (visual symbols), and so on, which when combined with a mouse, provide a point-and-click navigation approach. With the GUI, What-You-See-Is-What-You-Get (WYSIWYG, pronounced "Wiziwig") was born.

This same idea was later introduced to the PC with Microsoft Windows to provide the familiar look and feel that we see today in Windows 9x/Me/XP/NT/2000. When compared, both the PC and the Mac now offer a similar range of options, yet true

Mac enthusiasts constantly argue with PC devotees over performance and look and feel issues. So which is best? The answer really depends on what you want. Apple Macs have an obvious designer look and feel, are usually more expensive than equivalent PCs, and are often especially popular with artists and designers. In terms of performance, arguably the PC is currently winning the race.

Today, the PC installed with the Microsoft Windows operating system is by far the most popular platform. However, Apple's fortunes may change again – as the rising level of recent sales figures shows. Many more varieties of PCs are made than Apple Macs. Therefore, a wider range of software is available and prices are often cheaper all round.

If you really want to examine the computer buying business in detail, shop around. Ask friends who already use a computer – just appreciate that your friends are almost certainly going to be biased either for or against a specific type; this is natural, but read the reviews and see demonstrations before making your

> Get the fastest computer with the most amount of Random Access Memory (RAM) you can afford, to reduce the amount of time you need to spend finding, receiving and saving information. 32 MB is an absolute minimum, 64 MB is fine, 128 MB is better. And only buy a computer that allows you to upgrade/add more "standard" RAM modules easily. Get assurances that you can add more RAM in say 12-18 months, should you choose.

final decision. My own choice is the PC simply because it offers the range of software I want, to perform the tasks I need to complete.

The most essential component in a computer needed to use the Internet is a modem or equivalent device. Most new computers now come with a modem or Internet access device; however, you may want to add a new modem or install a faster model. Modems and other fast Internet access devices are covered in "Modems" on page 53 and "Speeding up your Internet connection" page 245.

Although you can probably browse the Internet with an older PC – for example, an IBM-compatible PC based on the Intel 486 chip – you may become frustrated with poor performance while viewing websites containing animations and self-running programs, and so on. Also if, like most people in the UK, you have to pay dearly for your Internet connection, a slower PC will almost certainly take longer to complete tasks

> **HOT TIP** The speed of a computer is only one component that helps determine how fast you can surf the Internet. If you have a slow connection to the Net, using a faster computer usually won't solve the problem – it will only allow interactive or multimedia components to play faster and run better. For faster Internet surfing, get the fastest connection you can afford: for example, leased lines, cable, ADSL and ISDN provide an Internet connection that is faster than a modem. For more information, see page 245.

WELCOME TO DELL

Choose A Country
United Kingdom ▶ Go

We Know How E Works

United Kingdom Customers

▶ **Home & Home Office**

▶ **Small Business**
Companies with 1-500 employees in the UK

▶ **Large Business**
Companies with 500-5000 employees in the UK

▶ **Large Accounts**
Companies with 5000 or more employees in the UK

▶ **Public Sector**
Healthcare, education, local and central government

▶ **Northern Ireland**
For all business customers based in Northern Ireland

▶ **Dell Factory Outlet**
Dell systems at discounted prices: The great majority are unused systems. They are all re-tested and backed by complete Dell service packages

and so probably increase your phone or Internet access costs generally. When buying a new or used computer, the two most important considerations that affect the speed at which you can use the Internet are:

- The **speed of the computer** (also known as the CPU speed).

- The **amount and type of memory (RAM)** installed.

These same performance considerations also apply to other devices that are used to access the Internet if these devices use a microprocessor and memory chips and other similar electronic components. The most important type of memory to affect the speed of your computer are the plug-in RAM chips your computer uses.

RAM chips hold information temporarily and lose their information when the PC is switched off. RAM is measured in megabytes (MB) or millions of bytes. Remember, in computer terms, a byte is simply eight bits of information. A fast PC with lots of RAM can help make your journeys around the Internet more enjoyable, more stable and interesting. Coupled with a reliable fast link to the Internet, you can then concentrate on the Internet content without getting sidetracked into looking for ways to speed up your viewing experience.

If you decide to opt for a second-hand PC, the best advice I can offer is to choose a well known brand name if possible, like Dell, IBM, Dan, etc., that is less than 2 years old. Why? Older PCs may not be able to properly cope with the current demands of the Internet.

Although you can "upgrade" some older computers by changing the main microprocessor (CPU) and perhaps adding more powerful RAM (memory) chips, check into the full costs of this option very carefully. After you consider the costs, benefits and drawbacks, as the price of PCs continues to fall, you may be better off simply selling your old PC and buying a new one.

Getting up to speed

The most important electronic chip in a computer is the main microprocessor – often referred to as the Central Processing Unit (CPU). The CPU performs the most important number-crunching operations and therefore makes an enormous impact on its overall speed. The rate at which a CPU completes a series of tasks is measured in **millions of cycles each second** – computer makers now use the term **Hertz (Hz)** meaning one cycle each second. A powerful computer today might work at 800 million Hertz – often shown in advertisements as 800 MHz – or 1 GHz (1000 million Hertz), 1.7 GHz, or even more.

How's your memory?

If you're upgrading, remember the absolute minimum amount of RAM you should aim for is 32 MB. Although 64 MB is better, ideally aim for 128 MB – or preferably 256 MB or more. Anything under 16 MB will probably cause problems for today's web browsers. As the web and television merge, sound, video and computer or Internet games and entertainment usually work much better with more RAM memory.

Hard drive café

To keep information intact even when you switch your computer off, on most computers you "save" your data to the computer's **hard disk drive**. A hard drive typically has several disks or platters that spin very quickly. The larger your hard drive, the more information can be stored and processed.

Current versions of web browser suites like Microsoft Internet Explorer need a considerable amount of hard disk space – typically 80 MB or more. Netscape web browser suites may need less while Apple Mac PCs generally need even less disk space. Check your web browser documentation for the computer you're using.

Web pages are becoming ever more animated and interactive and generally these types of web pages take up more storage space than that of a "simple" web page. It's amazing how soon you can fill a hard disk while regularly saving information from the Internet. Therefore again, aim to get the largest capacity hard drive you can afford: ensuring plenty of empty hard drive space also ensures that your computer runs better. Try to aim for a minimum of 5 GB (Gigabytes) – ideally aim for 30 GB or more, if possible.

If you are running out of hard drive space, you may be able to fit a second hard drive or install a larger capacity drive. If unsure of how to go about it, get advice from your computer dealer and if you want to know more about this topic, the plain English "Upgrading Your PC in easy steps" (Computer Step) has been designed to help anyone able to use a screwdriver.

Choosing a display monitor

Your computer's monitor is your window onto the Internet. The screen size of your monitor affects how you see some web pages – for example: if the screen is too small, you may be forced to use the horizontal scrollbars or keyboard more often which can become quite frustrating over time. Ideally, aim for at least a 17" screen minimum – as measured diagonally from corner to corner. But remember, web page scrollbars and boxes also take up space. Computer operating systems like Microsoft Windows and the Macintosh MacOS can use lots of boxes on the screen at once and web pages can contain lots of different components. Therefore, the "effective" screen size is only 15"!

Screen sizes smaller than about 15" can mean that you have to use your mouse or keyboard more often to complete your tasks. A 17" or 19" screen is ideal for Internet use as these can easily display most web pages properly and without the need for horizontal scrolling (if designed correctly). (For more information on web design, see "Web Page Design in easy steps" from Computer Step.) Your computer monitor also uses a special type of video memory so again, more video memory generally means items display faster. Try to get the fastest and largest amount of video memory you can afford.

Finally make sure your display monitor can display as many different colours as possible so that you can see images that use many colours and shades, like photographs, clearly as they should appear. In practice this means up to 17 million colours, however, you computer's operating system usually allows you to set the exact level. If this level is set too low at, say, 16 colours,

> **TravelMate 730 from ACER**

photographs on web pages especially will probably look patchy and flat.

Change your settings to display at least "256 colours" or "thousands" of colours and the quality of the display should improve considerably. Although often you can set your display to "millions" of colours, this option may cause some web pages to display more slowly as the monitor has to perform more work to meet the demands asked of it. Check your computer documentation on how to do this or speak to your computer dealer if unsure.

An ideal Internet-ready PC

Here's an ideal specification for a PC on the Internet today:

- **Computer speed:** 450 MHz or faster microprocessor (CPU).

- **RAM:** 128 MB of RAM upgradeable to four or five times that level.

- **Hard drive:** at least 4 GB capacity; 10–15 GB preferred.

- **Video card/video chips:** create the electronic signals to drive your display monitor. To view video clips and possibly 3D Internet displays clearly, try to get a video card with at least 8 MB of fast video memory, to help

RADEON™ 32MB SDR

minimise the amount of time your computer needs to spend processing these large routines.

- **Display monitor:** 17" or larger; 19" is a good option; 21" is pure joy.

- **Modem:** a 56 Kbps modem either built-in on-board, as a plug-in card or an external box. Most important: if you're buying a modem, make sure you choose one that is compatible with your computer and the phone system for the country in which you live.

- **DVD drive:** a Digital Video Disk (DVD) drive can also play Compact Discs for computers (CD-ROMs) as well as audio Compact Discs (CDs). As a minimum, a CD-ROM drive may meet your needs.

- **Mouse or equivalent point-and-click device:** a mouse is a small hand-held tool you use to move the mouse pointer or "cursor" around the screen. Although not absolutely essential to use the Internet, a mouse will almost certainly speed up your viewing.

- **Microsoft Windows-compatible keyboard**.

- **Sound card/sound capability:** a sound card – also called a sound board – or built-in sound capability allows you to hear and record high quality sound from the Internet, web pages, web radio and TV stations, music download sites, videos, and so on. A sound card plugs into a spare PC expansion socket and needs configuring in your computer's operating system software. To hear sound, you'll also need loudspeakers.

- **Loudspeakers:** convert the signals from a sound card or sound chips into sound. Loudspeakers plug into a sound card or connector that links to the appropriate sound chips on the main computer motherboard. Ideally choose compatible PC speakers that come with an amplifier built in to enhance the sound signals received from the sound chips.

- **Microphone/headset:** essential if you want to talk to others on the Internet.

> **HOT TIP**
> If you have some spare funds and want to get ahead of the game, consider getting a WebCam kit that combines with a microphone/headset, to build in basic video phone capability.

4
Modems

A modem is another essential electronic hardware device most people need to use the Internet today. But modems come in a variety of types and specifications. This chapter provides information you need to know about choosing and using a modem.

What is a modem?

A modem enables a computer to share information with other computers using the standard phone lines, and as such, for most current Internet users, is probably their most important electronic component. The word "modem" is made up from the two words: MOdulator and DEModulator – which is another way of saying: "Code the information, send it, then decode it at the other end." Modems are available in three main forms:

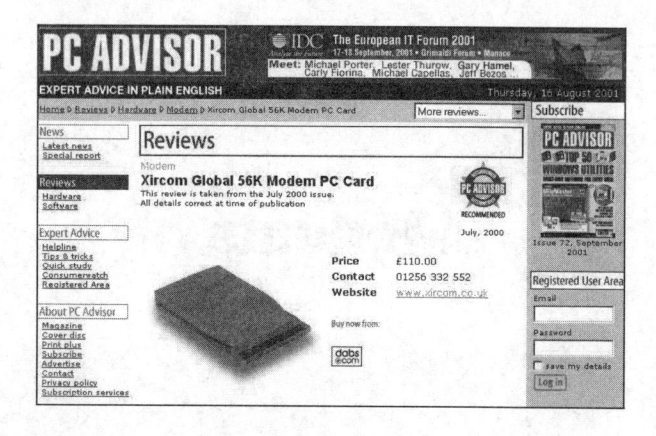

- An external "box" that connects to a computer. An external modem can connect to the serial, parallel or USB sockets (discuss these options with your computer dealer when buying your modem).

    Benefits: you don't need to remove the computer's casing to install an external modem. An external modem is often the best solution if you want to just get online quickly. You can also easily move it to another computer. Indicator lights show the status or progress of a connection and if you have a communications problem, the condition of these lights can help point to where an error might lie.

Drawbacks: adds more cabling at the back of the computer. Requires some desk space and its own power supply adaptor. Usually more expensive than plug-in card modems for desktop computers.

- A plug-in card modem installs into a spare slot inside the computer electronic box containing the main circuit board (motherboard). Follow the maker's instructions. As a general guide, you'll need to disconnect the computer from the electrical mains supply first, fit an antistatic wristband, then remove the computer casing and carefully install the card. Ask your computer dealer for advice if unsure.

Benefits: takes up no desk space, needs no separate power supply and doesn't add to the number of connection cables at the back of your computer.

Drawbacks: you need to remove the computer cover and understand how to fit the card. Once the computer casing is removed, there's an increased risk that electronic components may be damaged. Take care: electronic boards are fragile.

- For notebook computers, not desktops, a PC-Card – also known as PCMCIA – is a plug-in credit card-size module that installs into a special "expansion" slot on a computer's main circuit board (motherboard). No need to remove the computer casing.

    Benefits: most PC-Card modems can work with most types of notebook computer; however, do check if any special restrictions apply. Get advice from your computer maker or dealer. Small and compact and don't need an external power supply.

    Drawbacks: usually more expensive to buy and cannot work with desktop computers. A PC-Card must be installed into the correct slot otherwise permanent damage to the card and computer could result.

> When buying a modem, you may still be offered an older, slower modem running at 33,600 bps (33.6 Kbps). Buy the fastest modem you can afford that is compatible with the phone system in your country and avoid getting modems slower than 33.6 Kbps. 56 Kbps is the current standard.

Why do we need a modem?

Information in a computer when broken down to its most basic parts is essentially made up of a series of ones and zeros and is termed digital information. Phone lines were of course originally designed only to handle a range of varying values (voice) not just ones and zeros.

Therefore, to transfer computer information using the phone lines, a modem is needed to convert and prepare information correctly for sending through a phone line, and then reconverting and translating the incoming information to the digital format that a computer can understand.

Modems for networked computers

Most modems are designed to run on a single computer. However, if you have several computers linked together in a network, and want to provide Internet access to each computer, several options are possible:

- You could consider buying a **network-compatible modem.** A network modem installs on one machine but allows other computers in the network to use it as though it were connected to each networked computer. A network modem allows several different users in the network to access the Internet at the same time.

- Later versions of Microsoft Windows 2000 operating systems that have Windows Networking installed allow a modem to be shared across a network. See your Windows 2000 guide (or "Windows 2000 Professional in easy steps") for more information.

- Client/Server operating systems usually offer similar options. Check your documentation or speak to your computer dealer.

Modem speeds

Several years ago, once the value of modems became clear, many different modem manufacturers emerged across the world. To ensure modems could communicate properly with other modems, a set of standards became necessary so that all knew what was necessary. As a result, the "V" series of standards has emerged.

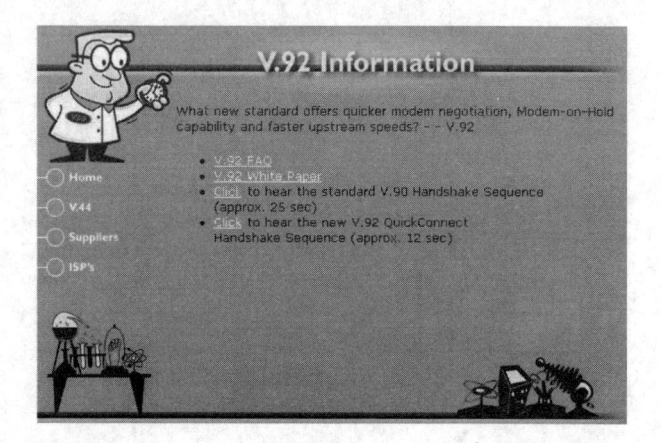

How fast a modem operates tells us how fast information can be sent and received. The faster the modem, the less time you need to spend online to retrieve the information you want – so if you have to pay for every second while online, a faster modem saves you money. **Modem speed is measured in bits per second (bps).** Current modems ideally run at 56,000 bps – often written as 56 Kbps (kilobits per second) or sometimes known as the V.90 standard. What this actually means is that a V.90 modem can receive information at up to 56 Kbps and send information at a speed of up to 33.6 Kbps. A more recent enhancement is the V.92 standard, which essentially provides better connection features than V.90 rather than faster overall speed.

Note these are maximum speeds quoted and in practice speeds are often somewhat lower. Why? Many modems still connect to the Internet using old copper-based phone lines – which were originally designed for voice communications, not computer data – even though a modem may be listed as 56 Kbps speed, for most people, that level of speed is rarely reached.

The actual speed at which you connect depends largely on the "quality" of the telephone line. As an Internet and computer author, I obviously spend a lot of time online and use a 56 Kbps modem often. Yet my connection speed averages at about 44 Kbps which is acceptable for general surfing.

Modems that shake hands

Before two modems can "talk" to each other, they perform a kind of electronic handshaking routine. A few basic tests are

USB Fax Modem

- Supports K56flex / V.90 56k for highest internet connection
- 56k data mode with automatic fallback
- Extended AT command set
- Fax service class 1
- V.80 Video mode
- Telephone line interface
- Pocket size
- Telephone Answer Machine
- Full 12 Mbps USB transmission

carried out automatically to ensure they're "speaking" the same language. Essentially, that's what a "handshake" is: after a successful handshake, the two modems must "agree" that they're compatible and how they will exchange or transfer information.

For example, one aspect that two modems must "agree" on is the speed at which to communicate. If one "talks" faster than the other can handle, confusion would result. Handshaking ensures that they "talk" at the same speed or that a faster modem slows down to match the speed of a slower modem – that's one of the reasons why sometimes your Internet connection speed may vary.

The entire **handshaking** process usually takes place very quickly so you probably won't even be aware of it happening. Indeed for most purposes, you don't need to know how it works, just that when things are running properly, it's an event that simply happens every time you connect to the Internet.

> **HOT TIP:** To ensure a modem can work properly with current modem speeds, make sure the computer/modem has a 16550 UART chip – ask your dealer if unsure. A UART electronic chip manages the information that flows into and out of a modem.

Squeezing the lemon and compressing data

To speed up the rate at which your modem sends information to another modem, the data or information can be compressed – a little like squeezing a lemon – so that the information takes up less space and travels across the Internet faster.

At the other end, the receiving modem automatically decompresses the information to its original size. Some types of files compress better than others. For example: a text file compresses much better than, say, a picture file. All new modems should now use data compression techniques so if you're buying, make sure that your intended modem uses the latest data compression technology for your country.

Zapping those pesky errors

Just like people make mistakes from time to time, so do modems. However, modern modems use some clever techniques to check for and correct any errors that may occur in the information being sent. Modem error control technology is another measure that helps ensure that information sent

Askey 56K PCI Rockwell Chipset

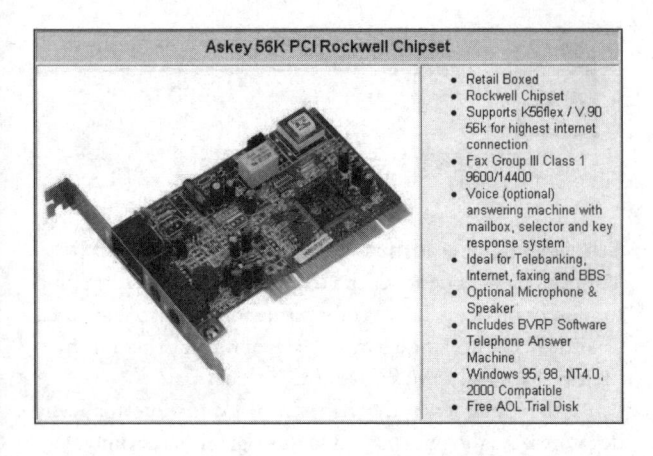

- Retail Boxed
- Rockwell Chipset
- Supports K56flex / V.90 56k for highest internet connection
- Fax Group III Class 1 9600/14400
- Voice (optional) answering machine with mailbox, selector and key response system
- Ideal for Telebanking, Internet, faxing and BBS
- Optional Microphone & Speaker
- Includes BVRP Software
- Telephone Answer Machine
- Windows 95, 98, NT4.0, 2000 Compatible
- Free AOL Trial Disk

arrives intact at the receiving end. The way error control works is to first break information into separate chunks or "packets" before sending the data.

At the other end, error control ensures that the receiving modem knows what the packets should contain and checks each one. If any damaged packets are detected, the receiving modem "asks" the transmitting modem to send another copy of the damaged packet. This process happens very fast and error control generally performs well.

A note about Call Waiting services

If you have a standard phone socket installed, you don't need a separate phone line for your modem: usually, you can connect your modem and standard telephone to the same phone line.

However, if you have a Call Waiting service set up on your phone system and your telephone and modem do share the same phone line, you may need to make sure that before using your modem, you turn off Call Waiting as these types of interactive services can cause connection problems. If in doubt, contact your telephone or Internet Service Provider for advice.

What else do I need to make my modem work?

Once you have your modem installed and connected to the phone line, every modem needs a software program to enable it to communicate with other modems and computers on the Internet and around the world.

Usually, compatible software comes with a new modem, or you can buy from a range of suitable off-the-shelf software packages to find one that matches your needs.

What else can I do with a modem?

One really useful feature of a correctly installed modem is that while travelling or if you're located away from your home or office – say on holiday or on business abroad – you can dial into your home or office computer or company network and access your information, just as though you were actually working at your home or office computer! If you do this while on holiday: shame on you, why not take a break instead?

Sending and receiving faxes

Many modems can also send and receive fax messages so you may not even need a separate fax machine (and therefore rolls of fax paper). Often a basic fax program may be included with a new modem but if you want more specific functions, upgrading to "Pro" versions is perhaps something to consider. If 24-hour fax capability is important to you, remember if you use a modem and PC, you may need to ensure your PC is either switched on permanently or can "wake up" on receiving a fax message.

To send and receive faxes, you'll need to have a fax program installed on your computer. Windows 2000 includes Microsoft

Fax so you may already have all you need – you'll only need configure your fax settings: see the Windows Help file. Alternatively, a variety of 'add-on' fax programs are available. You can do a search on the Internet, quiz your computer dealer, or perhaps even better, check whether your Internet Service Provider includes a free web-based fax service.

If your fax software is installed on your PC, when your computer receives a fax, the message is usually saved automatically. If you're working with some other software at the time of receiving a fax, often you can set your fax software to alert you to the fact that you are receiving a fax. You can then "switch" to the fax window and view the fax on-screen and optionally print it if you wish.

However remember that you usually can't edit a fax received in this way unless you have Optical Character Recognition (OCR) software installed and set up. Also, if you're using a separate computer display monitor, you don't need to have it switched on to receive a modem-faxed document as the information is already in the computer's main box – the monitor simply provides a way to view information stored on the computer's hard drive.

Internal modems for desktop computers

An internal "card" modem for a desktop computer is simply installed into a spare slot on the motherboard. Once installed and the case refitted, you'll be able to see the edge of the modem at the back of your computer (usually).

If you're doing the job yourself, learn how to install a modem before attempting this sometimes-tricky task, as circuit boards in computers are fragile. You can learn more in "Upgrading Your PC in easy steps" from Computer Step (www.ineasysteps.com). Or speak to your computer dealer.

To install an internal modem in a desktop PC, follow the maker's instructions. However, as a general guide, consider the following:

1. Make sure your computer and modem are both switched off and disconnected from the electrical main supply.

2. Unplug your existing phone lead from the wall socket.

3. Fit an antistatic wristband to reduce the possibility that static electricity in your body may damage sensitive electronic components.

4. Remove your PC's outer case and find a compatible empty slot for your modem card. If necessary, remove the blanking plate covering the slot you want.

5. Carefully remove the modem card from its packaging and install into the desired slot. Secure the modem edge with the securing screw.

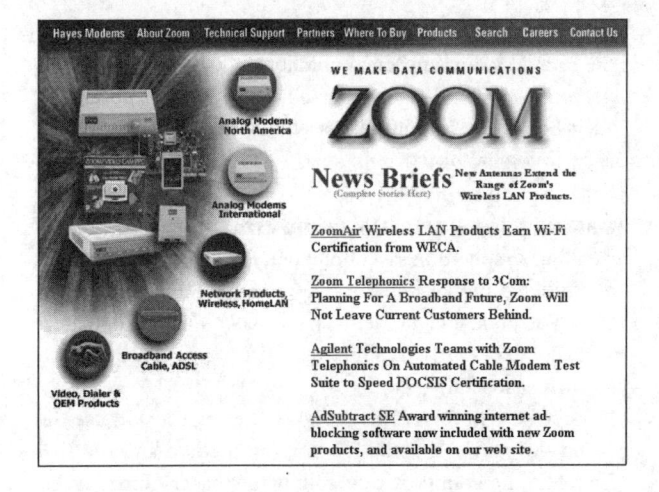

> **WE MAKE DATA COMMUNICATIONS**
>
> # ZOOM
>
> **News Briefs** New Antennas Extend the Range of Zoom's Wireless LAN Products.
> (Complete Stories Here)
>
> ZoomAir Wireless LAN Products Earn Wi-Fi Certification from WECA.
>
> Zoom Telephonics Response to 3Com: Planning For A Broadband Future, Zoom Will Not Leave Current Customers Behind.
>
> Agilent Technologies Teams with Zoom Telephonics On Automated Cable Modem Test Suite to Speed DOCSIS Certification.
>
> AdSubtract SE Award winning internet ad-blocking software now included with new Zoom products, and available on our web site.

6. Then, using the extra phone lead supplied, connect your modem to the wall phone socket.

7. Optionally, plug the lead from your existing phone into the correct socket on the modem card.

8. Carefully refit the PC case and reconnect your devices.

9. Switch on your PC. If you're using a later version of Microsoft Windows and the modem too is new, Windows should detect your modem and install the

software it needs for you. Watch the screen closely and follow any further instructions.

10. Install any additional related software following the supplied instructions.

Modems for portable computers

Installing a modem in say a notebook PC is much easier than for a desktop model and you don't need to remove the outer case. Notebook PC modems are usually small, completely encased, credit-card-sized modules that you simply push into the correct socket.

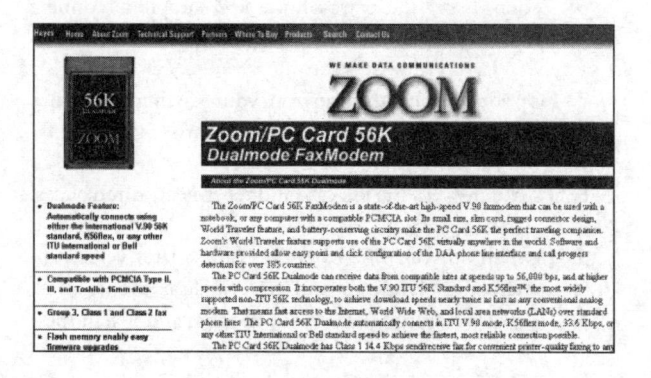

Make sure however, that you use the correct slot: use the wrong slot and you could destroy the modem and the PC! Therefore, most importantly, follow the maker's instructions throughout installation and get advice from your dealer if unsure. Mistakes with portable PCs can be expensive to correct.

Working with external modems

An external modem usually connects to an appropriate socket on the computer. External modems usually come with all the connecting leads and software you need to get up and running quickly, and so are usually easier to install when compared to fitting an internal modem. As a minimum, you'll have the connecting lead to the computer and the connecting lead that connects your modem to your phone socket.

Although an external modem can take up more room on your desk, usually a range of status indicator lights are present on the modem that can tell you what is happening while dialling your Internet Service Provider or when using the Internet. You might see the letters "RD", "SD", and "OH" to mean "Receiving Data", "Sending Data", and "Off Hook", to name but a few. When tackling Internet access problems that sometimes occur, your Internet Service Provider may ask about the condition of specific status lights, to quickly help determine where the problem lies. Also, you can easily move an external modem and connect it to another computer, whereas moving an internal card modem is more time-consuming and sometimes more tricky.

Remember, you don't need a separate phone line to use your modem and to make the job of connecting up even easier, most modems include a phone socket. To physically connect your modem, read and follow the maker's instructions. However as a general guide consider the following guidelines:

1. Make sure your computer and modem are both switched off.

2. Unplug your existing phone lead from its socket and simply plug this lead into the socket marked on the modem.

3. Then using the extra phone lead supplied, connect your modem to the wall phone socket.

4. Now plug in the larger lead that connects your modem to the computer. Usually, this lead will have moulded plugs each end with an 11-pin or 24-pin connector one end.

5. Connect the modem to its power supply and switch on.

6. Switch on your PC. If you're using a later version of Microsoft Windows and the modem too is new, Windows should detect your modem and install the software it needs for you. Watch the screen closely and follow instructions.

7. Install any additional related software following the supplied instructions.

5

Getting online

Once connected to the Internet, you can have a lot of fun, but probably the hardest part is successfully connecting for the first time. After all, if you're new to everything Internet, you don't know what to expect.

> Some of the most helpful people on the Internet are other Net users. For example, certain newsgroups are particularly valuable. Although this option is not much help until you're connected, if you do have a technical problem, perhaps you could ask a friend or colleague who already has Internet and newsgroup access to post your question and handle the replies.

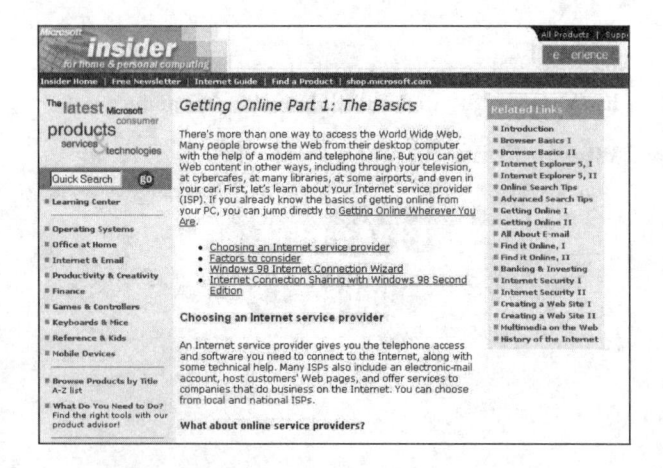

However don't be put off; the software that you'll use to connect to the Net is designed for anyone to use – not computer geeks – so take your time. Usually, you'll only need to install the software once so that getting online is then only a few mouse clicks away.

Getting set up to go online is not that difficult, especially since software is generally getting easier to install and use. Also, in the never-ending battle for customers, many Internet Service Providers now provide added help to get you up and running as soon as possible. After all, they don't benefit until you're connected, so if you do get stuck, I'll bet there's a contact phone number in your pack that you can call to get direct one-to-one help. If not, think twice about using that Internet Service Provider. When you're new to the Internet, you want help, not hassle. Good ISPs understand this important point.

What do I need to get on the Net?

To gain access to and use of the Internet, here's what you'll need:

- **An Internet-ready computer or other Internet access device:** an Internet-ready television or mobile phone for example. Whichever electronic device you choose, remember that the Internet software you choose gets the results you want. Therefore, make sure that the electronic hardware is powerful enough to properly drive your chosen Internet software – web browsers, web design software, email and newsgroup programs. If you're buying new equipment, don't forget, true audio/video-based email may arrive sooner than we might think – and will probably make extra demands on your equipment – so try to think at least 1 year ahead to get maximum value for your money.

- **Telephone or cable television connection:** this must be physically close to your modem, computer or other Internet access device. Remember, however, that, although most users opt for a physical phone or cable line, a "wireless" (remote) connection to the Internet is now also available.

- **Gateway connection to the Internet:** currently, there are two main ways in which you can get connected to the Net: 1) With a Dial Up device like a modem or ISDN Terminal Adaptor, or 2) Using what is known as a leased line. A leased line is a fast permanent but expensive connection to the Internet – and therefore tailored to Internet-oriented businesses. Most people connect to the Net using a Dial Up service through either an Internet Service Provider – like Demon for example – or a commercial online service like CompuServe or America Online (AOL). With these services, each time you connect to the Internet the only cost may be the equivalent of a local phone call, or less, or perhaps even completely free of charge (eventually). Many ISP choices are now available. You can search for "ISP" on the web to discover more or read the reviews in popular computer magazines.

> **BEWARE**
> At the very least, make sure any Internet provider lets you at least connect at the local telephone call rate or equivalent – ideally, check out free of charge packages in depth, especially the small print.

- **Internet software:** necessary to perform various tasks on the Internet, like using email and surfing the web. In addition, use up-to-date antivirus software to protect your computer while online. Software is available for both IBM-compatible PCs and Apple Mac computers. Most Internet access software is now available free of charge online. Or one of the best sources is your local magazine store: many computer and Internet magazines now include free CD-ROMs/DVD-ROMs that contain all the software you need to get started on the Internet. Once up and running, you can also download extra software or updates straight from the Internet.

> Remember to observe copyright, trademark and licensing laws when using or printing information and property "owned" by others – especially if used for commercial purposes.

Currently, computers or PCs offer the most popular way to access the Net. A typical Internet-ready computer is one that uses phone lines and an Internet Service Provider as described previously to connect to the Net. In practice, most types of modern computer can be used on the Net but older PCs will almost certainly struggle to properly display many current web pages – especially those that contain animated components. Older slower computers usually have to work much harder to display complex web pages, and generally put more strain on your computer's hard drive (a kind of semipermanent memory).

However, you can also use a growing variety of other Internet access devices including web-compatible TVs (WebTV), Palmtop PCs, Psion Organisers and mobile phones. But times are changing quickly. Perhaps sooner than we might think, television may become the most popular way to access the Internet.

Low-priced and free Internet access

Although much of what is available on the Internet may be free, unless you're connecting to the Net using work, University or library facilities, the chances are you'll probably have to pay some connection fees to an Internet Service Provider, local phone rate charges, and if using the faster ISDN, ADSL or cable connections, you may have further costs to pay. However, the cost of Internet access in many different countries looks set to keep falling: only time will tell whether a completely free system is sustainable.

In March 2000, Alta Vista started a promising new trend in the UK by announcing plans to offer low-cost access to the Internet for UK users through a freephone 0800 number for day-to-day use. Within hours of this announcement, NTL, another well-established Internet provider, and mobile phone chain Phones4U also announced plans to offer completely free Internet access for UK subscribers. However, since those developments, many such companies have been unable to maintain offering completely free access.

The battle for market share has only just begun as existing Internet providers will almost certainly announce plans to compete with these new services. At the time of writing this book, the well-known domestic electronics product maker Alba announced plans to provide a low-priced Internet-ready television. Almost certainly, many other manufacturers will follow soon with similar offerings. Developments like these

> **BEWARE**
> Free/nearly free Internet access is a new concept in the UK and many other countries. Therefore, be a little cautious at least in the early days. If you sign up for low-cost access, do check the small print to determine whether any hidden charges might apply. If fast, reliable and regular access to the Internet is particularly important to you, do remember that during the early development stages of "free" Internet access, services may become swamped with a high number of new subscribers, which may in the short term affect connection quality and reliability until the providers are able to upgrade their services to properly cope with the new increased demands.

> **BEWARE**
> With those Internet Service Providers that do charge outside of free access times, often the cost is the same as the local phone call rate, maybe even a little lower. However, some providers may charge more so do check your subscription small print to avoid getting large unexpected phone bills.

are set to completely revolutionise the way we currently access and use the Internet and probably the best is yet to come!

Modem roundup

Let's recap. Most people currently use an electronic device called a modem to access the Internet. A modem may come built-in to a computer or you can connect an external modem to your PC. Most new PCs being sold now do contain a modem either as a plug-in card or in the form of electronic chips built into the main circuit board (motherboard). Also, modem-like devices are likely to be used in the new generation of Internet-ready televisions and other Internet access devices currently being developed and soon to be on sale in the shops.

Most PCs over 2 or 3 years old, however, probably didn't come with a modem as "standard." Add-on modems usually come either as a plug-in card that is inserted into a special slot in the computer or motherboard, or as an external box that you can simply connect to your computer with all the necessary wires and connectors provided. Modems are examined in depth on page 53.

Using a printer

Although a printer is not essential to access the Internet, sometimes you may need to print Internet or web documents. Most printers today come in three main types: dot matrix, inkjet, or laser. If buying a printer, consider buying the best colour inkjet or laser printer you can afford. Dot matrix printers generally don't print graphics as clearly as an inkjet or laser printer.

Whatever type of printer you decide to buy, do consider the running costs – especially printing ink or laser toner, as these can deliver some nasty shocks. Colour inkjet printers especially can use more ink than you might imagine – especially black which is necessary in order to create a wide range of coloured tints and shades in photographic-type images.

WebTV: the future here now

Easy access to the Internet through television is almost certainly the way of the future for most Internet users. Using a special type of remote control handset, this approach allows you to view and "travel" around the web on your television screen at the same time as watching television programs, perhaps in a smaller window. Switching between "television mode" and "Internet mode" is available with a single press of a button!

Popular in the USA at the time of writing, Internet-ready televisions are now becoming more widely available in the UK and other countries. So why has it taken so long? Well for a start, WebTV and computer display monitors use different display technologies.

Computer monitors use the **Red-Green-Blue (RGB)** system to create all the colours needed by mixing varying amounts of red, green and blue light. Televisions, however, need to receive and recreate a wide variety of colours and so use the more complex types of broadcast systems (the PAL system in the UK and NTSC in the USA, for example).

Computer monitors and WebTVs also have different viewing dimensions. For example, a display monitor may be described as 4:3; this means, if 4 units make up the screen width, 3 units make up the height. A modern television may use a 16:9 ratio. Therefore WebTV usually uses a special type of web browser;

one that is designed to reproduce web pages for television rather than a computer.

The electronic circuitry necessary to link a television to the Internet may be available in two main forms:

- As a **separate add-on** box placed near to the television.

- **Components built in** as part of a television's electronics.

Whichever method is used, most should be able to accept standard devices like printers, scanners and so on, in addition to standard telephone and cable TV connectors. But if you're buying, certainly check these facts.

Internet kiosks and terminals

If you want to explore the Internet but don't have your own PC, WebTV or other Internet access device, consider using somebody else's – with their permission of course! A growing list of options is becoming available.

As ever-cheaper access to the Internet continues, all sorts of entry points to the Internet are expected to develop. In time, it's likely that you'll find Post Offices, shops, garages and even ferries may also provide email and Internet services as standard. Airports and train/bus terminals are also likely targets for more Internet terminals – in fact any place where people are likely to meet has potential for creating income from Internet services.

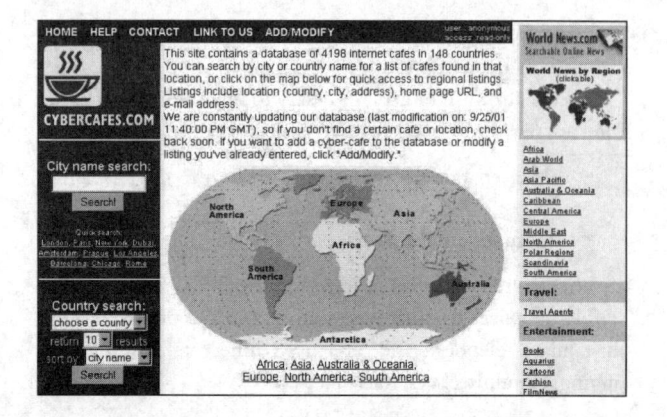

Cybercafés

If you live in or near many towns, you can escape from the office or home and visit your local cybercafé. There, you can enjoy light refreshments and optionally sit at a table that has a computer connected to the Internet. Often a great way to meet other users, perhaps enjoy a chat and have a fun time learning about the Net – especially if you're a new user.

Computer shops

Stores that sell computers often provide group demonstrations or presentations about using the Internet. Often, these kinds of promotion are likely to be biased towards the store's own products. However, you can learn much and perhaps get to try out those aspects of the Internet that interest you.

Public libraries and the Internet: perfect partners

Some public libraries in the know make Internet-ready computers available and even smaller local libraries can offer some free Internet access time. To use public library Internet computers, you'll probably need to reserve a time slot. The small public library in my own area – a suburb of one the UK's main cities – now provides free Internet access in prearranged 30 minute time slots; a wonderful way for anyone new to the Internet to experiment at their own pace.

Contact your local librarian for more information. Perhaps completely free Internet access will eventually become available, providing an entry point to the Internet for almost anyone. If you're completely new to the Internet, don't be afraid to ask for help; most library assistants are particularly helpful.

Don't forget trial Internet offers

If you're new to the Internet, reduced or free trial offers can be a great way to get started on the Net and try out different services. Most of the well-established Internet providers now offer a limited amount of Internet time free of charge.

However, do check the conditions: until completely free Internet access becomes available, you may still have to pay the local rate phone charges for every minute you're online. Again, check the small print in your subscriber agreements. Often, you can find the software you need to get on the Net free of charge from the cover-mounted CD-ROMs that accompany popular computer and Internet magazines. Using these options, you can try out a particular Internet service for about a month, and if you like their offerings, sign up.

Introducing Internet Service Providers (ISPs)

An Internet Service Provider is an organisation that can provide you with access to the Internet in return for a monthly or yearly fee.

Popular Internet Service Providers in the UK, for example, include BT click, BT Internet, Demon, Freeserve (Dixons), FreeUK, Global Internet and Netcom to name but a few. Until recently, some ISPs provided a limited number of free access hours each day or month. For a while, various Internet providers

Although as subscribers, we obviously want to pay as little as possible, remember subscription costs are only one aspect to measure the value for money you receive from an Internet Service Provider. Depending on what you want from an ISP, other considerations may be just as important – especially for business users who might stand to lose much if their Internet access or web presence is interrupted for any reason. In the following pages, we'll examine some desirable traits to look for in an ISP.

experimented with offering completely free Internet access – however, by 2001, most found this approach to be commercially unsustainable. Using the latest offers from some providers, you may only need to pay a small set-up or yearly subscription fee and use a freephone 0800, 0844 or 0808 number to get on the Net.

For example, BT Internet's "SurfTime" package provides completely free Internet access from 6pm–8am every weekday in addition to free weekend access – that is, midnight Friday through to midnight Sunday. During other times, only local call charge rates apply.

However, with BT's "AnyTime" package, you get 24-hour, 7-day dial-up modem-based access to the Internet for a monthly fee of about £15.

Looking for fast, 24-hour 7-day Internet access?

For users who may need to spend quite a lot of time on the Net, some providers offer continuous 24-hour/7-days a week unlimited Internet access for a fixed fee. However, always check any such agreement for any possible hidden charges or special limitations.

For example, at the time of writing, BT provide their "Home 500" ADSL package offering a maximum speed of 500 Kbps, and 24-hour/7-day Internet access for around £40/month for home users. ADSL is a technique often referred to as broadband, which essentially allows more information to travel across the Internet at the same time.

If we make the simple comparison with water pipes, ADSL/broadband is like a large diameter pipe, compared to a 56 Kbps modem which is like a small diameter pipe. A range of equivalent and faster options is also available for businesses. For more details, visit: www.btopenworld.com/

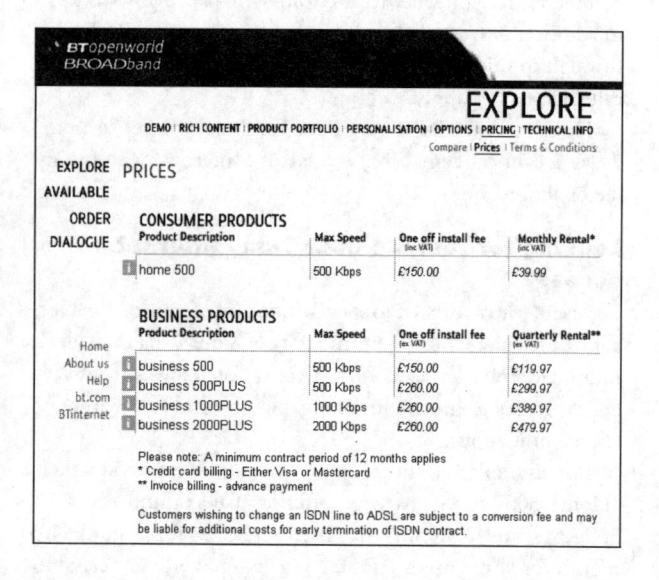

BTopenworld
BROADband

EXPLORE

DEMO | RICH CONTENT | PRODUCT PORTFOLIO | PERSONALISATION | OPTIONS | PRICING | TECHNICAL INFO

Compare | **Prices** | Terms & Conditions

EXPLORE PRICES
AVAILABLE
ORDER
DIALOGUE

CONSUMER PRODUCTS

Product Description	Max Speed	One off install fee (inc VAT)	Monthly Rental* (inc VAT)
home 500	500 Kbps	£150.00	£39.99

BUSINESS PRODUCTS

Home
About us
Help
bt.com
BTinternet

Product Description	Max Speed	One off install fee (ex VAT)	Quarterly Rental** (ex VAT)
business 500	500 Kbps	£150.00	£119.97
business 500PLUS	500 Kbps	£260.00	£299.97
business 1000PLUS	1000 Kbps	£260.00	£389.97
business 2000PLUS	2000 Kbps	£260.00	£479.97

Please note: A minimum contract period of 12 months applies
* Credit card billing - Either Visa or Mastercard
** Invoice billing - advance payment

Customers wishing to change an ISDN line to ADSL are subject to a conversion fee and may be liable for additional costs for early termination of ISDN contract.

Commercial online services

Commercial online services provide a range of their own information services and areas of special interest, like forum and Chat rooms, and access to the Internet. Examples include CompuServe, America Online (AOL) – who now own CompuServe – and the well-established and respected Computerlink Information Exchange (CIX).

> CAUTION: Using the Internet increases the risk of picking up a computer virus or of someone breaking or "hacking" into your computer: see www.grc.com/ for more information. Although the virus threat is often over-hyped with many so-called viruses found later to be hoaxes or easily removed minor viruses that do little damage, the threat nevertheless is real. If your computer becomes infected with a virus, at worst you could lose your entire data store – possibly a devastating blow to anyone in business.

CompuServe is popular with business and, to a lesser extent, individual users, whereas AOL provides content that is arguably more oriented towards individual users and families. Often, commercial online services supply their own software or customised versions of existing software, to provide access to their services or to use the Internet.

Online services like to promote the view that getting online is easier with them for new Internet users. Currently, like many Internet Service Providers, commercial online services usually allow you to try their service for free for a limited time, after which – if you decide to subscribe – you may have the option of a limited number of hours for free.

You may pay a fixed fee each month or year and outside of the free times you may only have to pay the equivalent of the cost of a local rate for each minute you're online. However, at the time of writing, some Internet Service providers have started offering low-cost or possibly free Internet access here in the UK. Similar moves may also start to affect other countries in Europe too. This trend may therefore soon change the nature and pricing of existing commercial online services in a variety of countries around the world.

> If you're in business and looking for free or cheap Internet access, check subscriber application conditions carefully to make sure that as a business, you're not excluded or have to pay extra charges. Some new free Internet access plans at the time of writing apply to non-business customers only.

Introducing domain names

In the same way a postal address ensures mail reaches a specific building, a domain name is an address of a computer somewhere on the Internet. Although sets of numbers are really used to indicate an Internet address, we humans much prefer words.

88 > Getting online

For example, for the full web address: www.ineasysteps.com, the domain name is ineasysteps.com This is much better than trying to work with something like 267.43.97.84, for example. The four sets of numbers make up what is called the Internet Protocol (IP) address. When you choose an Internet Service Provider, your web address and email address use their domain name.

Finding and choosing an Internet Service Provider

To gain access to the Internet, most people use an Internet Service Provider and connect using standard telephone lines or cable television services. Therefore, depending on your particular subscription package, you may have to pay for telephone charges or have other fixed or variable charges. Like the differences in people anywhere, Internet Service Providers are many and varied and can be found in many countries around the world.

> Some Internet Service Providers may offer unlimited Internet access in return for a fixed cost. Nevertheless, always check if any special restrictions or hidden charges may apply.

Until recently, local ISPs or ISPs based in your own country would have generally offered the most cost-effective Internet access. However, where an ISP is located is now not necessarily the most important choice factor! For example, the well-known Californian company Alta Vista recently offered low-cost Internet access to residents of the UK.

So how do you find the best ISP? Use the web and search for "ISP" or "internet service providers". You can also find regular reviews of ISPs in popular computer and Internet magazines – usually offering an excellent source of up-to-date information. Often, magazines might list what they consider to be the Top 10 ISPs, so perhaps by making comparisons across several magazines, this approach can help you come to a quick and reliable decision.

> If after trying an online service for a while you then decide to switch to another Internet Service Provider, don't forget to cancel your subscription with your original online service provider – otherwise you may still have to pay for something you're no longer using.

Alternatively, you can do your own in-depth investigation. Below is a checklist to help you choose an Internet Service Provider that meets your needs. If this seems long and detailed to you, remember that a little extra knowledge gives you power – it's then unlikely that a poor Internet Service Provider can fob you off with excuses if they don't meet their obligations. Consider making a list of what you want from your ISP, then compare what's on offer from a range of ISPs. Discover the differences and weigh up the pros and cons of each provider.

- **Dial-up cost:** if you're paying for every minute of Internet access, the dial-up access number your Internet Service Provider provides is important. Ideally, choose one that uses a local dial-up number (for example 0345 and 0845 in the UK). Often, a completely free Internet Service Provider may offer a better choice if available.

- **Internet time:** discover how much Internet time is available in the package you're considering. Some ISPs provide a fixed amount of free Internet time, beyond which local rate call charges may apply. Other ISPs give 24-hour / 7-day free access for a set monthly fee, or for a fixed yearly set-up charge.

- **Range of services:** covers the kinds of things an ISP provides – email, Internet access, newsgroups, FTP (page 409), web space, mobile phone links, automatic virus scanning, and so on. Some provide full access to all services; others may limit certain aspects like the kinds of newsgroups you can visit. Some newsgroups, for example, contain material that is intended only for adult participation (for example: porn sites). If you have children, you may prefer to have only a limited number of newsgroups available: ask ISPs about their policy and what options are available for control in these areas.

- **Connection options:** although for many users modem access may be fine, some business users may need faster access through ISDN, ADSL or cable modem access (page 245 onwards). With these more expensive connection options, compare and evaluate costs and benefits.

- **Set-up charges:** some ISPs may still charge a "registration" or "set-up" fee to cover the cost of establishing your account. Others provide all you need for no extra cost. The cheapest options may not necessarily offer the best overall value when all terms are considered.

- **Regular running costs:** once your account is set up, discover if you have to pay any regular running costs and if so, what are typical costs.

- **Modem-to-subscriber ratio:** the greater the number of modems an ISP has available at any one time, the more subscribers can connect at the same time. If the modem-to-subscriber ratio is too low, you might have to endure irritating delays when trying to connect. A ratio of 20–30 users to 1 modem may be reasonable;

15:1 is better. An ideal minimum is 10:1 and a good ratio is about 5:1.

- **Internet software:** the most well established Internet access software like Internet Explorer and Netscape Communicator/Navigator is now available free of charge. However, some providers may include their own customised software and charge a small fee on sign-up.

- **Access speed:** Internet access speed determines how fast you can view information and complete tasks on the Internet, so it makes sense to opt for the fastest speed you can afford. An Internet Service Provider determines overall access speed; therefore, choose an ISP that offers the fastest access speeds. Why? Even if you're using a standard 56 Kbps modem but your ISP only supports speeds up to 33.6 Kbps, your overall access speed slows down to match that of your ISP.

- **Technical support:** sometimes, you may need help to solve an Internet connection problem. If you're new to the Internet, it's not unreasonable to need extra help until you're more familiar with the Internet and getting connected. The better providers appreciate new users' needs and make email and phone support available to match. Email support is little help with an Internet problem if you can't get on the Internet in the first place, so 24-hour, 7-day, 365-days a year telephone support may be an important condition for you. Also, check at what phone rate technical support is charged: some provide freephone 0800 numbers, others charge local or even national call charge rates, and some charge more expensive Premium rates.

- **Get testimonials:** one of the best sources of information on an Internet Service Provider is its existing customers. Ask users of a service what they think about their Internet Service Provider. Visit support newsgroups (page 367) and read some posts.

> **HOT TIP**
>
> A particularly good test is to call an Internet Service Provider's technical support line at peak times to evaluate their response under those conditions. The best ISPs plan ahead and make provision for changing conditions.

- **Additional services:** some ISPs also provide extra services sometimes free, sometimes chargeable, which may interest you, for example, the provision of free fax services.

Website hosting Internet Service Providers

If you plan to create your own website, consider the following guidelines to help get the best value for money:

1. **Technical support:** 7-day, 24-hour email/live support with reply in less than 24 hours – under 12 is better.

2. **Contract duration:** ideally, get a no-minimum contract deal so that you can cancel without penalty at any time if they don't live up the their promises or if you're not happy with the service. To discourage you from cancelling, some providers may offer discounts if you sign up annually.

3. **Mirroring and peering:** applies particularly for those with websites hosted by an Internet Service Provider. Mirroring and peering ensure that your website provides the fastest connection speeds available.

4. **Email addresses:** you may think you'll want just one, but if you have a family, the chances are that at some stage everyone in the household might like an email address! Also, business website users may ideally need "unlimited" (or enough) email addresses or "aliases" to ensure you they can provide for services like:

orders@mycompany.com, support@mycompany.com – and so on.

5. **Autoresponders:** an autoresponder provides an automatic reply when an email is sent to a specific email address. Ideal for businesses, for example, to handle general sales enquiries or provide some clearly defined information without the need for people to be on-hand. Business users should try to get "unlimited" autoresponders, as they are now an almost essential Internet marketing tool.

6. **Downtime:** for website owners particularly. During "downtime", your website is not visible. A good web hosting company has 99% or more "uptime": 1% downtime is reasonable – though even 1% downtime can mean your website is invisible for over 3 days a year!

7. **CGI-bin:** no it's not an exotic dustbin, rather a CGI-bin provides special scripts and forms that web businesses will probably need.

8. **E-commerce compatibility, capability and support:** essential for web businesses that want to accept payments online 24 hours a day.

9. **Check 'em out live:** visit some websites hosted by an Internet Service Provider to evaluate their claims. Check things like speed of access, loading time, how helpful they are, and so on.

What happens when you connect to the Internet?

Once you have the necessary electronic hardware to connect to the Net, you'll need special software to do you want, for example: use email, browse the web, visit newsgroups, copy and download files. We'll examine the software you need in each chapter that covers the topic. Before we cover how to install your Internet access software, to help you know what to expect when you do connect to the Internet, the following paragraphs outline what happens.

Although many email programs can be set up to automatically disconnect once all new email messages have been downloaded to your computer and you have sent your messages, usually however, you can change the default settings so that once connected to the Internet, even if you choose to close your email program, you can still remain connected – an ideal way to free up resources on your computer to browse the web, visit newsgroups, chat online, and so on.

> If you choose different settings, you may not be able to connect properly to the Internet until the settings are correct for your particular Internet Service Provider.

Most users who access the Internet currently use a modem and the services of an Internet Service Provider. The modem dials a special phone number provided by the Internet Service Provider. This type of access is sometimes referred to as a dial-up service. Here's the sequence of what happens:

1. You **choose the command to dial your Internet Service Provider.** The software you install uses a special program to dial and connect you to the web.

2. Following the prompts that appear on screen, once connected, you may be asked to **supply a user name and password** – very often you can set up your software to remember this key information so that you don't have to keep entering these details every time you want to go on the Internet.

> Don't share your user name and password Otherwise, someone else can access all your email and use your web account. If you only have a limited amount of free web time, anything over and above this limit may be chargeable – to you. So if someone else is using your settings – and therefore your account – you'll get the bill!

3. Once **logged in**, you can use any of the various software applications to use the Internet. For example, you can answer email, browse the web, take part in newsgroups, chat online, and so on.

> Once you've connected successfully, consider keeping a written record of user name, password, access phone number, and other details. Then, if you need these details later, you have them to hand. Caution: just make sure you keep your record in a secure place. With these details, anyone can gain access to your Internet Service Provider account. One solution: Password Keeper from Gregory Braun at Software Design: www.execpc.com/~sbd.

Most email programs also allow you to set them up to dial-up, send and receive any emails and disconnect automatically, to save time and money if you have to pay for Internet access.

Connecting for the first time

If you've not installed Internet software before, don't worry if much of what follows in this chapter doesn't make much sense to you. Unfortunately, some jargon is unavoidable when discussing the options that get you linked to the Internet – the hardest part is connecting first time successfully. OK, let's get started. Before connecting to the Internet:

1. Always, always, always have installed **an effective antivirus program** that is kept up to date. Ideally, choose an antivirus program that scans email messages before downloading. For more information about antivirus programs, see also page 182.

2. Ideally, have your **antivirus tables updated at least every 2 weeks** especially if you use your computer often and reliability is critical to what you do.

3. Make **regular backups** of your data, ideally at least 2 copies, so that if a virus does get past your protection – no antivirus protection is 100% effective – you always have a copy of your up-to-date information intact. You may lose some information but at least you'll still have most data available to reinstall once your system is "cleaned."

As a general rule, always follow the guidelines provided by your Internet Service Provider for getting connected first time. If you have Call Waiting active on the phone line you're using, usually you'll need to turn it off as Call Waiting can confuse a modem.

You may not need to know some of the information provided in these paragraphs, so the process of getting connected should be easy. However, we've covered the business of getting connected for the first time in more detail here, just in case you come across problems and need to know a little more about what's going on.

Also, many Internet Service Providers include key information on their websites – not much help if you can't connect in the first place, I know, but in that event, maybe ask a friend who is already up and running to visit your Internet Service Provider's website and have a pen and paper handy. If you do come across problems, any Internet Service Provider worth doing business with wants you to get connected as soon as possible and as painlessly as possible. So if you're stuck, do give them a call: they are there to help.

> If you're new to the software procedure for setting up your Internet software, changing settings incorrectly can prevent you from getting access to the Internet temporarily – until the correct settings are reinstalled. A good guide is to write down original settings before making any changes so that, if the latest change causes problems, you can easily re-insert the original information.

OK, let's examine the "nuts and bolts" of connecting to the Internet. Computers use two types of software to get up and running on the Internet:

- **Internet access software:** actually gets you connected to the Internet. In your Internet documentation that accompanies your Internet package or computer, you might see this labelled as Dialler, Winsock or TCP/IP Stack software. Don't let the jargon worry you: in most instances, you don't need to know about the Winsock or TCP/IP Stack – just respond to the prompts your Internet software provides.

- **Internet application software:** lets you use the Internet once connected. Examples include web browsers, email programs, newsreaders and online Chat software.

Internet access software: a closer look

Your Internet access software component must be properly installed and set up before you can access the Internet. Internet access software is itself made up of 2 components:

- **Dialler software:** dials the correct phone number at your Internet Service Provider, and provides information to verify to your ISP that you are an authorized user. Microsoft names this component Dial-up Networking (DUN) software.

- **TCP/IP software:** once the dialler software has enabled a valid connection, the TCP/IP software ensures that your Internet applications can communicate properly with other computers on the Internet.

Microsoft Windows 9x/Me/XP/NT4/2000, and current versions of the Apple Mac, include Internet access software either directly or as an easy add-on component. When you install Internet application software like email readers, web browsers, and so on, usually you can set up the software so it automatically uses Dial-up Networking (DUN) to dial in to the Internet.

Checking your Windows 9x (and later) TCP/IP settings

Most Internet access packs perform most of the set up for you. However, for Microsoft Windows 9x and later users, you can make sure you have TCP/IP active by performing the following steps.

1. On the desktop, right-click the Network Neighborhood icon and select Properties.

2. With the Configuration tab shown, check that "Client for Microsoft Networks" protocol is listed (installed).

3. Also check that "Dial-Up Adaptor" is also installed.

4. If both are listed, click the OK button to close the dialog box.

HOT TIP While you're prompted to connect in Windows, you'll see an option to "Save password." Once you know the correct password, if you choose the option to remember your password, you won't have to keep entering your user name and password details every time you want to connect to the Internet. However, if you want to ensure maximum security do not choose the option to save or remember your password.

5. (Optional) If the items in steps 2 and 3 are not installed, click the "Add" button and install them one by one.

6. In the Primary Network Logon box, choose "Client for Microsoft Networks".

7. Click the "File and Printer Sharing" button to clear it. If either check box contains a tick, click the box to erase the tick. The only time you won't want to clear these boxes is when you want to share your computer information with other users on the Internet – usually you'll want to protect your files, so this area is an obvious security risk.

8. Click OK to confirm your settings and close the dialog boxes.

9. Close down and re-start your computer to enable your settings.

HOT TIP Also make sure you have the correct modem driver and the latest version installed. The author found that an updated driver not only cured intermittent dropped connections but also boosted Internet access speed by about 25%! Speak to your Internet Service Provider or modem dealer.

Installing Internet software from an Internet Service Provider

Simply follow the instructions provided in the set-up software or Wizard and respond to the various prompts. You'll probably need your user name, password details, dial-up number, and various other pieces of information.

In most instances, wizard-based software provided by your Internet Service Provider should make installation straightforward, but you will need some key information they provided to create your account. When finished a few minutes later, the end result is that you can successfully connect to the Internet with just one or two mouse clicks.

Some common terms you may come across when establishing your Internet settings

Below are some settings that you may need to install or change sometimes, in their usual sequence:

TCP/IP settings: in Windows 95/98/Me, if you connect to the Internet using a dial-up phone number and modem, each connection you set up is placed in your Dial-up Networking box. Here's how to get to it. For Windows 95/98, on the Windows desktop, click the "My Computer" icon, followed by "Dial-up Networking". For Windows Me, on the "Start" menu select "Settings" then "Dial-Up Networking". Then, for Windows 95/98/Me, in the "Dial-up Networking" box, you can make a new connection by choosing the "Make New Connection" icon to start the wizard and answering the questions it provides.

Or if you want to change or check the settings of an existing connection, right-click the icon you want and choose the "Properties" command.

If you're using Windows XP, you can simply run the Network Connection Wizard and answer the prompts to help get connected quickly.

If you're using an Apple iMac, use the following sequence to get connected: on the Apple menu, open the "Internet Access" folder and choose "Internet Setup Assistant", then follow the prompts.

Server Types: in Windows 95/98/Me, you can view the Server type for a specific connection. Here's how. For Windows 95/98, click "My Computer", followed by "Dial-up Networking". For Windows Me, on the "Start" menu select "Settings" then "Dial-Up Networking". Then, for Windows 95/98/Me, right-click on the desired connection and choose the "Properties" command. Click the "Server Types" tab.

Now under the "Types of Dial-Up Server" category, you'll probably see a "PPP" connection. Typically this might read: "PPP, Internet, Windows NT Server, Windows 98". Therefore, unless your Internet Service Provider tells you otherwise, choose "PPP" as your connection method. Why? This option usually provides the fastest Internet speeds for modem-based connections. To help speed things along, under the advanced options if your Internet Service Provider instructions allow (check first), choose the following options:

- Disable (no tick mark in the box) "Log on to Network" (unless you're told otherwise by your Internet Service Provider).

- Enable (click to place a tick mark in the box) "Enable Software Compression."

- Disable Require encrypted password.

Under the "Allowed Network Protocols" category, for Internet access, enable (place a tick mark in) the TCP/IP box.

Internet dialler software

When you sign up with an Internet Service Provider, they provide you with a user name and a password. Therefore, keep your user name and password details secure.

Earlier in this chapter, I mentioned dialler software. In Windows 95/98/Me, here's how to view, insert or change your dialler settings. For Windows 95/98, on the Windows desktop, click "My Computer", followed by "Dial-up Networking". For Windows Me, on the "Start" menu select "Settings" then "Dial-Up Networking". Then, for Windows 95/98/Me, right-click the connection you want and choose the "Connect" command. In the "Connect To" dialog box, you can enter or change your "User name", "Password", the "Phone number" you're using to dial your Internet Service Provider that gets you on to the Internet, and the "Dialling from" location.

Setting up your email and newsgroup software

The following settings need to be correct if you're to be able to send and receive email and visit newsgroups.

Microsoft Outlook Express: Here's how you can view and change these settings. First open the "Tools" menu and choose the "Accounts" command. In the "Internet Accounts" dialog box, click the "Properties" button. In the "Properties" dialog box, under the "General" tab, you can specify your name, organisation (optional), your email address (for example: joe@mysite.com) and include a reply email address if you want replies to go to another address.

Click the "Servers" tab and you can enter or change other essential settings. Two main types of email system are usually available to handle all email sent to you (incoming mail): POP3 or IMAP. For our purposes now, we don't need to know how they work, just which one your Internet Service Provider uses.

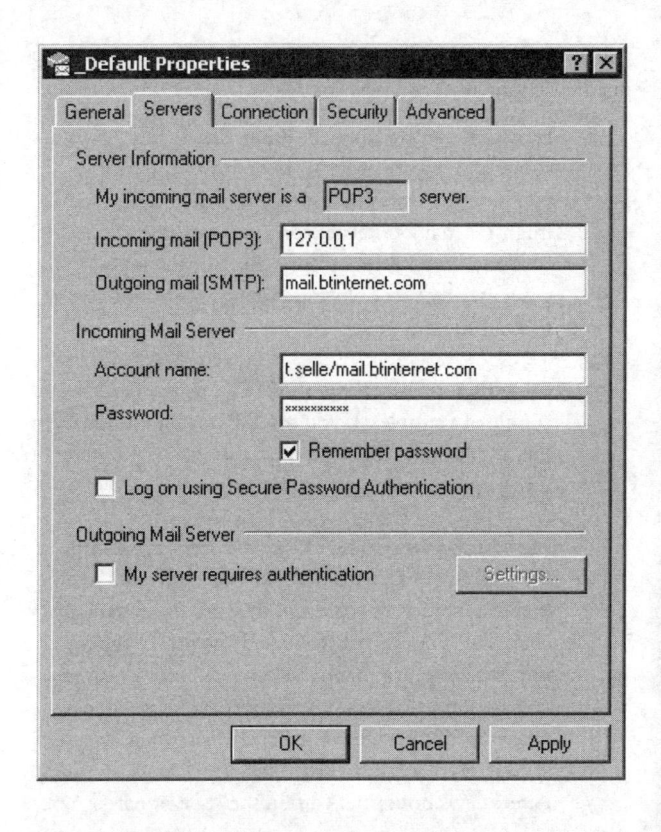

Most currently use POP3 but IMAP is growing in popularity. To recap, a mail server is a powerful computer that handles email. You'll need to know the name of the server for incoming mail, outgoing mail and newsgroups:

- **Incoming mail setting (POP3 or IMAP):** to give you some idea of the pattern, here are two examples. If you're a BT Internet subscriber, the POP3 setting might be: mail.btinternet.com; or if you have a LineOne account: pop3.lineone.net (the illustration on the previous page uses a Norton antivirus protection setting, so is a little different).

- **Outgoing mail setting (SMTP):** again, here are a couple of examples. If you're a BT Internet subscriber, this might be: mail.btinternet.com. Or if you have a LineOne account: smtp.lineone.net.

- **Newsgroup server (NNTP):** to access newsgroups in Outlook Express, with the "Internet Accounts" dialog box displayed as described in the previous paragraphs, click the "News" tab followed by the "Properties" button. Using the "General" tab, you can set up your newsgroup access in a similar way to your email set-up. Click the "Server" tab to enter or change your newsgroup server. BT Internet subscribers for example, might enter: news.btinternet.com in the "Server name" box.

Setting up other Internet software

If you're using Netscape Messenger, you can gain access to similar settings as previously described for Outlook Express. In the main Netscape Messenger window, open the Edit menu and choose the "Preferences" command. Under the settings in the "Mail & Newsgroups" category, you can insert or change existing settings.

For Eudora Pro, as a general guide, look under the "Special" menu and choose the 'Configuration' or 'Settings' command – depending on the version you're using. Other Internet access software provides similar options to those discussed in this section, so you can follow the pattern.

Dialling the Internet

Here we really mean dialling your Internet Service Provider – which is the same thing. However, if successful, the result is the same: a connection to the Internet. OK, let's cover this topic. Usually, when you install the Internet access software provided by your Internet Service Provider, once you answer the prompts that ask for the essential information listed in the previous paragraphs of this section, when you dial the Internet you can connect.

Now, the question you might ask is, how do I dial? In Microsoft Windows, usually, every time you start up your email program and choose the command to check your email box, the Internet dialler starts dialling automatically. Likewise, when you start up your web browser, the Internet dialler can be set up to dial automatically. Also in Windows, you can:

1. For Windows 95/98 click on "My Computer", or for Windows Me from the "Start" menu select "Settings".

2. Click "Dial-up Networking".

3. Then click on the dial-up icon you want in the Dial-up Networking box.

4. Finally click the "Connect" button.

To help make the process even easier you could even create a shortcut of the desired Dial-up Networking icon and place this on your Windows desktop. So next time, you could avoid steps 1 and 2 above. Once you start dialling, if you have a sound card and speakers installed, or equivalent, you can hear the modem make some strange noises – a little like fax machine tones. As you're connecting, you should also see some small dialog boxes appear on the screen telling you what is happening.

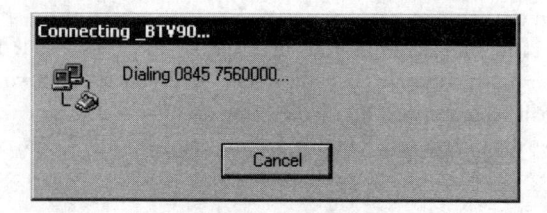

Also, if you haven't set up your system for automatic user name and password identification, before you can connect properly to your Internet Service Provider, you'll need to enter the correct user name and password for the account you're using.

Once connected, by default in Windows, you'll see a little icon appear in the lower right corner of the screen showing two computers connected or situated close together. You can double-click this icon at any time while online to view the speed at which you're connected, to see how long you've been online and there's an option to disconnect too. You can now check email, use the web, read from your favourite newsgroups, and so on.

What if I can't connect using a dial-up modem?

Usually, modems are quite reliable: the problem is more likely to be related to basic software settings and physical connections you've established. So always check the simple things first like:

- Is the power on?

- Are the connecting leads installed properly?

But if you still have problems, let's go back a couple of steps and try to analyse what's happening. If you have sound capability on your computer or Internet access device, listening to the sounds that are made can tell you quite a lot about what is going on and if you use this option regularly, you'll get to know the sounds that should occur when your connection is successful.

Here's what I mean in more detail. Before dialling, switch on your speakers and turn up the volume, then try dialling again. Usually, when you dial in successfully: the first thing you should hear after you choose the Connect button or equivalent is a brief dialling tone which sounds exactly like the tones your hear when you pick up a phone before dialling a number. Soon after, you should hear the different phone number tones being dialled – this is the dialler software performing its role. Usually, these may sound clearer when connecting using PPP rather than the older, slower SLIP system.

Now after the few dialling tones have completed, you'll hear some fax machine-type tones. What's happening here is your Internet Service Provider trying to recognize your account; this stage is sometimes called "handshaking". So at this time or soon after, you may be asked to enter your user name and password. If all is well, you'll get connected.

If you can't connect, considering the above sequence, try to discover where the problem might lie. Also, do remember, especially at busy times – certain times of the day and perhaps weekends – some Internet Service Providers may have too many users trying to dial in for their systems to cope with. However, you shouldn't come across this problem often.

If you do, contact your Internet Service Provider and try to get a guarantee of improvement or consider changing providers.

If you get a line-engaged tone, disconnect, and then try again a few seconds or minutes later. You may need to repeat this sequence several times at peak usage times. Here are some general suggestions if you still can't get connected:

1. **Are you getting a dialling tone?** If not, make sure that the modem phone lead is plugged into the computer or modem and the phone socket at the other end – and that your phone line is working of course.

2. **Is your modem dialling?** If not, if you're using an external modem, make sure that it is powered up and is in the "ready" state. One option to try is to turn off "Wait for dialling tone before dialling" in the modem settings. Here's how to get to it: Control Panel > Modems > General tab > Properties button > Connection tab. If the phone number does not appear to be answering or not responding properly, make sure you have the correct dial-up number. Try dialling a known voice phone number with someone available to answer. With sound switched on in your PC, if the modem is dialling properly, when the recipient answers, you know the modem and dialler software are working correctly, so the problem lies elsewhere. If all the above are fine and you're using an internal modem that is not dialling, it's possible the modem may be faulty. Read your modem documentation and contact your Internet Service Provider for advice.

3. If you get a dialling tone and the modem dials, but the software rejects your **user name and/or password**, first make sure you have the correct details entered. If you misspell just one character, the "handshaking" sequence as explained earlier will fail – it's an easy mistake to make – after all, passwords are often designed to be difficult to copy and remember as an added security feature. If you know that your details are correct, contact your Internet Service Provider – if your account is new, perhaps it has not yet been made live or some sort of mix-up may have resulted.

4. If your telephone connection keeps breaking while online, first, check whether you have Call Waiting active on that phone line – if yes, then an incoming call will probably break your connection – the modem may think a disconnect command has been entered. One remedy is to disable Call Waiting. Other possible causes for dropped connections include poor telephone line quality (a crackling line), too many extensions from one phone line and other people using phones connected to the same line at the same time you're connected to the Internet. If necessary, consider checking the TCP/IP settings and Server settings as explained earlier in this section. To access the Internet remember, your modem must also be properly installed in your Microsoft Windows or other operating system.

To check your modem settings, open the Windows Control Panel and click the Modems icon. Click the Diagnostics tab, select the modem you want to check, then click the "More Info" button. After a few seconds, Windows tells you if any problems are detected here, otherwise the "port information" is displayed.

If you can connect to the Internet but can't use one of your Internet programs, your modem is fine; the settings in the software may be incorrect. Try uninstalling the software and reinstalling once more or, if you're feeling really downtrodden, you might need the help of your Internet Service Provider.

Introducing Internet software to get things done

The Internet has many "faces" each fulfilling a different role. The software necessary to use these aspects of the Internet is often available free of charge. However, do check with the software owner or supplier on conditions of use, especially if being used for commercial purposes. To make full use of the Internet, you'll probably need the following kinds of software:

- **Email:** to send, receive and manage your email messages (pages 257, 301 and 345).

- **Web browser:** required to explore the web (page 119).

- **Newsreader:** most ISPs allow access to thousands of newsgroups (see also "Internet newsgroups", page 367).

- **FTP (File Transfer Protocol):** enables you to upload and download files to and from the Internet (page 409).

- **Web design:** If you want to create your own web pages, you'll need a web design application and probably a basic graphics touch-up program like Paint Shop Pro. (See also "Creating your own website" on page 439.)

A simple trick to (sometimes) boost connection speeds

Remember, the speed at which you connect to the Internet determines how fast you can send and receive email, how fast web pages display and so on. For 56 Kbps modems, typical Internet access speeds might reach 44 Kbps or more.

Once connected in Microsoft Windows, you can easily tell what speed you're connected at: by default, double-click the little icon of 2 connected computers in the lowermost right corner of the screen when you're connected to the Net. In the small window that appears, view the connection speed.

If you think your connection speed is slower than it should be even though you're using the correct and most up-to-date software drivers for your modem, here's one option to consider: tell your phone line provider you're getting a slow connection to the Internet and ask them to increase the **line gain**. In the UK, British Telecom currently provides this service free of charge (dial 151). Then try restarting your PC and connecting again to see if you now have an improved connection speed.

6
Exploring the web

So now you're up and running on the web. Doesn't it feel great? Like over 145+ million other Internet users worldwide, suddenly you have access to an awesome amount of free information from millions of web pages located on tens of thousands of computers around the world! My guess is you're just going to love having the keys to a million new doors. OK, let's have some fun.

The web (or if you like detailed explanations, the World Wide Web) is now one of the most important "faces" of the Internet. If the Internet is a large sprawling oak tree, the web is one of its strongest, most important branches.

Web browsers: windows on the web

To view the web, you'll need web browser software. You can then view web pages and discover new websites. Several software producers have created web browsers, including two of the most popular free-of-charge browsers today: Microsoft Internet Explorer and Netscape Navigator. Currently, the more popular of the two is Microsoft's Internet Explorer, which is now included as part of the Microsoft Windows operating system and more recently sold with new Apple Mac computers.

> **HOT TIP** You can have more than one web browser installed – you'll just need to make one your default browser.

Most web browsers operate in a similar way to each other, using menus, toolbars (rows of buttons), dialog boxes and windows appearing on the screen at various times. Using a browser's commands, you can move around a web page and navigate across a website or move to another website and start all over again. Or you can search the web for specific information (see also "Finding what you want on the Net", page 191).

Both Microsoft Internet Explorer and Netscape Navigator are often included on free CD-ROMs that accompany many of the popular computer magazines. Or you can download the software from the Internet ready for installation later – however, be warned that larger software products can take a long time to download using a modem connection. Once you have a web browser installed, whenever a new version becomes available, you can install the upgrade to keep in step with the latest web developments. Microsoft Windows can make browser updating for Internet Explorer even easier through the Windows Update command provided on the Start menu.

> Your browser software usually contains commands that let you change which page appears as your default Home page. Hint: look under the program Options category in your web browser software.

What happens after I connect?

After you've installed the Internet access software usually provided by your Internet Service Provider, when you first connect to the Internet, your web browser starts and you're usually automatically connected to your Internet Service Provider's Home or Index web page. If you imagine you have just opened the front door to a large house, a Home or Index page is like the first room or floor space you see. The default Home page usually takes a few seconds to appear – but might take a while if, at the time you connect, the Internet is busy. Popular times include, of course, weekends.

A typical web page contains text and images and is often designed like a printed magazine – except that, with a web page, you "turn the pages" by clicking on special links. More on this later.

> **HOT TIP** If, while navigating the web, you feel lost, you can usually display your default Home/Index page easily: click the "Home" button on your main browser toolbar. You can identify what each button does simply by holding the mouse pointer steady on top of a button for a few seconds.

What can I do on the web?

Once you are connected to the web and have a web browser available at your fingertips, you have access to an incredible range of choices. What's more, the web is easy to use: just move your mouse pointer where you want to go and click. Here's just a taster of what you can do on the web:

- Visit your favourite web pages.

- Search for specific information.

- Beat the traffic and the queues: visit your bank and pay bills online.

- Visit your supermarket and do your grocery shopping.

- See what's on offer for a great holiday – and order your tickets online!

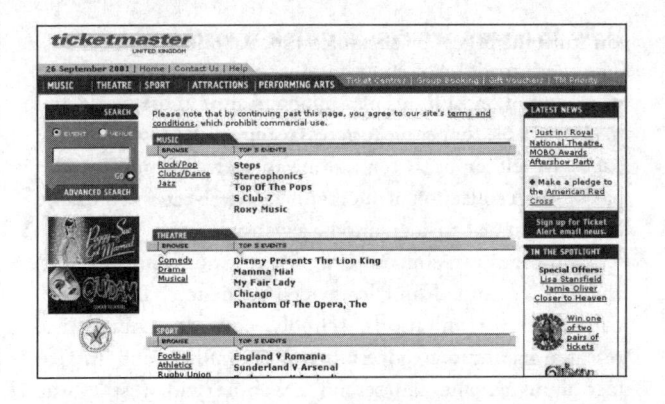

- Check out your investments online – and make some money!

- Watch your favourite TV show.

- Listen to radio.

- Play and download some music and video clips.

- Find a new job.

- Create your own web pages.

How the web works: a quick overview

The web is made up of a huge number of documents called web pages stored on millions of computers around the world and made available for people to access using a web browser. These pages are either open for anyone to view or you'll need a password. A collection of interconnected web pages at the same location can be considered to be a website.

Web pages can contain text, pictures, animations, sounds and both recorded and live video sequences. Individuals, companies, organisations, schools, colleges, universities, research institutions, governments, the military and, in fact, just about anyone can set up a website with just a little knowledge and some know-how – and this book can show you what you need to know.

Physical distance or location is not really relevant on the web in terms of navigation, so you probably won't know if the page you're viewing is located on a computer a few blocks away or half way around the world. But the point is, it doesn't matter where the original web page is located.

The web offers easy, low-cost (and more commonly now, free) access to an incredible ever-growing variety of information! One of the great things about the web – and the key to its amazing rate of growth – is that it is so easy to use. Users don't need to know much about computers – that's the web's great advantage. You simply get online and in your web browser, either:

- Enter the web address you want in the "Address" box or "Go to" box above the main browser window pane, and press the Enter key or…

- Move your mouse pointer to a web page link you want and click it. In seconds – usually – your desired web page is displayed on your screen, providing the web address you choose exists and is available online. More on this topic later.

Although the web is not owned by anyone, key organisations help it develop and improve, to meet ever-growing demands from users. One of the most important steering bodies is the World Wide Web Consortium (W3C) – a group of companies and organisations that help develop new standards for the web. The W3C is actually run by the Laboratory for Computer Science at the Massachusetts Institute of Technology (MIT).

Introducing hyperlinks: the invisible thread that binds the web

The single most important component that makes the web so powerful is the link to other pages. Links are sometimes known by other names, for example: hyperlinks, hypertext and hot-links (but let's use the word links).

A link can be made up of text, a picture or another object and can easily be identified. Some text links are shown highlighted in bright blue and underlined. With another type of link, when you place your mouse pointer over it, the link changes colour.

With some text links and all graphically-based links, the mouse pointer symbol usually changes to a pointing hand as soon as you place the mouse pointer on a link object. Also with most browsers, while your mouse pointer is placed on a link, the web page address to which the link points is also shown in the display bar at the bottom of your browser window.

If you click on a link shown on a web page, the contents of the web browser window changes to display the contents of the page you chose. In this way, you have moved from one web page to another position on the same web page or to an entirely different web page. To recap, a web page link can point to another:

- Position on the current web page.

- Web page at the same website.

- Web page stored on a separate computer (web server) at another website – which may be local to you or situated on the other side of the world! Remember, distance doesn't really matter on the web!

More on the Home or Index page

When you first reach a website, you know one of the first pages you usually see is the Home or Index page. Traditionally, non-business oriented websites usually refer to their main entry page as the Home page. Business websites often prefer the more formal Index page. Some mainly business-oriented websites use an introductory page that is displayed before the main Index page appears. An introductory page links only to the Home/Index page either automatically after a preset time delay, or when a visitor clicks the only link on the page. From the Home/Index page, you can usually gain access to all other pages on the website – although some pages may require a password.

> **HOT TIP**
>
> If you want to start your web browser without being prompted whether you want to connect to the Internet, you can change your default Start-up page to a blank page rather than any particular web address. In Internet Explorer v5.0 and later, you can choose the Internet Options command in the Tools menu to display the Internet Options dialog box, and with the General tab displayed, click the Use Blank button, followed by OK to have a blank page displayed when the browser starts.

How do I change my Home/Start page?

You can change the Home page that usually appears first every time you connect to the Internet. Do remember, however, that your default Home page probably contains information that is useful and helpful to new users especially. However, before changing the Home page, it's worth making a note of its web address, so that if you change your mind, you can always reinstall your original Home page easily.

Here's what to do. Get a pen and paper and look in the Address box usually just above the main web browser window. Here's an example of a web address – also called a URL: www.ineasysteps.com (To build in more impact, this domain

> **HOT TIP**: Today's web browsers are "clever"! Often you may not even need to type any web address, instead just click the links you want on a page to move around a website and around the web. The point is, where a web page is located is not usually relevant to your web browsing session.

name could also be promoted as: www.InEasySteps.com – web browsers treat them exactly the same.) So write down the address of your default Internet Service Provider's Home page. Every web page on the Internet has a web address.

In Internet Explorer, the web page address is placed in the box immediately to the right of the word Address. In Netscape Navigator, the Address box is usually labelled either "Location" or "Netsite" when a web address is present. If the box is blank, Netscape changes the box label to "Go to". Alternatively, you can just save your original Home page. Internet Explorer calls a web address that is saved for access later a Favorite, while Netscape uses the term Bookmark. See page 152 for more information on working with Bookmarks and Favorites.

> **HOT TIP**: Individual web page names usually end with .htm, .html or .shtml. However, some newer database-driven websites may use other filename extensions, like .asp and others.

Introducing the HyperText Markup Language

HyperText Markup Language or HTML is the basic computer language used to create web pages. However, HTML has already been available for several years with at least three revisions to-date: v2, v3.2 and v4. The latest advances have resulted in the development of Dynamic HTML (DHTML) to provide a much richer and more animated web environment.

Dynamic HTML allows self-running programs on a web page to operate in various ways even after a web page has fully downloaded. In an HTML-based page, once the page has downloaded, usually what you see is what you get. Entirely new changes only happen when the user clicks a link or performs an action on the page. However, sometimes "richer" web pages may take longer to download and some visitors may not be prepared to wait.

In a DHTML page, an animated component, for example, can "play" even after a page has fully downloaded into a web browser. DHTML is not just a single development but rather several technologies combined that allow events to happen without needing to communicate with the web server (the computer that makes a web page available to anyone) or have a user perform any steps to complete the action. JavaScript – another basic computer language – is one of these key technologies used in DHTML. However, to "view" JavaScript your web browser must have this option turned on.

What you need to know about URLs

Each web page needs to have a unique address and in fact a more formal name for a web address is a Uniform Resource Locator (URL). A URL can also tell us quite a lot about that particular page. Here's an example of a web address (URL): http://www.ineasysteps.com. This web address points to Computer Step's Home or Index page – the full address might be: http://www.ineasysteps.com/index.html – however, most web servers nowadays are set up to need only the basic web address.

In most modern web browsers, you don't usually even need to enter the "http://" component if you're entering a web address. For example "www.ineasysteps.com" is usually enough. Also, most current browsers assume the web address you're entering ends in ".com", unless you enter another type of ending address (like ".co.uk", for example). Therefore, continuing the example above, most current web browsers need only: ineasysteps.com to find this website.

Don't worry if this makes web addresses look confusing: they're really no harder to understand than a postal address, just a little different. So let's recap and take a closer look at what's actually in a web address in more detail:

- Traditionally, web addresses are written using lower case letters, but most web browsers now accept upper or lower case letters.

- Every web page contains the first part "http://" which stands for HyperText Transfer Protocol. The colon (:) and two forward slashes form the last essential part of the protocol. If you omit http:// when entering a web address, most browsers are now intuitive enough to include it automatically, so usually, you won't need to enter http://

- The following three letters: "www" stand for World Wide Web. Most web pages also will have "www" included. A full stop always follows "www". If the web address you're looking for ends in ".com" (and sometimes .org and .edu), again, with most modern browsers, you may not even need to enter "www". For example, to find Computer Step at http://www.ineasysteps.com, often you only need enter: ineasysteps.com – as we use the default .com domain name extension. **Key point:** this is one reason why dotcoms are currently considered the most valuable domain names and perhaps why currently there's a shortage of good quality cheap dotcom names.

- The third part of a web address is the host name of the particular website or page, often referred to as the domain. In our example above "ineasysteps.com" is the domain name that points any web browser to the first page in the Computer Step website. Host names can use upper or lower case characters, so "ineasysteps.com" and "InEasySteps.com" are considered to be the same. Note that no spaces are allowed here and a full stop is always placed between the host name and the domain name extension (".com" in this example).

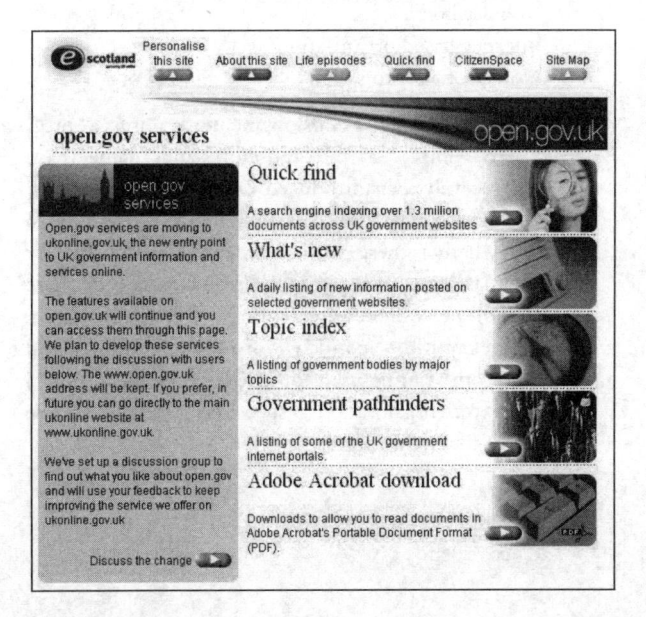

- Finally, the last component – the domain name extension – identifies the kind of website to which the page belongs. In our example, ".com" stands for a company or other commercial organisation. Here are the most popular current choices:

Academic institutions:	ac
Company or commercial organisation:	com
UK or New Zealand company:	co (.uk/.nz)
Educational institution:	edu
Government establishment:	gov
Military body:	mil
Internet-based organisation:	net
Non-profit organisation:	org

Some new domain extensions including: ".info", ".pro", ".aero", ".biz", ".coop", ".museum", and ".name" have also recently been introduced. Other proposals include: ".firm", ".banc", ".ltd", ".eu" and so on. It's too early to tell whether these will become well established or popular. You can also mix and match extra codes here to indicate your website's country of origin if desired. For example, ".co.uk", ".org.uk", ".ltd.uk", and ".uk.com" can be used for UK-based companies and non-profit organisations respectively. Below is a sample list of the main countries:

Australia:	.au
Canada:	.ca
Cocos Islands	.cc

Denmark	.dk
Germany:	.de
Spain:	.es
France:	.fr
Israel	.il
Japan:	.jp
The Netherlands:	.nl
New Zealand	.nz
Norway:	.no
South Africa	.sa
Taiwan:	.tw
United Kingdom:	.uk

Note: the USA is omitted as any domain lacking an individual country identifier suggests that the web organisation may be US-based. However, in practice ".com", ".net". and ".org" can also suggest an international organisation.

Finding a web page quickly

Often, if you know the full web address of a specific page, you can enter it into your web browser Address box instead of navigating to the Home/Index page and clicking on the various links to arrive at your desired page. For example, imagine I wanted to move to a page at Computer Step's website that described a book on web page design, I need only enter the following in my browser: "www.ineasysteps.com/ineasysteps/web-page-design.html". Quite a lot to remember.

However, there's an easier way. This imaginary example shows that a web page named "web-page-design.html" is stored in a web folder called "ineasysteps" that is accessible from "ineasysteps.com". Once you have found a page you want in this way, you can save it for easy access later as a favorite in Internet Explorer or as a bookmark in Netscape Navigator. Then, next time you want to return to this page, you won't need to enter the full web address; simply click the favorite or bookmark link.

Working with non-web based URLs

To gain access to parts of the Internet other than the web, you'll need to change the first part of a URL (http://) and replace it with something else:

- "ftp://" followed by the remaining part of the address, points to a File Transfer Protocol (FTP) site. For example: ftp://ftp.computerstep.com/books/pdf/wpd/chapter1.txt

While downloading software and information from the web, long download times may be acceptable if you have lots of free or low-cost access to the Net, but probably completely impractical if you have to pay for every second while online. In that event, check whether any free CD-ROMs from computer magazines may contain what you want.

Key point: you may not even need to enter ftp:// as most browsers today know that what follows is an ftp-related address (for more about FTP, see also page 409).

- "news:" is used to access newsgroups. Note, you don't need to include the two forward slashes (//) – only the colon (:) – to enter a newsgroup name. For example, if I wanted to go to a gardening newsgroup on orchids, I only need enter "news:rec.gardens.orchids"

Web portals: information magnets

During the 1990s, lots of new buzz-words began to appear about various aspects of the Internet: web portals, web communities and hubs are three of the more popular labels for example. A web portal is really a fancy name for a website that offers a doorway to information about a specific topic – not necessarily the Internet either – although a portal can form an ideal starting point to discover all about the Internet.

By grouping information topics together in this way, website providers can make things easier for web users – and anything that does this always get attention, doesn't it? The idea is to provide quick access points to the popular themes. Many also offer extra features, for example:

- Free web-based email services, so that wherever you are in the world, providing you can gain access to the web, you can use email.

- The ability to customise your own portal Home page so that you can work with only the kinds of things that interest you every time you switch on your computer and log on to the web.

- Chat services enable you to talk with other subscribers from around the world live (sometimes referred to as "real-time") on topics that interest you!

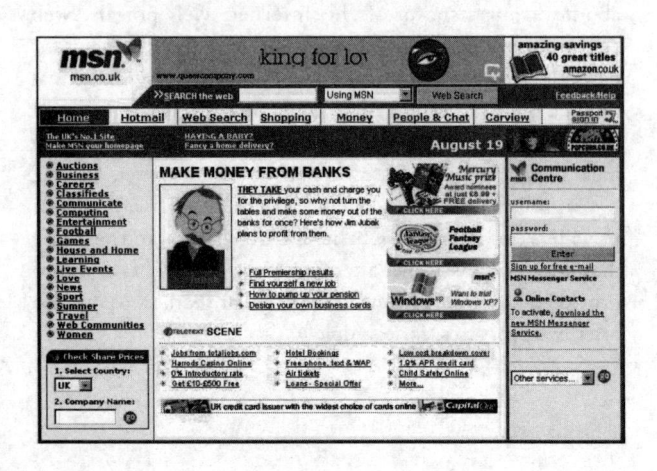

- Key information like national and world general news and sports news, and finance information to help you closely monitor financial markets, track your favourite shares, etc., and generally see what's happening around the world.

Web portals, search engines and directories have much in common as most web portals also provide fast search facilities. Popular examples include Yahoo – www.yahoo.com (and .co.uk), MSN – www.msn.com, Excite – www.excite.com and Netscape – www.netscape.com.

Streaming multimedia fun on the web

We live in a world that is dominated by our five senses with colour, movement and sound playing a central role. On the web, designers can entertain or entice through the effective use of text, pictures, sounds, animation and moving video images. The combination of any or all of these components is what we call multimedia.

Business websites especially sometimes like to use multimedia to help sell their products and services – after all, video can be highly enticing can't it? Or you can hear simple sound clips or sound sequences on a web page or listen to your favourite pop, rock and classical works.

If you need a lift, why not visit the movies: hear your favourite movie sound tracks and gripping video clips. With streaming live multimedia, perhaps you can still see that "must have" concert or sports event for which you just couldn't get the tickets this time. Discover what's going on in the world: watch your favourite news program on the web or play back video sequences of your favourite celebrities.

To play streaming multimedia, you'll probably need an Add-on program if it doesn't come with your browser. Two of the most popular are RealPlayer from RealNetworks (www.real.com) and NetShow from Microsoft (www.microsoft.com/netshow/vxtreme/plugin.htm).

7

A closer look at web browsers

Your web browser is your own powerful doorway into the amazing World Wide Web and other parts of the Internet. Today, although several types of web browser are available, the vast majority of Internet users choose either Microsoft Internet Explorer or Netscape Communicator/Navigator. So in this chapter we'll mainly examine these browsers in more depth.

At the time of writing, Microsoft Internet Explorer is by far the more popular of the two. Internet Explorer is considered by many to be closely linked with the Microsoft Windows operating system, and like Netscape Communicator/Navigator, Internet Explorer (IE) is available free of charge, so perhaps this too has been a major factor in its amazing growth take-up.

However, bucking the trend for ever-larger memory demands is Opera, a slick web browser, email program and newsreader suite from Norway that makes surprisingly light demands on a computer – unlike the two generally larger heavyweights Microsoft Internet Explorer and Netscape Navigator. Opera v5.x now also comes free of charge; you can install a copy from: www.operasoftware.com However, earlier versions of Opera might have problems handling some JavaScript in some websites: check the relevant documentation.

What's in Microsoft Internet Explorer?

Internet Explorer allows you to not only browse the web but can also closely integrate with your Microsoft Windows Desktop and help manage a company network if required.

Both Internet Explorer and Netscape Navigator have grown from a single product (web browser), but which now includes several other add-on programs that handle: email, newsgroups, web page creation, Internet telephony, online Chat and various multimedia enhancements including:

- **Microsoft Outlook Express:** one of the most popular email programs and Newsreaders. For information on newsgroups, see page 367.

- **NetMeeting:** a program that allows you to communicate live with another person on the Internet. For more information about Microsoft NetMeeting, see page 397.

> Modern web browsers are amazingly powerful tools and like powerful software everywhere can sometimes be confusing to use. However, don't forget lots of online Help is usually available through the Help menus and at the websites of the various web browser providers.

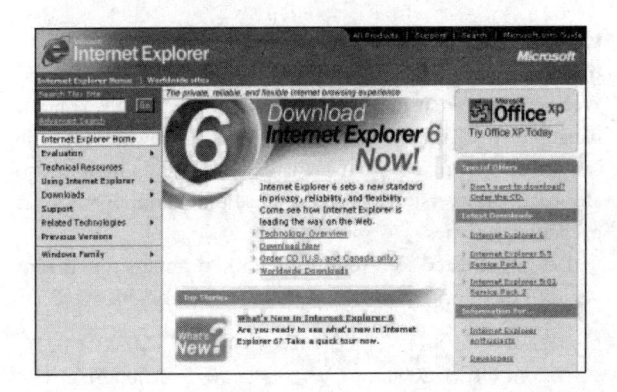

- **Microsoft FrontPage Express:** a basic web page creation program. For more information about web design, see page 439.

- **Windows Media Player:** ideal for playing many popular video and audio clips that are included on many websites – including of course, Microsoft's own streaming media files.

Internet Explorer includes some helpful additional features including IntelliSense, which can "remember" various settings and complete common entries for you. For example, with IntelliSense turned on, when you enter a user name a second time, IntelliSense can automatically insert the accompanying password for you in the relevant box.

Identifying your Internet Explorer version number

Web browsers are usually updated at regular intervals. You can usually identify the version of your current browser from the "About…" command often available on the Help menu. Also any particular version might have a build number to cover particular varieties.

Below are listed some common build numbers for current versions of Internet Explorer 5.0, 5.5, 6.0 and Netscape 6.x:

IE5.0:	5.00.2014.0216
IE5 in Office 2000:	5.00.2314.1003
IE5 for Windows 98 Second Edition:	5.00.2614.3500
IE5.01:	5.00.2919.6307
	5.00.2920.0000
IE5.5 Developer Preview (beta):	5.50.3825.1300
IE5.5 with Internet Tools beta edition:	5.50.4030.2400
IE6.0:	6.00.2462.0000
IE6.0:	6.00.2600.0000

So by looking at the build number, you can identify your particular version more accurately – which is sometimes useful for problem solving: your Internet Service Provider may ask for this information. At the time of writing, Internet Explorer has reached v6 moving up from v5.5. If you're using versions earlier than 4.0, your browser may struggle to properly display many of the web pages today.

My advice is to upgrade to the latest version as soon as you can. Internet Explorer v5.0 and later versions also make fewer demands on the operating system of a computer and so are arguably more stable, although a few strange quirks have been identified in the different "builds". Nevertheless, the general development trend is that newer browsers can be more demanding, so if you're using an older computer, your web browsing sessions may perform better with an older browser.

Tuning in to your own channel on the web

A striking feature of Internet Explorer is that you can also view "channels" covering a wide range of information topics. A "channel" website can automatically deliver only information that you're interested in at specific times. You simply "subscribe" to a specific channel and set the times you want. Channels can cover a wide range of topics, for example: travel, business, news, finance, stocks and shares, entertainment, computing, Internet, movies, etc.

Checking Internet Explorer browser security

Although recent versions of Internet Explorer have included additional security updates to further protect users when buying online, some browser weak points have also been identified. The latest updates and patches are usually available from the Microsoft Update website. For more information and access to the latest upgrades, bug fixes and updates, see: www.microsoft.com/ie/

You can also use the "Windows Update" command. If your version of Windows followed the standard installation route, click the Windows Start button and Windows Update should be installed on your Start menu.

Alternatively, in the Internet Explorer v5.0x/6 main window, Windows Update is also available in the Tools menu. However, do remember that web browser software can now take up megabytes of hard drive space, so downloading and performing updates while online can take quite a while. Unless you have uninterrupted cheap 24-hour Internet access, a better option might be to use update options that are often available on a CD-ROM or DVD.

Once you disconnect from the Internet, when you reconnect again, your browser doesn't remember the previous Forward/Back sequence. The Forward/Back buttons work only for the current session.

What's in Netscape Communicator/Navigator?

Both Internet Explorer and Netscape Navigator have grown from a single product (web browser) several years ago, to now include several other add-on programs which handle: email, newsgroups, web page creation, Internet telephony, online Chat and various multimedia enhancements.

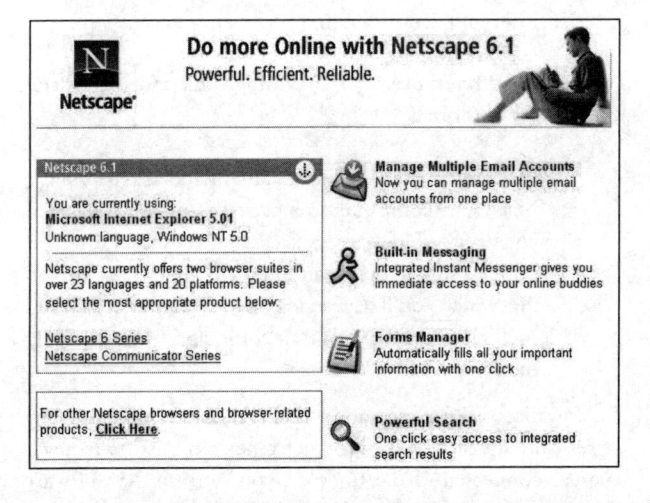

> **Netscape**
>
> **Do more Online with Netscape 6.1**
> Powerful. Efficient. Reliable.
>
> ---
>
> Netscape 6.1
>
> You are currently using:
> **Microsoft Internet Explorer 5.01**
> Unknown language, Windows NT 5.0
>
> Netscape currently offers two browser suites in over 23 languages and 20 platforms. Please select the most appropriate product below:
>
> Netscape 6 Series
> Netscape Communicator Series
>
> For other Netscape browsers and browser-related products, **Click Here**.
>
> **Manage Multiple Email Accounts**
> Now you can manage multiple email accounts from one place
>
> **Built-in Messaging**
> Integrated Instant Messenger gives you immediate access to your online buddies
>
> **Forms Manager**
> Automatically fills all your important information with one click
>
> **Powerful Search**
> One click easy access to integrated search results

Amazingly, most essential Internet and web software is now available free of charge today! Netscape Communicator is the name used to describe a suite of programs that include the web browser Netscape Navigator. Netscape Communicator comes with a range of utilities, including:

- **Messenger:** a powerful email program and newsreader.

- **Composer:** a basic web page editor.

- **Netscape/AOL Instant Messenger:** a live/instant Internet Chat program.

- **RealPlayer:** plays live streaming audio/video clips and other formats.

- **NetWatch:** a tool that is now also included as part of the Netscape Communicator package and is available if you want to block access to certain websites. However, unlike a similar option in Internet Explorer, to turn on NetWatch you'll have to log on to the Internet first and then choose the NetWatch command from the Help menu.

For more information and access to the latest upgrades, bug fixes and updates, see: www.netscape.com Also, whenever you're connected to the Internet, you can use the Software Update command in the Help menu and follow onscreen instructions. However, again, do remember that downloading and performing updates while online can take quite a while.

Unless you have uninterrupted cheap 24-hour Internet access, a better option might be to use update options on a CD-ROM or DVD.

Earlier versions of Netscape Navigator

At the time of writing, the latest version is 6.1. Earlier versions worth mentioning include: 4.6, 4.5x, 4.08, 3.x and 2.1.

If you have an older version installed, consider upgrading as soon as possible to the latest stable web browser version, as earlier versions may not be able to handle some current web pages properly. However do remember, modern web browsers usually include several other add-on programs and therefore may need a surprising amount of storage space on your computer.

Web browsers: the menu bar

With the main web browser window visible, at the top of the window just underneath the Title bar is the browser menu bar. Here all the commands you need to set up your browser and surf the Internet are available.

Toolbars and buttons

The commands you'll probably use most while using the Internet are easily available in the form of buttons usually placed just below the menu bar. So instead of having to open the menu you want and choose your command, you can instead simply click the button you want.

Usually, you can quickly discover the name or purpose of a button simply by placing the mouse pointer on the button you want briefly – the program then shows a text description next to the button which disappears when you move the mouse.

> The standard Copy and Paste commands are usually available in browsers if you want to copy information into another program. However, do remember copyright and laws that may apply.

Forward and Back buttons

The Forward and Back buttons usually allow you to navigate to pages you have visited while online during the current browsing session. To go back to a previously visited page, simply click the Back button, as many times as necessary until you see the page you want. Likewise, you can move forward through a sequence using the Forward button.

The Home button

Whenever you want to return to your browser Home/Index or Start-up page, click the Home button – which in both main browsers can easily be identified with a house symbol/icon.

Stop and Refresh/Reload buttons

Sometimes after you click a link to move to another page, the page you want may not appear, display too slowly, have errors, and so on. Or you may change your mind and decide to visit another page. The Stop button allows you to cancel an action.

The Refresh or Reload button allows you to re-display a page with the most up-to-date information. Some pages contain information updated every few seconds; Refresh lets you see the latest display. Refresh actually causes an older version of a page that may be stored in your browser's cache memory, to be replaced by the most recent version. Also, Refresh is sometimes useful if a page fails to load properly.

The Address or Go to box

The Address or Go to box holds the web address of a web page. You can enter a web address in this box or if you click a link on a web page, your browser software places the destination web address of the page you want in the Address or Go to box. Internet Explorer v5.0 (and later) uses IntelliSense – a software tool that, when turned on, attempts to guess what you're entering as you type a web address into the Address box.

IntelliSense examines your History list and Favorites as you type, so you may not even have to enter a full web address before IntelliSense finishes it for you. Netscape Navigator versions also use a similar approach by examining your browser's History list.

The right mouse button short-cuts

IBM-compatible PCs can make use of an extra set of menu command short-cuts only available when you press the right mouse button – by default. The actual commands presented depend on which part of the browser window your mouse pointer is on when you click the right mouse button. For example, in Internet Explorer, using the right mouse button commands you can quickly choose the Add to Favorites command. Or you can place the mouse pointer on an image and choose the Save Picture As command.

Bookmarks and Favorites

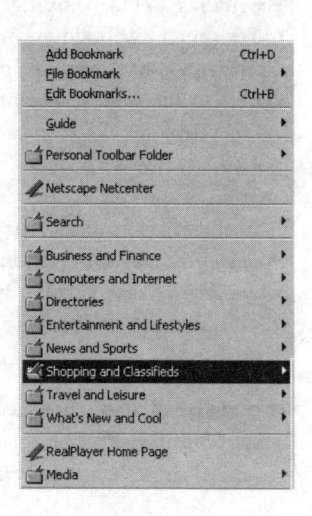

Web addresses or URLs are not the easiest of entries to type: enter one character incorrectly or insert a space where there shouldn't be one and the web address will be incorrect – probably forcing an error page to be displayed instead of the page you want. To help make the task of entering web addresses easier, web browsers let you save the web addresses of the websites you like best or want to visit frequently so you won't have to enter an address next time. Internet Explorer calls these Favorites – note the US spelling convention is used here. Netscape Navigator uses the term Bookmarks, but both names essentially fulfil the same purpose.

In Internet Explorer, the Favorites command is available as a button on the main toolbar or from the Favorites menu. When you opt to save a website as a Favorite in Internet Explorer version 5.0x/6, you can also check the "Make Available Offline" check box, to save the desired website and those pages linked to it, so you can browse the site content offline.

Also, at specific intervals, you can set up Internet Explorer to check for any changes and update the copy stored on your computer to match. You can also rearrange Favorites using the Organize Favorites command on the Favorites menu.

In Netscape Navigator, you can find the Bookmarks button on the Location toolbar usually directly under the main Navigation toolbar; or the Bookmarks commands are available from the Communicator menu. Netscape Navigator provides the Edit Bookmarks command from the Bookmarks command or the button on the Location toolbar to rearrange bookmarks. Also, Update Bookmarks from the Edit Bookmarks command allows you to check for bookmarked sites that have changed since you last saved them.

The History list

As you move from page to page while browsing the web, sometimes you may want to return to a web page that you visited some time ago. The best web browsers record the websites you visit and make these available in the History list.

You can then easily gain access to the History list using the History button or its equivalent command. Although in some instances, you can use the Forward and Back buttons to find a page you visited previously, the History list is much more powerful. In Internet Explorer, the History command is available from the History button, and in older versions as a command in the File menu. In Netscape Navigator, open the Communicator menu, followed by the Tools menu.

Even though a History list can be really useful, the best way of recording a web address for easy revisiting later is to save the page as a Bookmark or Favorite. Why? From time to time, you'll probably want to flush out old, no longer required web addresses and files that may slow down your browsing and this action usually means deleting the current History list.

> If your History list gets too large, your web browsing may become slower. Use the Clear History command in Internet Options (Internet Explorer) or Preferences (Netscape Navigator) to empty your History list. You can also change the default number of days when History clearing automatically occurs.

Cleaning out your web browser cache

For web browsers especially, regular housekeeping is a worthwhile activity to perform to help web pages display more quickly and for your browser to perform more efficiently. Both

Microsoft Internet Explorer and Netscape Navigator provide commands to empty the cache using the Internet Options (IE) and Preferences (Netscape Navigator) dialog boxes.

Weaving an easier web with AutoComplete

Internet Explorer versions 5.0x and later include AutoComplete that can remember essential but boring information for you like user names, passwords, web addresses and web forms. So if you regularly access a password-protected website, with AutoComplete turned on you won't need to repeatedly enter your passwords, etc.

Usually, you can turn AutoComplete on or off using the Internet Options command in the Tools menu and check either the General tab or the Content tab – depending on your particular version.

Saving a web page

You can save a web page using the Save As command from the browser File menu and in the Save dialog box you can usually choose whether to save the page as plain text or HTML format. If you choose plain text, you can view and work on the page text in any text editor. Although you can't save the images using this option, you can still save individual images separately (see the following page). If you choose to save in HTML, you can view the page later in any web browser – saving both text and images.

Internet Explorer v5.0x/6 goes one step further and allows you to save an entire web page complete or as a single web archive file. A web page complete option saves the page images into a different folder from the main page. A web archive single file option saves everything on the web page into a single folder – great if you want to share the web page contents with friends or colleagues – but they'll also need Internet Explorer v5.0x or later to view a page saved in this way.

Saving a web page as a desktop shortcut

In Internet Explorer, with some free desktop space visible and the page you want shown in the main browser window in the Address bar, drag the page icon immediately to the left of the web address onto the Windows desktop. In Netscape Navigator, in the same way, drag the icon on the Location toolbar (placed immediately to the left of the word Location or Netsite) on to the desktop and drop it where you want it.

Saving parts of a web page

Often, you won't want to save an entire web page, just one of its components: say an image or some text. To save an image, click the image you want using the right mouse button to display a floating menu, then choose the Save Picture As or Save Image As command. Windows 9x/Me/XP and later web browsers also allow you to save an image as desktop wallpaper. Click the right mouse button on an image and look for the Set

As… or Save As Wallpaper command. You can also save sound, music/video clips via the Save Link As or Save Target As commands.

Printing a web page

With the web page you want on view, simply choose the Print command from the File menu (or the Print toolbar icon) and choose the options you want then click OK or Print.

Changing your browser default options

When you first install and set up your browser, the software enters some default settings to enable your browser to work. However, once you become more familiar with how to use your browser, you may want to change some settings. So here's how: in Internet Explorer, look for the Internet Options command in the View or Tools menu.

You can also change Internet Explorer options by right-clicking the Internet Explorer program icon on the Windows desktop and choosing the Properties command, or using the Internet or Internet Options icon in the Windows Control Panel. In Netscape Navigator you can change the default options using the Preferences command usually found in the Edit menu.

Typical categories in Internet Explorer include General, Security, Content, Connections, Programs and Advanced. Netscape Navigator typically includes: Appearance, Navigator,

Mail & Newsgroups, Roaming Access, Composer, Offline and Advanced. In Internet Explorer Internet Options dialog box, if you use a newsreader other than Outlook express or Internet Mail & News, remember you'll need to enter its name in the correct box usually found in the Programs category options. You can also change entries for your default HTML editor (web design), email program, and others.

Turning images off and on

Why might you want to elect not to see images? Well, one reason is that pictures and other images can take a while to display in your web browser.

If you have a slower Internet connection, an older computer, or if you're only interested in the text content of websites you're currently visiting, then one powerful way of speeding up your browsing is to change the default settings to turn off images. You can easily change them back again later. This command option is usually found under the browser Options category.

In Internet Explorer v5.0x and later, choose Internet Options from the Tools menu and click the Advanced tab. Under the Multimedia category, click the box to clear a tick mark from the Show pictures option. Once images are turned off, every time you move to a web page that contains images, a bounding box with a thin perimeter line appears to show where the image would have appeared. Also, if a web page has been designed properly, within these bounding boxes, you should see some text briefly describing what the image is about. More on this surprisingly important point later in the chapters about designing your web pages.

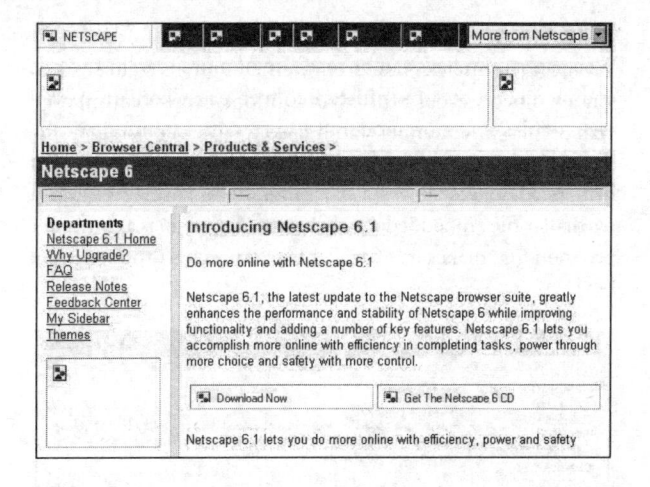

With images turned off, if you want to view an image, place the mouse pointer on the image you want, and in Internet Explorer, right-click to display the floating menu and choose the Show Image command. In Netscape Navigator, choose the Show Images command from the View menu. When finished, you can turn all images back on again, by reversing the commands, closing the browser and then restarting.

Plug-ins and Helper applications

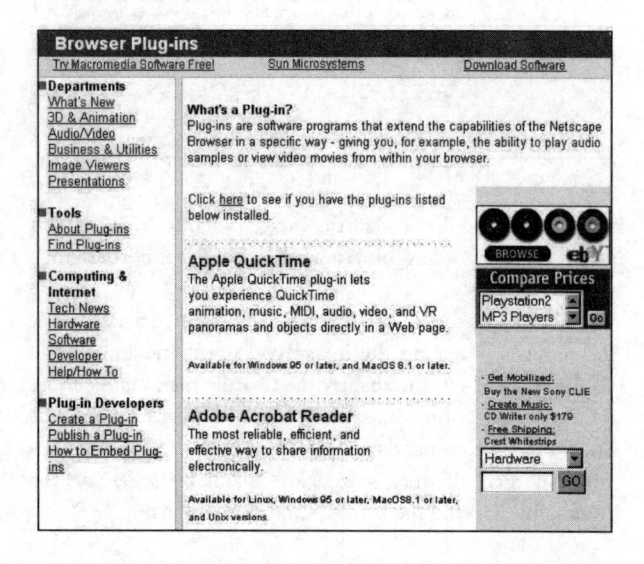

Web pages nowadays can be made up of more than just words and pictures. Lots of sophisticated web pages contain special types of files, and most modern web browsers can automatically display a wide range of file types. However, sometimes you may need to install a special program to display or use a particular file embedded in a web page. A plug-in is a computer program that makes itself available to your web browser when needed. An ActiveX control is another type of program that works with your web browser.

Usually, the website provider includes a link that installs the plug-in or Helper application you need, or links to another website that makes what you need available. You just follow the onscreen instructions to install the plug-in or Helper application. Sometimes you may be asked to accept a software Certificate – if you trust the Certificate source completely you can click OK, if not refuse to accept the Certificate.

The reason I suggest caution here is that anything which directly interacts with your computer from the Internet is an obvious security risk: viruses, hoaxes, etc. So you need to be sure that the Certificate provider is trustworthy.

Java, JavaScript and ActiveX

There's a never-ending demand for interesting animated and colourful ways to make a web page more attractive, compelling and interesting. Java is a programming language used to create highly animated and interactive web pages. However, for a Java component – sometimes called an applet – to work, it must first be downloaded fully and run in the web browser.

JavaScript, a much simpler language than Java – and arguably now more popular – is also a web language that can be used to create attractive and powerful web pages. JavaScript is also part of the latest variety of web language used to create web pages: DHTML (see also page 464). The main difference between Java and JavaScript however, is that JavaScript information is understood by current web browsers directly. Popular JavaScript examples include animated images, fade-ins and fade-outs and scrolling messages.

AcitveX is a Microsoft development designed to make using web pages easier and to provide more flexibility in design options. ActiveX controls are modules that are installed to work with a browser, for example: RealPlayer (examined later in this chapter).

Downloading files from the Net

One of the great benefits of using an up-to-date web browser is that often you can start the operation to download a file simply by clicking a link on a web page. For example, you might want to download a software upgrade, an ebook (electronic book) or even an entire software program. Internet Explorer and Netscape Navigator both include the tools you need to download files in the background while still using the web. So even though you may be downloading, you can still perform other web tasks. However, if you have too many web tasks running at the same time, instability may result or the speed at which a file downloads may fall. And when you download a file, you'll usually be prompted to enter the location you want to download the file to and to provide a name for the download.

Downloading files using a web browser may work OK for smaller files, but if the item you want is a large file size, you're usually better off using a dedicated FTP program like GoZilla! to download the file for you. For more information about FTP, see page 409. The main benefit of using a dedicated FTP program is that if you lose your Internet connection while the download is in progress, most FTP programs can reconnect and continue downloading the remaining part of the file. While using a browser however, usually you'll have to start the entire download again! Not a fun way to spend an afternoon!

Viewing and listening to multimedia content

Many websites provide popular sound and video clips including many tracks available in the popular MP3 audio format. Internet Explorer comes with Media Player – this can interpret many types of new media formats. However, often better players are available. For example, to view and listen to lots of sound and video clips on the Internet today, you'll almost certainly need the RealPlayer ActiveX/Plug-in installed. RealPlayer is a software tool that allows you to play RealVideo and RealAudio clips.

If your browser does not already have the RealPlayer installed, you'll probably find a link on a website that already provides RealPlayer content or if not, visit: www.real.com

The big benefit of RealAudio is that it offers a way to provide music clips, both recorded and live, that can start playing while downloading to your web browser – a much better option when compared to the older type of discrete audio clips that had to be downloaded completely before they could start to play. In fact, lots of radio stations from around the world are now broadcasting on the Internet using this "streaming" technology. For example, if you're into relaxing classical music, take a look at: www.classicfm.com/

Microsoft too have also realised the scope for radio on the Internet. To discover more, in Internet Explorer v5.0x and later, right-click anywhere on the main toolbar then choose the Radio command. A new Radio toolbar then appears just below the main toolbar. When you next go online, you can click the Radio Stations button > Radio Station Guide to see what's available and check it out. To discover more, consider visiting:

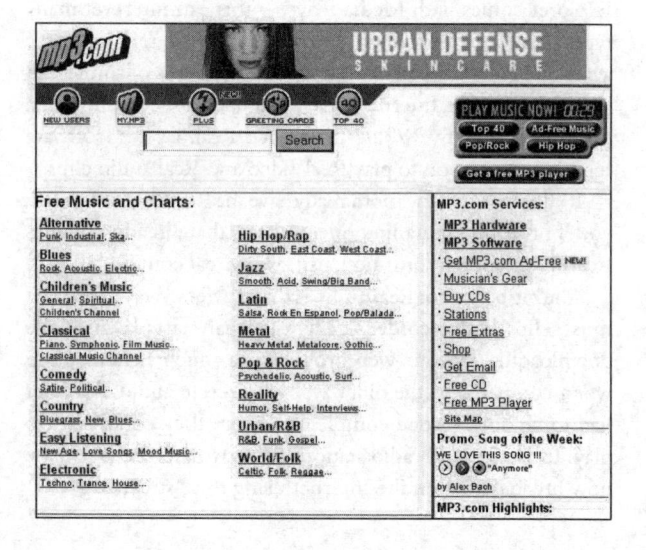

- www.mp3.com

- www.msn.com

- www.microsoft.com

Viewing special effects and animated content

More and more stunning animation routines are becoming commonplace on sophisticated websites. Many of these now use fast-loading cutting-edge animation clips that employ ShockWave and Flash technology.

Shockwave and Flash animations can be likened (in a basic way) to self-running television advertisements. However, the real key to their obvious success is that they're quick to download and play at average connection speeds.

To view these kinds of compelling sequences, you'll need to have the correct Shockwave and Flash ActiveX/plug-ins or "players" installed in your web browser. Currently, the Shockwave and Flash players are free for anyone to download. Usually, they're made available from reputable websites that include this kind of content in their web designs. Or you can get more information from: www.shockwave.com An excellent example that demonstrates the power of Flash animation is available at: www.eye4u.com

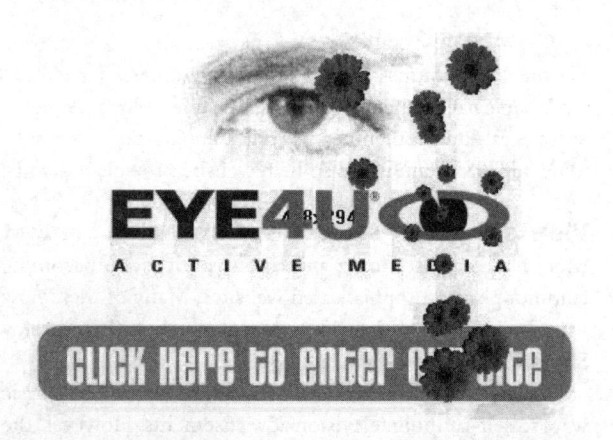

Computer cookies

The best ones are superb biscuits that perhaps bring back colourful childhood memories – just one more from the cookie jar! However, sorry to burst your bubble but in this context we're really discussing something with a less crunchy nature.

The cookies we're interested in here are small computer files that are often copied to a visitor's computer when they first visit a website. Then, when a user revisits the website that originally copied the cookie, this website can identify the web browser used at the time the visit was made.

A popular application for a cookie is to personalise a web visit, so that when a visitor returns to a website, a message like:

"Welcome back John…" appears. So that when we revisit a website three months later, we're suitably impressed that these nice people have remembered our first names. Not quite right: web pages don't remember us, but a cookie can remember some key information and so help website providers identify some basic characteristics about their customers, for example:

- Types of web browser being used.

- Which pages are visited.

- Where customers are located.

- The URL of the website visited immediately before the current one.

- And so on…

Sometimes website providers may ask for more detailed information about you to help you and them next time you visit. If you decide to provide this extra information, the website provider can build up a more accurate picture of what you want from their site and this information helps them provide the most appropriate kind of advertising, and so on.

> A cookie can only really identify a web browser, not a person – unless you decide to provide extra information like your name, email address, and so on.

Viewing web page source code

If you're interested in web page design, you can usually view the HTML code that helps make up a page. Viewing the source code of a web page can help you understand how the page works so that you learn more about web design.

In Internet Explorer, with the web page you want on display, choose the Source command from the View menu, or right-click somewhere on the page you want and choose the View Source command. In Netscape Navigator, choose the Page Source command from the View menu or right-click somewhere on the page and choose the View Source command.

```
<!-- $RCSfile: index-us.html,v $ $Revision: 1.405 $ -->
<!DOCTYPE HTML PUBLIC "-//W3C//DTD HTML 4.0 Transitional//EN">
<html>
<head>
<script language="Javascript">
<!--
var CTCcookieget='';
var playurl = getplayurl();
if (playurl) {
  document.write('<META http-equiv="refresh" CONTENT="0; URL=' + playurl +'">');
  //location.href=playurl;
}
function playcheck(theURL) {
  var referring = refurl();
  var modurl = theURL + '?refer=' + referring + '&js=1&brwsk=ie.m3u';
  location.href = modurl;
  return false;
}
function setCookie(name, value, days) {
  millisecs = 1000 * 60 * 60 * 24 * eval(days)
  expire = new Date();
  expire.setTime (expire.getTime() + millisecs);
```

Viewing web pages offline

If you have to pay for every minute spent online, one way to save money is to first go online and visit each web page you want. Wait until each entire web page has fully displayed, then choose the Work Offline command usually found in your browser's File menu. When you view web pages in this way, once a web page has fully displayed, all its contents are stored in a temporary area of your computer's memory, called:

- Temporary Internet files in Internet Explorer.

- Cache memory in Netscape Navigator.

Once you've visited the pages you want and you've disconnected from the Internet, you can then usually use the Forward, Back and History buttons to visit the pages again to examine the content at your own pace without worrying about online charges. Next time you go online and visit the same page, usually your web browser first chooses the "cached" version, unless the page has been changed or updated. (The new version usually overwrites the old version in the cache memory area.)

You can change the rules of how your browser treats cached web pages using the Internet Options command in the Tools menu, followed by clicking the Temporary Internet Files Settings button. In Netscape Navigator, choose Preferences from the Edit menu, followed by Advanced, then the Cache command. Then enter the changes you want in the boxes.

Key web browser Tips

Let's recap and look at some ways to enhance your web viewing:

- If your time is precious or you have to pay for every minute spent online, if possible plan your Internet sessions in advance. If you know what you want before going online, you'll save money and time.

- Depending on how busy the web is when you go online, you may meet delays when trying to access some web pages. Rather than wait for each page to display fully, if you have other tasks to complete like answering or sending email, use your computer's power to perform those tasks while waiting for the page you want to display.

- If you're browsing the web for text-based information only, you can speed up your browsing by turning off images in your Internet Options (Internet Explorer) dialog box, usually from the Advanced tab – multimedia content too – or Preferences (Netscape Navigator).

- The more windows you have open and the more programs you're using concurrently, the greater the demands on your computer. Therefore, before web browsing, ideally save any open documents and close any programs that you don't need.

- If your computer becomes unstable while several large programs are active, the chances are that your computer is getting low on memory or resources. Save open documents immediately and close any unused open program windows – if you're unlucky, you may even have to close down and restart your computer to cure the problem.

> **HOT TIP**
> In the author's experience, Windows NT/2000/XP is much better at handling memory and resources, compared to earlier versions of Microsoft Windows.

- If a web page is not displaying fast enough for you, click the Stop button, then re-click the link but – this time – choose the command to open the page in a new window. Then at least while the page is being displayed you can continue to work with your original web page.

- If you find web browsing slow and sluggish, consider flushing out your Cache memory or Temporary Internet Files and History lists.

172 > A closer look at web browsers

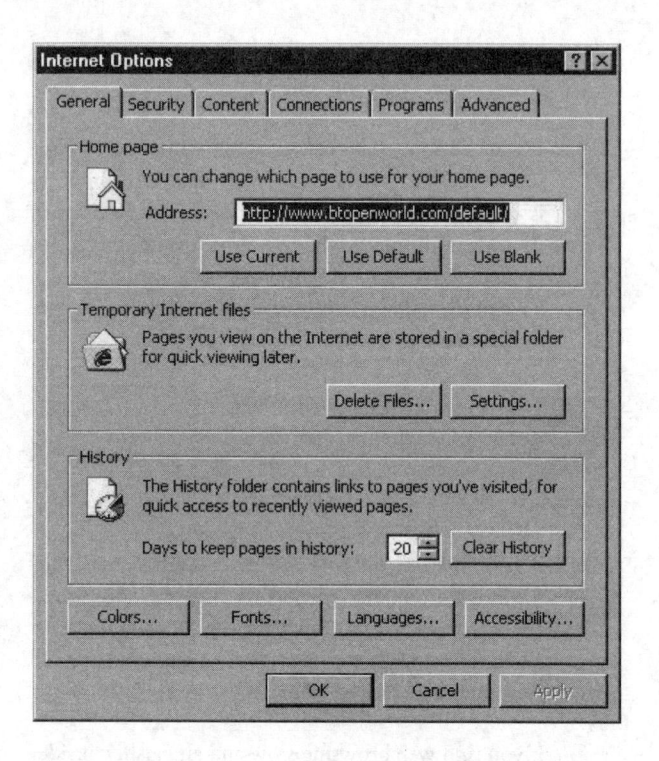

8

Maintaining your security online

The Internet is essentially a vast network of computers connected together creating enormous opportunities for those few people who simply want to cause havoc and steal information. Let's examine a few simple steps you can take to defend your online activities from attack.

Dealing with Internet pests

Once you get an email address and optionally a web address, take part in newsgroups, online chat and discussion lists, your online "identity" becomes available to anyone with an Internet connection. Sometimes, interaction with others can result in being pestered or harassed by inconsiderate Internet users. So what can you do to stop this kind of unwelcome activity? Consider the following guidelines:

1. If possible, try to ignore any email messages you receive from unknown sources. Most pests are seeking a reaction. Don't give it to them.

2. Keep all email messages received from a pest in a separate folder – just in case your harasser doesn't stop. In extreme situations, you can then provide these as evidence in a court of law – every email contains code that can be traced to a computer somewhere on the Internet, so in the worst of circumstances, a harasser can probably be traced even if they try to cover their tracks!

3. If ignoring the pestering doesn't appear to be working, contact your Internet Service Provider and send copies of the emails you have received. Internet Service Providers usually don't want Internet troublemakers working from their servers and so, in mild cases, may send a warning to the originator, or if the offence is more serious may simply close down the perpetrator's account without warning, or even take more serious legal action.

4. Be careful if playing Internet pranks: what you may consider a joke may be interpreted by others in an

entirely different light. An email death threat sent to ex-US President Bill Clinton resulted in a jail sentence for the originator!

Avoiding hoaxes and scams on the Net

Occasionally, someone sends a false message to many people on the Net, with instructions to pass the message on to as many other people as possible. These hoaxes and chain letters can include the usual drivel; for example:

- How to make "free money": of course we know that nothing is ever really free; a price has to be paid by someone somewhere. Usually, these kinds of emails are targeting people who genuinely could use some extra cash quickly. However, like some envelope addressing scams, the offer is often not genuine. Sending out these kinds of bulk email broadcasts is also a great way for scamsters to harvest new genuine email addresses, which then get sold as part of a "new" email list. So my advice is simply not to reply to this kind of rubbish, just delete the message. Or expect to get a lot of junk email in the future.

- Dire warnings about opening emails: especially if they contain specific words or phrases in the Subject box.

BEWARE If you think an offer is too good to be true, you're probably right and it probably is. This is your intuition trying to warn you. However, if you do want to follow up, check them out; get independent opinions; do some research before signing up. Here's a common warning sign: most scamsters don't like to include a genuine phone, fax and mailing address on their website. But don't assume that because they do include these verifiable details, they're genuine. This may still form an elaborate con trick.

- The lowest of the low: sending out urgent appeals to raise money for a child dying of cancer.

However, genuine appeals for help are made, so don't automatically assume all such emails are false. You can do a lot to check if an email is genuine. To discover the latest hoaxes and scams, visit your antivirus program's website: many include information about hoaxes in addition to genuine computer viruses. Or you can check out renowned independent sources like:

- www.fsa.gov.uk/
  (The UK Financial Services Authority).

- www.fraud.org/
  (The Fraud Information Centre).

- www.scambusters.com (Scambusters).

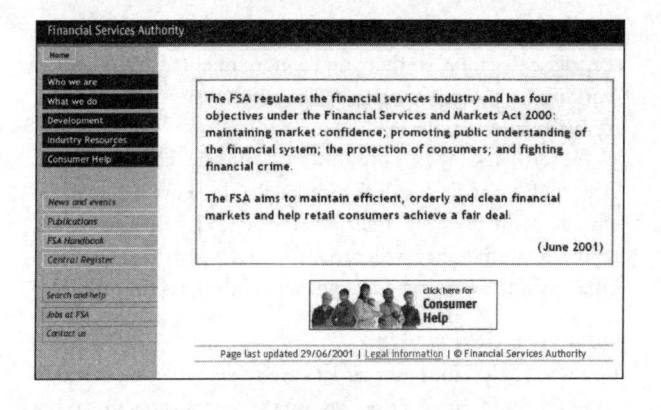

- www.urban-myths.com/

- www.kumite.com/myths/

- www.scamfreezone.com/

- www.onelist.com/subscribe/net-alert (email newsletter).

Computer viruses

To some people, the entire topic of computer viruses has been over-hyped by the media. Others consider viruses a real threat exacerbated by widespread Internet use. There's some truth in both of these views. The Internet is an absolute dream for virus writers. However, this real threat has made most people more security conscious, so that you're more likely to catch a virus working on a company/organisation/university network than from the Internet directly.

Nevertheless, always use antivirus software with up-to-date virus tables installed – ideally updated at least every 2 weeks – whether you use the Internet or not, and run virus scans regularly. Remember, you can still catch a virus from sources other than the Internet – friends and colleagues for example.

How to catch a virus

Unfortunately, computer viruses are an ever-present threat to computer and Internet access users everywhere. Once we connect a computer to others to form a network, a virus can spread more easily. As the Internet is the ultimate network, the potential for virus infection is much increased. For Internet users, a virus can be caught from various sources. The risk is dramatically increased if you're unprepared, or do not use up-to-date antivirus software. For example, consider: common virus sources include the following:

- An attachment to an email message (high risk). Until you're 100% sure, consider all Microsoft Excel/Word/Access documents sent to you with caution, especially if they contain macros, a perfect home for viruses.

- Downloading an unknown program from a newsgroup (high risk).

- A routine embedded in a website (lower risk – but higher if you're using an older web browser). Most websites want to keep customers, not kill any chance of doing business, and so in practice most websites and Internet Service Providers provide high levels of protection.

> **HOT TIP** Get into the habit of not opening any attachments until you have scanned them using an up-to-date antivirus program. And even if your software does not find a virus, an attachment can still be infected: the software may only detect those viruses that it knows about. So keep your antivirus program up-to-date: regularly download updates from your antivirus provider's website.

Email viruses: a special threat

Most email viruses come as attachments to plain text email messages. Providing you don't "open" or run an infected attachment, you probably won't catch a virus. Remember, in most email programs you only need click an attachment to open it, so beware.

However, recent virus scares that don't involve attachments have been shown to exploit weaknesses in certain email programs confusing the issue still further to many. So what do you do? First, don't accept any email attachments from someone you don't know. I choose to immediately delete all attachments I receive from any unknown source, period! Friends and colleagues are often the most common way to spread a virus – they may not even know their system is infected. So again beware.

At the time of writing, email viruses still circulating the Internet include: Happy99.exe (Trojan Horse), CodeRed.A (worm), and VBS.xxxxx (worm). A Trojan Horse is a program with another program hidden inside – and often the one inside is out to cause trouble. A worm virus repeatedly attempts to copy itself. A Trojan Horse can't do any harm until you open the attachment and run the little critter. If you receive an email with this program (or any other Trojan Horse) attached and if your antivirus software has not already picked it up, DO NOT

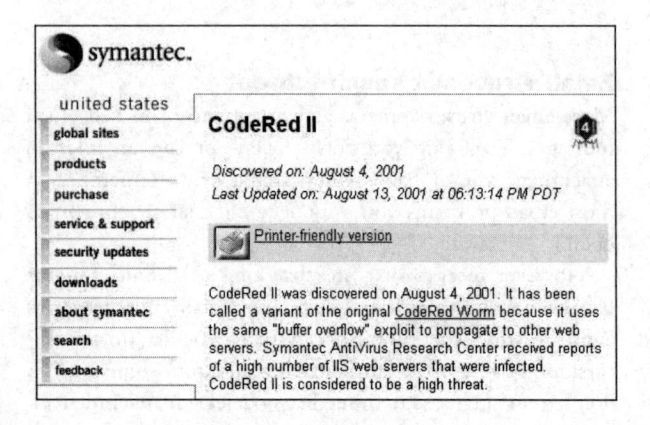

OPEN THE ATTACHMENT, simply delete it. Then reply to the sender and let them know that their computer has been infected with this virus.

Recently, a new kind of email worm-type virus has emerged that at first glance appears to be activated as soon as a plain text message is read. Bubbleboy was the first example of this new strain of havoc. What really happens, however, is that a script file is embedded into the email message that can write a file to the recipient's hard drive if:

- They're using certain types of email programs, and...

- Those email programs have not been updated with a patch to fix the security "hole" or bug. For example, some versions of Microsoft Outlook may still not have received the patch to fix this error even though it is freely available from Microsoft.

If the worm file does get written to the hard drive, providing the virus file is immediately deleted, the problem may be solved. However, if the worm file remains, when the computer is next switched on or re-booted, the virus can again run unhindered to cause havoc.

The Loveletter/Love Bug virus, classified as VBS/LoveLetter.A by Symantec (www.symantec.com/) also emerged around the world with unexpected amazing speed. However, a fix became available within hours from Symantec: hats off to them! The following paragraphs include some pointers to help you avoid catching a computer virus and action to consider if you do.

Are HTML emails safe?

No, absolutely not! Remember HTML is the language used to build web pages. An HTML email can contain malicious virus components that can overload a computer. Nevertheless, HTML-derived viruses do not appear to have presented a major threat (yet). Just remember, vigilance and an active up-to-date antivirus program are your best defence against any computer virus.

Antivirus software on the Net

Some of the more popular and well established antivirus programs are:

- InnoculateIT from Computer Associates is available free for personal users and home businesses at: antivirus.cai.com/

- Norman Virus Control: www.norman.no

- McAfee: www.mcafee.com/

- Norton Antivirus: www.symantecstore.com/

- The AntiViral Toolkit (free trial software): www.avp.ch/

- Panda Antivirus: www.pandasoftware.com/

- Sophos Antivirus: www.sophos.com/

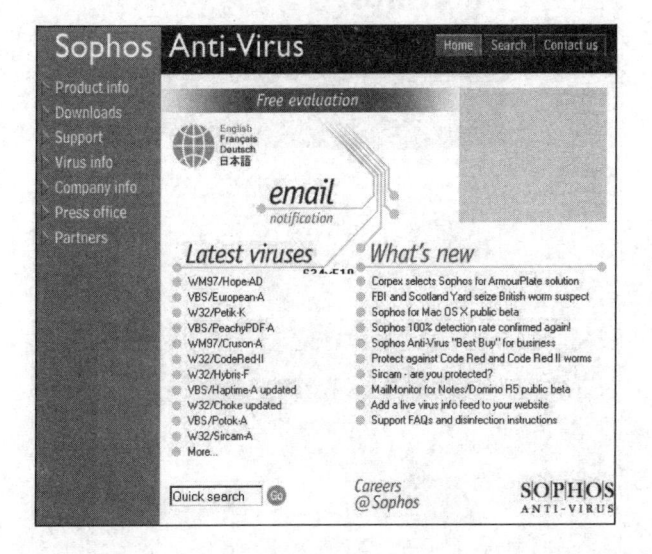

- F-Secure from Data Fellows is designed for corporate use or large computer networks: www.datafellows.com/

- For Mac users, consider Norton Antivirus Mac at: www.symantec.com/nav/nav_mac/

184 > Maintaining your security online

Avoiding virus infections

To minimise the chances of catching a computer virus, let's group the most important antivirus points in this chapter. Consider the following powerful guidelines to help keep your computer virus-free:

1. Always have installed an effective antivirus program that is regularly updated. My own Norton Antivirus (from www.symantec.com/) is automatically regularly updated at least every 2 weeks online to cover the latest virus threats. Lots of free antivirus programs are available online (for example: antivirus.cai.com/) or consider shareware or full-blown retail copies from well established companies like McAfee and Symantec.

2. **Never, repeat never** open any email attachments that you're not already expecting – especially if received from friends, family or work colleagues. If in doubt, contact the source and confirm that they did indeed send it to you, then virus scan it anyway. If you still have doubts, simply delete it.

3. Back up your essential files regularly – if all else fails, this step alone can "save the day" – and your sanity! You can use tapes, zip disks and jaz disks, recordable CDs or at a push even floppy disks.

4. Question whether using a popular email program is justified – to create maximum impact and spread a virus quickly, virus creators often target the most popular software like Outlook Express. Only you can decide what is best for you, but alternatives can be viewed at popular download sites like: www.download.com/

> **HOT TIP**
> The approach outlined on this page may seem extreme, but a computer virus can be devastating! It's not a bad idea to assume all macro-based documents DO contain a virus – until you're proved wrong! Next, don't accept any macros from anyone unless you know and trust them and they have assured you that the document has been virus scanned before sending to you. Then, still use your own up-to-date virus scanner to check it anyway.

Virus infection and remedies

Sometimes, even the best laid plans are still not enough to prevent infection. Therefore, if you do catch a computer virus, consider the following steps:

1. Don't panic! Easy to say, I know, but it's crucial that you remain as calm as possible. If you're still able to use your computer, don't send any email messages to anyone; don't copy or send information on floppy diskettes, zip

disks, jaz disks, backup tapes or CD/DVD-ROMs until you're sure the virus has been deleted.

2. At this point, what you don't do can be more important than what action you do take. In other words, don't make any changes unless you know what you're doing and why you're doing it.

3. If you have antivirus software installed and have kept it up to date, there's a good chance that the software has detected the little nasty. So, your antivirus software may have a remedy or offer suggestions. Follow the prompts and instructions carefully.

4. If your antivirus program cannot offer a cure, read the user guide and program Help file to better understand what action you should take.

5. Ask a friend or colleague if you can use their (virus-free) computer to access the newsgroup "alt.comp.virus" to get (usually) quick and helpful feedback and advice – possibly by people who may also have been infected so who know exactly what you're going through. Key point: online folks can be amazingly helpful when you're in trouble.

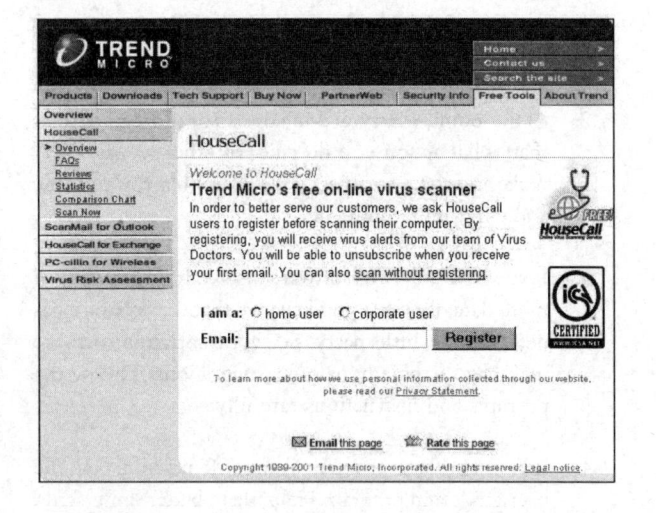

6. If you can still get online, some antivirus program providers make antivirus detection software available online for use in emergencies. For example: check out HouseCall at: www.housecall.antivirus.com/ or the McAfee Online Clinic at: www.mcafee.com/ can help check for viruses live on your computer.

7. If the virus problem remains, your data is valuable and you haven't got any backup copies, consider contacting reputable professional experts to recover your data and clean your system.

8. In extreme circumstances, the only option may mean completely wiping your computer's hard drive and reinstalling the operating system, software applications and data (if available). After which, scan all other disks that you have or use to make sure the virus has not been transferred.

Protecting your PC from hackers

Use the generous free tools and guidelines provided by Steve Gibson's superb "Shields Up" site at www.grc.com/ to test online just how vulnerable your computer is to hackers.

Shields UP!

Internet Connection Security for Windows Users
by Steve Gibson, Gibson Research Corporation

Pressing these buttons grants your formal permission and requests our connection to your computer for the display of data that can be gained by anyone across the Internet:

Test My Shields !   **Probe My Ports !**

Information gained will **not** be retained, viewed or used by us in any way for any purpose whatsoever.

TWO NOTES: Shields UP! benignly probes the target computer at your location. Since these probings must travel from **our** server to **your** computer, you should be certain to have administrative right-of-way to conduct probative protocol tests through any and all equipment located between your computer and the Internet.

ALSO: If you are using a personal firewall product which LOGS contacts by other systems, you should expect to see entries from this site's probing IP addresses: 207.71.92.193 and 207.71.92.221. These are (obviously) not any form of intrusion attempt or attack on your computer, so please do not be concerned with their appearance in your firewall logs.

If you use Microsoft Windows and have not checked your security before, trust me, surprises and shocks are almost guaranteed! Make use of the currently free tools and know-how at GRC.com to help protect your files in a network.

Plus, you can get lots of superb information about how to prevent the uninvited from trying to gain access to your computer while online. To provide maximum security, install a good "firewall" program like Zone Alarm from www.zonelabs.com ZoneAlarm is free for personal use, while for business use, a business licence costs only a few US dollars and provides great value! Key point: a good firewall is, I believe, an essential defence product for active Internet users everywhere.

9

Finding what you want on the Net

The Internet is like a huge library in which some books move around, others disappear without warning and new ones are continually born seemingly out of nothing and without pause or reason. A vast collection of information on almost every topic imaginable is emerging that grows ever larger every second of every day – with a pace of growth still increasing! Today in the 21st century, we're seeing only the first shoots of an enormous tree that one day will truly cover the entire earth and probably far beyond!

But until then, how do we mere mortals find what we want on the Internet today under these ever-changing conditions? Answer, we do what anyone does when travelling in a strange land: we use maps and guides – or to be more precise, search tools. Today, most are still free of charge – although as Internet growth starts to settle down into a more predictable rhythm, that may change. The Internet is rich in the variety and number of free tools that you can use to search for information. Some tools however, stand out more than others in their awesome power and flexibility. The web in particular contains many superb search tools – also known as search engines and web directories – and it's mainly these little beauties that we want to cover in this chapter.

Types of web search tools

Specific tools on the web are used to collect, store and logically arrange key information about web pages around the world to make the job of finding specific information easier. The most important search tools available today include search engines and web directories and their various spin-offs. So what's the difference?

Essentially, search engines are computer-run, whereas a human operator usually compiles information made available in a directory. Below is a list of the most popular and most important search engines and directories available on the Internet today. In fact, most searches come from the most important search engines and directories including:

- **About.com:**   www.about.com

- **AltaVista:** www.altavista.com or www.av.com

- **Ask Jeeves:** www.askjeeves.com

- **Copernic:** www.copernic.com

- **Direct Hit:** www.directhit.com

- **DMOZ Open Directory Project:** www.dmoz.org

- **Dogpile:** www.dogpile.com

- **Excite:** www.excite.com

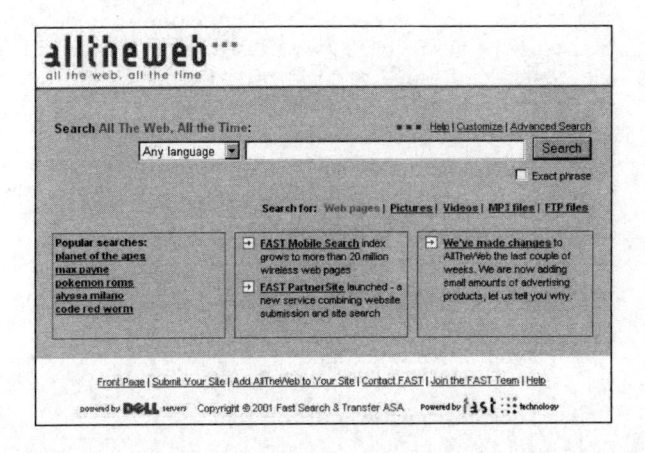

- **Fast/All the Web:** www.alltheweb.com

- **Google:** www.google.com

> **HOT TIP** Google is a relatively new kid on the block dreamed up by some rather clever folks at Stanford University and probably set to be a big player! Why? Google uses robot programs to scan and explore the entire web – just like many other search engines. However, results returned for any particular site are determined by the quality of each resulting link to that site and the quality of the other sites that link back to it. In Google, the only way a website can improve its ranking is to have more good quality websites linked to it. A superb idea that helps improve the quality of the Internet for all of us.

- **GoTo:** www.goto.com

- **HotBot:** www.hotbot.com

- **InfoSeek:** www.infoseek.com

- **Iwon:** www.iwon.com

- **LookSmart:** www.looksmart.com

- **Lycos:** www.lycos.com (UK: www.lycos.co.uk)

DON'T FORGET: Even though the cataloguing of websites is happening continuously, finding all websites can take time. So if what you're searching for is not listed, it doesn't mean that it's not available on the Internet. Remember, a similar check done a few days later may provide different results.

- **Magellan:** www.mckinley.com

- **Metacrawler:** www.metacrawler.com

- **MSN:** search.msn.com

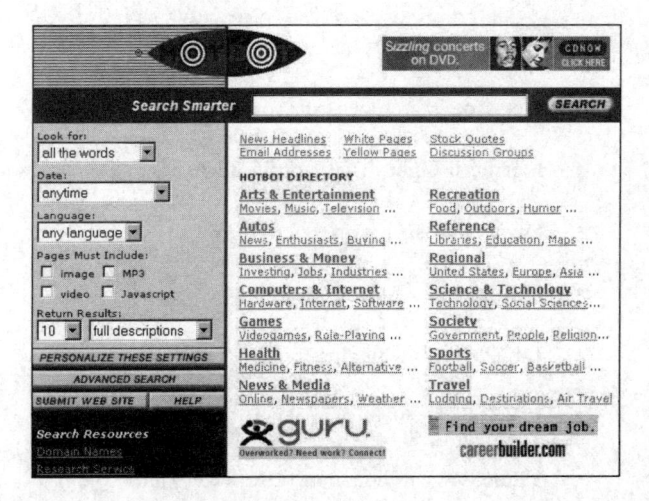

HOT TIP

Whatever tool or method you choose to use, plan what you want to do in advance before starting your search tool. Read the quick guides usually provided on each search tool: as search tools get better, how best to use them changes. Consider using several search engines/directories for detailed results, and try performing several searches using different words on your search topic/theme.

HOT TIP

A new more specialised breed of Internet shopping-related search engines is emerging, that can find and compare prices and availability for various products. For example, take a look at Shopper.com on www.shopper.com

- **Netscape:** search.netscape.com

- **Northern Light:** www.northernlight.com

- **Snap:** www.snap.com

- **Sprinks:** www.sprinks.com

- **UK Plus:** www.ukplus.co.uk

- **WebCrawler:** www.webcrawler.com

- **Yahoo:** www.yahoo.com (UK: www.yahoo.co.uk)

> **HOT TIP**: Some search engines, like Metacrawler, Dogpile and Copernic, are especially powerful and can search the databases of multiple search engines all in the same session.

How search engines work

Some search engines automatically and regularly send out search agents – also known as spiders, web crawlers or "bots" (from the word robot) – which are amazingly clever software applications that continually scan the web and report back the information. These intelligent agents continually roam the web in search of information, log what they find and report the information back to their source. Remember, this sequence happens very fast and is a continuous nonstop activity.

So most search engines have three main components:

- One or more intelligent agents.

- A database to hold information received from the intelligent agents.

- A search tool that allows users to search their database of websites.

In this way, search engines try to map the web. I say "try" because the amazing pace of change and relentless growth and unpredictable nature of the web have defeated all attempts at cataloguing every single web page! The task is probably impossible. However, intelligent agents never stop trying. Search engines also collect key information when someone has published a web page or website and submitted details manually to a search engine.

Some search engines automatically record every word on a web page; others may record only basic information like web page titles. You can learn lots of key techniques about submitting a website to search engines and directories by reading "Search Engineering your Website" (Computer Step).

Because individual search engines work differently, they return different results. Some concentrate more on website titles, others use the first few sentences; others use keyword density, and so on.

Often, the method a search engine uses to map a website also changes without warning to keep fair play for everyone. Also, several search engines use the same tools. For example, the Inktomi system is currently used by GoTo, HotBot, MSN

> If you're really into web searching, you could consider making your favourite search engine's start page as your web browser's Home page. That way, as soon as you connect to the web, your search page automatically displays ready for searching. On your Search engine entry page, look for a link that says something like: "Make this my Home page", or change your browser settings yourself (hint: look for the Options dialog box).

and Snap; therefore, entering the same word or phrase into these search engines will probably return similar results.

Searching for what you want in a search engine

To find specific websites, you'll need to enter a word or short phrase into the search box and click the Submit or Go button. (Search engines usually treat upper case or lower case text in the same way, so you don't have to be concerned with entering capital letters.) Before you do so, however, note down several different key words or brief phrases covering the topic you want.

For example, let's assume you want to search for websites covering classic cars. If you enter "classic cars" (without the quotes), your search might result in all websites containing the words "classic" and "cars" – which could amount to hundreds or even thousands of web pages! You might even end up with irrelevant pages about classic history, classic jokes, classic novels, and so on.

If your search returns hundreds or thousands of pages, then clearly, checking each web address manually is simply not worth the time and effort. Most people may only examine the first 10 – 30 websites listed anyway. Therefore, one workable solution is to fine-tune your search so that only the websites you really want are returned.

Examine the search rules and options for the particular search engine you're using. The better search engines however, let you at least specify whether to search for any word, specific sequence of words or an exact phrase. Various methods might be called for. As a general guide though, consider the following examples and relate these to your own searches. To search for websites:

- On Australian wines, enter:
  +Australian +Wine

- About any types of wine except Australian wines, enter:
  -Australian +wine

- Containing the word "Australian" or "wine", enter:
  Australian OR wine

- Relevant to high-tech investments, enclose the search phrase in quotes: "high tech investments" or "high-tech investments".

In the search examples above, note the use of the capital letters OR. In search engine terms, essentially, OR means one or the other; AND means this one plus the others.

When entering search words and phrases, consider the different ways a word might be spelt by people in different countries, for example: "organization" or "organisation".

Making sense of Search results

Once you've entered your search requirements and clicked the button, if your topic is rare you might get just a few web pages listed. However, for many topics, you'll get hundreds or thousands of web page "hits" returned. Usually each hit lists some basic details about a web page or website.

For example, in AltaVista, Computer Step appears as:

1. in easy steps computer books by computer step
Computer Step, top British publisher of computer books. Our in easy steps series uses concise language and has an easy to follow layout....
URL: www.computerstep.com/
Last modified on: 12-Aug-2001- 30K bytes - in English (Win-1252)
[Translate] [Related pages]

Or, from HotBot:

1. Computer Books Direct, Books Online Books, in easy steps computer books and manuals
Computer Books Direct To You: in easy steps are reference guides for computer software and hardware users.
8/14/2001 http://www.ineasysteps.com/
See results from this site only.

The first line usually shows the name or **title** of the website, followed by a **description**. Usually the description is extracted from information that the website designers provide, or the search engine may attempt to form its own description from the web page contents.

The following line may contain a **percentage score figure** that indicates how relevant a web page is to the search word or phrase entered. The higher the percentage figure, the closer the search engine considers the web page matches what you want. You can also see the date this page is found, its file size, and a full link to the site.

> When you decide to visit a website found from your list of search "hits", whatever search tool you decide to use, rather than just click the relevant link, right-click the link you want and choose the command to open the destination site in a new window. This way, you always have your original list of search results handy in the original window. Then, if the latest search result proves not to be relevant, close the second window and repeat the tactic to visit each relevant web page listed in your search results.

Web directories

Search engines can return a list of websites based on what you ask them to search for. Web directories like Yahoo! and Yell work differently: they store web information under relevant categories and sub-categories.

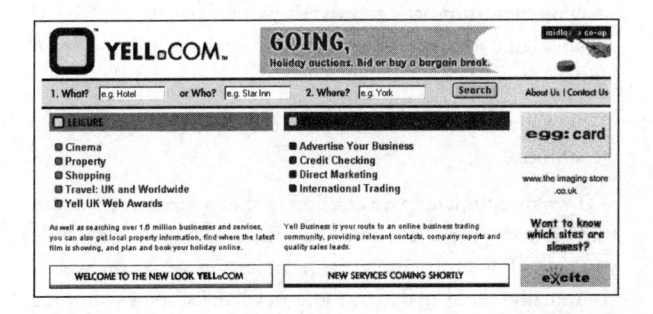

These categories might have headings like: Business, Arts, Science, Language, Internet, Computers, and so on. Under each main category is usually a list of sub-categories. Under each entry in a subcategory, there may be a further list of categories, and so on. In this way, a web page or website is placed into the most logical location.

Finding what you want in a directory

The best directories provide a search box in which you can usually enter the word/phrase you want to find. You could start at the "top" (main entry page) and navigate "down" through the relevant categories until you find the group/single category you want. That's where your desired web pages should lie.

Finding a lost web page

Imagine some time back you saved a particular web page "deep" within a large website. For example, imagine the link you saved pointed to:

> www.ineasysteps.com/books/ineasysteps/miniguides/uti.html

Two months later, you connect to the Internet and want to find that same page. But when you click the bookmarked link, you get a "File Not Found" error message page. As the web is continually being updated, these dead links are a continual problem; however, sometimes a few minutes' investigation may be all that is needed to find what you want.

If a website provides a search engine to help find the product or page you want, then usually that offers the best search option. If not, one sometimes-quick remedy is to simply edit the web address provided in the web browser Address bar. Using our example above, we start by removing the last one or two components to display:

www.ineasysteps.com/books/ineasysteps/miniguides/

From that resulting location, we may find the new link that points to the page we want. If not, we edit some more:

www.ineasysteps.com/books/ineasysteps/

Then, if necessary, edit further still to display:

www.ineasysteps.com/books/

And so on. These steps take only a few minutes but if you're still left empty handed simply email the website and ask for what you want – this can be a good way to check out how helpful they are and how fast they respond.

Email address locators

Finding the email address of someone on the Internet is a little like performing some detective work. The most obvious places to look in include email address directories – providing the person you want has agreed to have their email address listed in a public directory. Also, if necessary, check out options for finding individuals in the web search engines and directories.

Direct links to various email directories are available from the Address Book command in Outlook Express and Netscape Messenger. In Outlook Express v5.0x onwards, click Tools > Address Book, then click the Find People button. In the Find People dialog box, under the Look In drop-down list, you can gain access to various email locators. Choose an option and enter your search details. The most popular email address locators include:

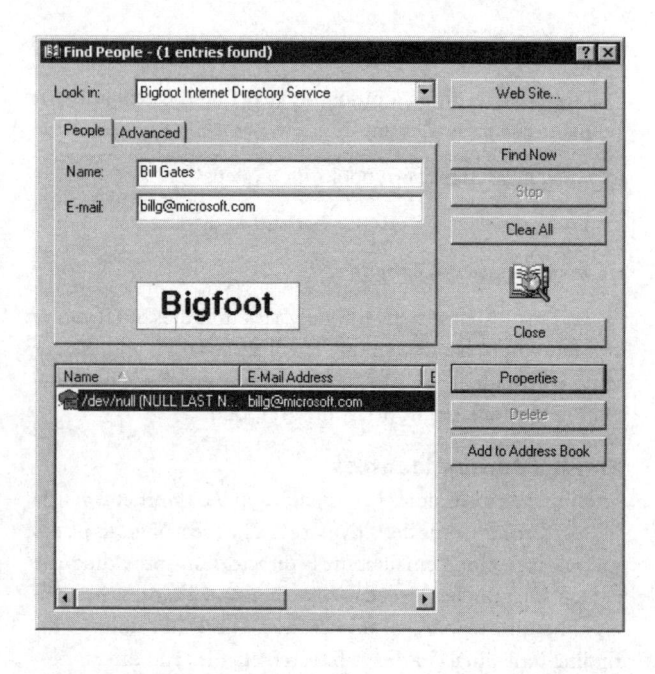

- Bigfoot: www.bigfoot.com

- WhoWhere: www.whowhere.com

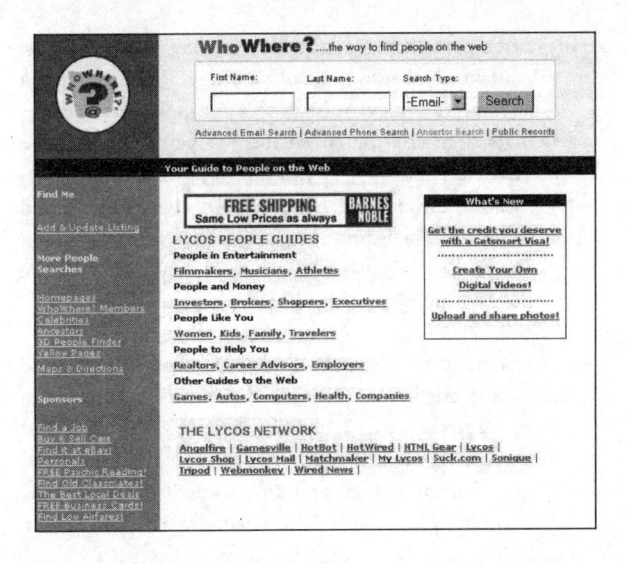

- Yahoo PeopleSearch Directory: people.yahoo.com

Internet search tips

1. When you find pages that interest you, save a copy of the page on your computer, so that when you disconnect from the Internet, you can access the information when you want.

2. After performing a search, you may be given a list containing of hundreds of websites. Rather than just clicking the relevant links to examine some of these, instead choose the command to open each link in a separate window – so you'll always have the original "search results" page handy. In Internet Explorer and Netscape Navigator, you can right-click a link and choose the command: "Open in New Window", from the floating menu that appears.

3. Often, during a search, if you're really only interested in text information, consider turning off graphics in your browser. Remember, by default, when you visit a page your browser attempts to show everything on the page. Turning off graphics speeds up browsing as only a bounding box and some associated text may be shown.

4. If you pay for every second while connected to the Internet, you can often save money by connecting at off-peak periods – in the evenings or at weekends – with some payment plans.

5. If the website you're visiting is based in another country and the site is particularly busy – you may have access delays or Internet "traffic" jams. Consider coming offline and reconnecting again during the night hours of the relevant country: access speeds may then improve

if fewer people are using resources relating to that part of the Internet.

6. When using Internet search tools regularly, consider briefly noting down the best and worst times to use specific search engines or directories.

7. Save each of your favourite search engines as a Bookmark or Favorite, for quick and easy access later (for more information about Bookmarks and Favorites, see page 152).

8. Don't forget some great printed Internet directories and month-by-month guides are also available, for example: "5000 Brilliant Websites" (Computer Step) or magazines like ".net". These can provide an ideal start especially if you're new to the Internet. Do remember, however, that as the Net is continually changing, some information in a printed Internet directory may be out of date as soon it's published.

9. If you're not quite sure what you want but merely want to find out more about a topic or theme, here's a neat strategy to consider. If you enter "FAQ" (without the quotes) as the word to search for in your favourite search engine, you'll get many topics returned all about Frequently Asked Questions. You can fine-tune your

FAQ search by entering one or two more words about what you want. For example, "FAQ dogs" would return all listed entries that contain a Frequently Asked Question file on dogs. Spend some time experimenting to locate the best way to find what you want, so that the next time you want to search for a different topic you'll know the best way to proceed.

Open Directory Project Help Central

Got a question or comment about the **Open Directory Project (ODP)**? Want to find out more about us? Click on one of the links below for more information.

ODP Information

- About Us
- Sites Using ODP Data
- Linking to the ODP
- ODP in the Press
- Social Contract
- Free Use License
- Terms of Use

FAQs About the ODP

- General Info
- Submitting/Updating Sites
- Special Categories
- Becoming an Editor
- Existing Accounts
- Get ODP Data

Editing Guidelines

Send Feedback to ODP Staff

10

Shopping online

A recent Durlacher report suggests that about half of all UK Internet users believe the Internet will change how they shop within 2 years. Online shoppers can save money, have more choice and don't have to brave the traffic jams, fight for a parking space and spend ages queuing in one form or another. But like any new system, there are teething problems, risks and drawbacks. So let's take a closer look at what's possible when you shop on the Net.

Why shop online?

The main value of being able to shop on the Internet is that you can choose and pay for products and services using your computer or other Internet access device and suddenly have a much wider choice of where to buy your goods and services. However remember, you can also pick up some superb last minute bargains on the Net! You no longer need to accept what stores in your local or national shops provide and if you don't like queuing or getting stuck in traffic jams, maybe online shopping – at least some of the time – might be for you.

What's more, an Internet shop or store often doesn't need an expensive high street building with all the incredible extra costs that are associated with providing a public access resource.

Therefore, as costs are cheaper, Internet businesses can often afford to sell their products and services for less – potentially saving you money. Already in the UK, at the time of writing, there's been much talk in the media about the amazing savings car buyers can get simply through buying online (or from mainland Europe), for example:

- www.carbusters.com

- www.enterprisecity.co.uk

- www.bizweb.com

- www.shoppingsearch.com

Is it safe to shop online?

Any company or organisation that is serious about doing business on the Internet must take into account the security of your credit card details while online. Currently, the most popular way the best companies protect your sensitive details while online is to use an encryption technology called Secure Sockets Layer (SSL) with several additional levels of security being considered. Breaking into an SSL secure transaction is extremely difficult and requires a huge amount of computing power.

All the best security systems work by simply deterring criminals and, in essence, this is the strength of SSL: for those who are bent on crime, there are simply easier ways. As a result, millions of shoppers now accept that online transactions performed in this way address their concerns. This new confidence is demonstrated by the massively increasing amounts of money changing hands online around the globe in the last year – a trend set to continue.

Some things to check before buying online

On the Internet, in theory, it may not matter where you live, right? After all, let's say your want to buy a DVD or CD-ROM product online from a company based in the USA, and which is designed for the UK market. The product may essentially be the same item that you buy from your local computer store. However, by buying online, if we compare the value of the UK pound against the US dollar, we would currently expect to save money. However, in practice, the transaction may not be quite so straightforward.

For example, always check out delivery costs and whether you may need to pay VAT and import duty when the goods arrive in the UK – these costs coupled with any extra hassle can make the entire experience simply not worth the trouble; you could even end up losing money!

Therefore, if buying goods online that are to be imported, first check your country's policy for handling online purchases. UK users can find more information at HM Customs website: www.hmce.gov.uk/ Currently, goods costing more than £18 may have VAT and import duty added. However be warned, the rules and guidelines vary for similar products and can be confusing. Also, you can look for Which?, the Consumers' Association Web Trader logo. To display this logo, Internet shops are investigated by lawyers from the Consumers' Association and website members must follow the Web Trader code of practice – which covers important things like following consumer laws, displaying prices clearly with no hidden extras, delivery obligations, dealing with complaints properly, and so on. For more information, see: www.which.ent/webtrader

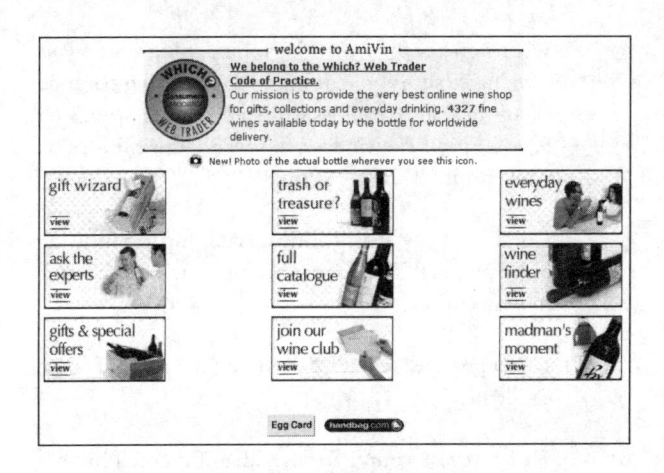

Consider the following 10 key guidelines to help you shop online safely:

1. When you pay for something online using your credit card, make sure you're using a "secure" payment page – look for a closed padlock icon somewhere in your web browser payment window, or a web address that starts with "https://" instead of "http://".

2. Don't send any sensitive financial information using ordinary email. Web forms that use "https://" are much more secure.

3. Never provide credit card details online as proof of age or identity.

4. Never reveal your Personal Identification Number (PIN) number to anyone (both online or offline).

5. Don't ever give out your credit card details in Chat rooms, newsgroups or discussion forums (also known as bulletin boards).

6. Get suppliers to confirm delivery and guarantee details by email.

7. Discover refund and goods return policies before buying.

HOT TIP Here's one strategy that might save UK buyers money when buying online. Whenever appropriate, buy products in bulk online from sellers in your own country to get the best prices. Don't forget, if you want to import products you buy online that are worth more than £18 (currently), ask the supplier about delivery and import charges. If you wish to continue, first buy a single product and wait until the product arrives to check if any extra charges apply on that product.

8. Keep copies of all email communications used in Internet transactions.

9. When you receive your credit card invoice, if you see any transactions listed that you did not make, contact the online retailer and your credit card company immediately. If you do get conned, most banks now limit your liability to about £50, but do check these terms.

10. In my opinion, genuine "etailers" should display a real mailing address (not a Post Office box) and include contact phone and fax numbers. If you don't see these, be especially cautious.

What can I buy?

Thousands of different items from smaller products like music CDs, books and videos to a growing range of larger goods. You can also buy or use a wide range of services on the Internet: house and car insurance, holidays, business services, online banking and property buying and selling to name but a few. You can get an in depth look at what's available when shopping online by reading: "5000 Brilliant Websites" available from www.ineasysteps.com

If you want to make the online shopping experience even easier, you may prefer to do your shopping all from one location on the web using a shopping mall in which a range of different companies offer their products and services all conveniently in one place. Web shopping malls are particularly popular in the USA with a growing trend now becoming evident in other parts of the world including the UK.

How do I buy online?

Often, smaller websites may use basic web forms in which you enter product details or make a selection, and in which you add your name, address and payment details. When ready, you click the "Send" or "Submit" button and the form information is almost immediately emailed to the company or organisation.

Sites that have many different items, sizes or varieties for sale usually use a more sophisticated shopping cart system in which you can search categories of products and choose the ones you want as you shop by clicking the "Add to basket",

"Add to cart" button or equivalent. When finished, usually you'll go to the "Checkout", confirm and optionally change any entries.

The shopping cart software then usually calculates your total order and optionally adds any sales tax, handling and delivery charges. At some stage in the Checkout stage, you'll need to enter payment information – the favourite usually

in easy steps

Your shopping cart

order no. 3915

Continue Purchase Cancel

Qty :	Item number :	Product Description :	Price :
▲ 1 ▼	1840780398	Web Page Design in easy steps (2nd edition)	£ 8.99

Total without shipping
£ 8.99

Continue Purchase Cancel

being credit card details. When you are satisfied, you'll click the button to complete the order. Once payment is cleared you should receive a receipt or invoice by email.

Internet banking and online trading

The cost of completing a commercial transaction using a walk-in high street bank in the UK is currently about 50p; online it's about 0.5p. So it's not difficult to see why the major banks are investing millions in development costs to create secure ways of doing business on the Internet. Soon we can probably expect further banking savings, as banks will probably start to transfer credit card statements and other similar financial documents to customers using the Internet.

11

Children and the Internet

Although the Internet is, without doubt, an amazing development offering enormous opportunities, possibilities, remedies and solutions in many forms to millions of users, it can also be a wild "land." Freedom always carries with it a high price and the uncontrollable nature of the Internet can bring additional problems. Parents therefore, naturally want to protect their children from unsuitable parts of the Internet.

If you're a new Internet user with a sensitive nature, if you go on a random voyage of discovery around the web, be prepared for some shocks! At some stage, you'll almost certainly come across introductory pages to sex sites or porn banner adverts in other websites in an attempt to get you to click. OK, let's tell it like it is: the plain truth is that more money is made

> ## Welcome to KZuk.net
>
> KZuk.net is a free ISP created just for kids aged from 4-12, which provides interactive games and activities to help them learn whilst having fun.
>
> Sign-up for your **FREE CD-ROM** and give your kids a place where they can learn and play in complete safety.
>
> **zones**
> quiz
> homework
> mind blowing
> music
> magazine
> chat
> penpals
> art
> games
> fun
>
> **software**
> KZsurfer
> KZmail
> KZmail monitor
> Comic Chat
> Control Panel

from the sex industry on the Internet than from any other single source!

If you do not want to see any of that side of the Internet, you'll need to know in advance the web address of where you

222 > Children and the Internet

want to visit each time you use your web browser, or consider installing and setting up web filtering software. However, filtering software is not a perfect solution and tends to err on the side of caution, so may block sites that might be perfectly acceptable to you.

Nevertheless, those who do break their country's decency laws – even on the Internet – stand to get caught, as some have already discovered to their cost. With the right equipment, almost anything is traceable – and the tools are getting better and more sophisticated every day. A key question is, will staying anonymous on the Internet become a thing of the past soon?

Although a variety of filtering tools and methods are available as covered later in this chapter, probably none are completely 100% reliable. The only sure method for protecting children while they use the Internet is for a parent to be with them 100% of the time while online – a clearly impractical option for most parents today.

Identify the key danger categories

Arguably, the web, Internet newsgroups and FTP download sites probably rank highest as the most controversial areas of the Internet, especially for parents. However also remember that there may be other areas to which your child could gain access. These may contain material that at one end of the scale parents might consider mildly inappropriate or others areas that are absolutely off-limits to minors! For example, parts of the web contain pictures, text and video information that are intended only for adult viewing. The most responsible website providers of these materials ensure that adult verification procedures are in place to stop children gaining access. However, these systems may not be adequate in every instance to stop under age users accessing these sites, and often such websites

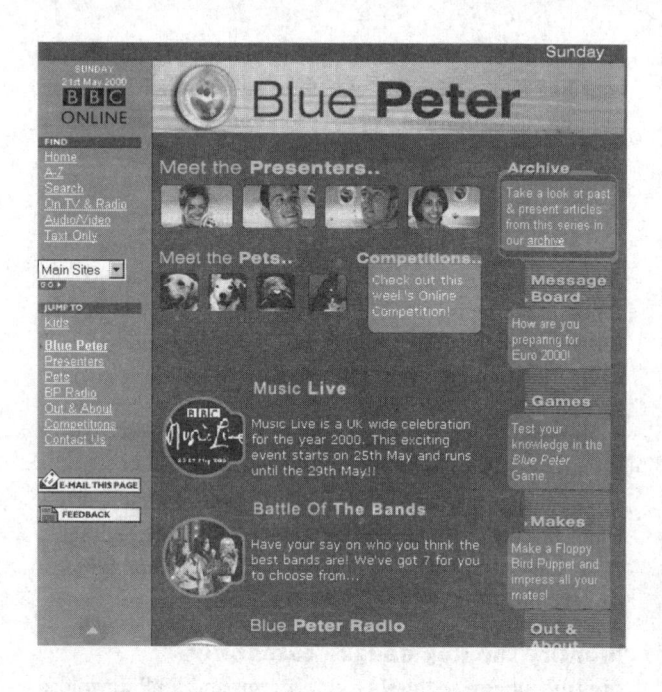

224 > Children and the Internet

may include "sample" material on their "introductory" pages anyway – clearly irresponsible! So why do they do it? For many web businesses, an important way to earn extra income from advertising starts with being able to demonstrate high numbers of visits. As a result, the largely unregulated nature of the Internet means that some website providers are simply not concerned about who accesses their site.

What about porn, drugs and other dangers?

Older children especially are naturally curious and can be exceptionally resourceful. Anything with the slightest hint of "no, you shouldn't go there", and we've got their attention: their minds are already working out "HOW TO go there." I suspect readers like myself who have children especially understand the strong urge for the new, the curious and the driving force for independence as our children start to grow into young adults.

Here's a startling statistic: probably about a third of all websites that make up the Internet include some adult sex-related content! Without filtering software in place, children can easily access sex sites and other websites of "questionable intent". However, even with filtering software in place, resourceful children may still work out how to "beat the system."

The problem does not end with access to pictures, sound and video clips intended only for adult use. All sorts of documents can be made freely available on the web to anyone who wants to read them. For example, some extreme web pages may show how to make poisons and home-made guns, and so forth.

Others may show how to just play relatively harmless but possibly expensive pranks. Those that show how to make atomic bombs and so forth hardly present a problem as, in practice, the process is almost totally impossible for anyone who does not have access to all the right components, which is why the same information is probably already available in many other higher educational establishments in one form or another around the world.

As the Internet is essentially an information store, children can find out about drugs if they're persistent enough. They can also see lots of instances of how abuse of drugs has ruined the lives of other people and of course there's no access to drugs simply by viewing on the Internet. Those who do "push" drugs, usually prefer the up-close, one-to-one, in-the-shadows contact, rather than the anonymous and "open" Internet in which anyone can be traced.

So what's the answer? Well unfortunately, there is no easy, simple quick-fix answer. What may work for one parent may not be appropriate for others and different people have different levels of tolerance. However, the following paragraphs can help you develop a strategy for minimising Internet dangers and helping your child get the best from the Internet.

Getting involved

For parents who have children with access to the Internet, the most essential advice I can offer is to get involved. If computers are new to you, why not put some time aside to learn – ideally side-by-side with your child – about computers and the Internet, if only for their sake? It's a perfect opportunity.

You can learn from each other but, in the crucial early stages of your Internet experiences, you're present and can monitor what your child is viewing immediately. To help learn more about the Internet, you can read books, magazines, take evening classes and so on. Lots of options are available; somewhere there is probably an ideal solution to suit your situation.

Ideas for creating boundaries & rules

As a parent of two teenage children myself, I appreciate that it's not always possible – or desirable – to be with your children all the time while they are using the Internet. They too need to learn independence and responsibility. And of course, as children get older, most let their parents and guardians know in plain English about their need to do their "own thing." Some parents may not want to tightly control their children's use of the Internet. Parents may consider they have a trusting relationship with their child and so are quite happy to work out a system on that basis. This is the route our family follows and it works well in practice for us. You pay the phone bill and your Internet Service Provider's fees and you probably provided the computer or WebTV, so you can set the rules. Therefore, as a start, consider the guidelines below:

1. If you have to pay for your Internet connection, agree times for your child to use the Internet and put a strict time limit for use. The animated nature of the Internet can become addictive.

2. No visiting X-rated or adult-themed websites. Period.

3. No intentionally visiting sites containing bad language or including material that your children know you don't approve of.

4. No giving out their (or your) personal information, email address, phone numbers, mailing address, personal photos, and so on, to anyone you don't personally approve of, especially in "live" areas like Chat rooms. Put a big "No" on this one – permanently!

5. Get agreement on the kinds of newsgroups your child can visit. Certain "alt..." newsgroups again contain material that deals with adult themes and some material may be highly illegal in your country.

6. Explain to your child that they should not send emails to anyone that you don't know/don't approve. On the Internet, someone with paedophilic intentions, for

example, can easily assume the identity of another child who is also keen to meet others on the Net.

You can also explain to your child that, whatever they do on the Internet, a record is stored on the PC or at your Internet Service Provider and that you as the parent may be held accountable – or that, in the case of older children, they may to have to answer questions they might prefer not to answer ever!

Discuss content control and filtering options with your Internet Service Provider

If you're concerned about what your child may access on the Internet, consider seeking an Internet Service Provider that promotes a child-friendly policy and includes appropriate options. Some provide added security with downloadable free blocking software tools. Some providers can ensure that access to certain newsgroups is refused; for example: alt.sex…, alt.binaries… and so on. In combination with other methods like web blocking software, this approach could provide a lot of protection from much of the pornography on the Internet.

Changing your web browser settings

The best web browsers include options that allow you to change or restrict the kinds of websites that a user can visit. Both Microsoft Internet Explorer and Netscape Navigator can let users control access by using a rating system.

This approach offers one way to restrict the kind of information your child can access on the Internet. This approach can work with the ratings labels that may be installed on certain websites by responsible providers as outlined in the following paragraphs.

The PICS approach

A group called the Platform for Internet Content Selection (PICS) have established a set of standards that can classify the content of a website into different categories. Any compatible web browser – like Internet Explorer, Netscape Navigator, and other compatible software – can then be configured to use the PICS standard as a guide to Internet content.

Any or all the categories of language, nudity, sex and violence (from mild to extreme in each category) can be set. In Internet Explorer v5.0x/6.0, you can set your preferences using the Internet Options command in the Tools menu. Then in the Internet Options dialog box, click the Content tab and examine options in the Content Advisor. In Netscape Navigator v4.5x onwards, go online then choose the Netwatch command in the Help menu to make your changes. In later versions you may need to search for "Netwatch" on the Netscape website to install Netwatch. This approach offers a great way to protect children from accessing inappropriate websites, or to block out certain categories of website – for example, some companies and organisations may not want employees accessing information that is not relevant to their industry during working hours.

However, PICS and other similar blocking systems are arguably far from perfect. Within a PICS-enabled web browser, perfectly "acceptable" websites may get blocked simply because the software detects a word that is used out of context or if a website does not have any rating label, as indeed many perfectly reasonable sites don't. Also, as content controlling software has to first examine a website, usually browsing speed overall slows down and so web pages may take longer to fully appear compared to a browser with no filtering active.

RSACi

Many responsible website providers rate their websites in a similar way to that which is done for television and videos. Several methods exist and one of most well known is the RSACi system. RSACi-rated sites should include the RSACi logo somewhere on the Home or Index page.

Web filtering and blocking software

In addition to built-in web browser tools for controlling access to the Internet, you can also buy software that can detect a website's content and block access to it if necessary. Filtering software can use a combination of tactics.

- Examine in advance web page wording and block those pages that contain suspect words.

- Block known sites.

- Ban other sites.

However, web filtering and blocking software usually does slow down browsing – there's usually a time delay while a website's content is being "checked."

So using the full options in blocking software can result in frustration. However, this is an issue that only you and your child can resolve. Some of the most popular filtering and blocking software include Net Nanny, CyberSitter and CyberPatrol. Most blocking programs include regularly updated lists of websites considered unsuitable for children to visit. Popular filtering programs include:

- CyberNanny: www.cybernanny.net/

- CyberPatrol: www.cyberpatrol.com or www.cyberpatrol.co.uk

- CyberSitter: www.cybersitter.com/

- Cyber Snoop: www.pearlsw.com/

- Net Nanny: www.netnanny.com or www.netnanny.co.uk/

- SurfWatch: www.surfwatch.com/

- Some ISPs – BT Internet for example – provide free web filtering software to help parents set up safer web viewing for their children. Customised blocking software providers like, for example, CompuServe, AOL and Prodigy provide their own tools for blocking access to certain websites or other dubious Internet content.

Using the Internet for homework and adult research projects

The Internet can be an incredible aid to children seeking to complete their school homework, or simply to help make homework more enjoyable, and indeed for anyone wanting to carry out basic or in-depth research.

A variety of free and "free-for-a-while" encyclopedias are available online; for example, check out:

- **Encyclopedia Britannica:** www.eb.co.uk

- **Free Encyclopedia:** freeportal.virtualave.net/FreeStuff/FreeBooks/encyclopedia.shtml

- **Encyclopedia.com:** www.encyclopedia.com

- **How Stuff Works:** www.howstuffworks.com/

- **InfoPlease:** www.infoplease.com/encyclopedia.html

- **Microsoft Encarta:** encarta.msn.co.uk

- **Mythology:** www.pantheon.org/mythica.html

- **Discovery School:** school.discovery.com

- **Spartacus Educational:** www.spartacus.schoolnet.co.uk

- **Works of J R R Tolkien:** www.glyphweb.com/arda

Or you can simply use your browser to search online with the search term "encyclopedia" plus "your topic" to find more focused information on the subject you want.

12

On the road and using the Net

Ahh... A laptop and an open road winding around a stunning Mediterranean coastline. Not a care in the world. The wind rustling through your hair on a fine summer's day. OK, enough... I just wanted to get your attention and dream a little myself. People across the world are moving around now more than any other time in history. It's perhaps not surprising, is it, when we consider all the modern gadgets, tools and different kinds of vehicles that are now commonplace in many countries?

You can also access the Internet from almost any country in the world, but once you move away from your base, you need to plan in advance and be prepared for the unexpected to minimise disruption.

With all this movement, people still need Internet access or to at least use email and a growing number need access to the web while on the move in order to perform their work tasks or just to have fun. To use email anywhere in the world, you only need a phone line – just start up your web browser and log on to your web-based email box.

Choosing and using a portable computer

The pace of development of computers is simply amazing and perhaps even more so with portable computers that have to perform the same kinds of tasks as their desktop counterparts and yet occupy a fraction of the physical space. Often when price comparisons are made, equivalent mobile computers are not as powerful as their desktop cousins. Obvious essential features include:

- **Weight:** as light as possible but balanced with what you want. Sizes range from laptops, notebooks, sub-notebooks, down to palmtops – or you may need only something like a Psion Organizer, Personal Digital Assistant (PDA) or even an Internet-compatible mobile phone to use email and basic web facilities.

- **Superb warranty:** consider what might happen if you're in Afghanistan and your notebook PC dies. If, under those conditions, a replacement computer can be sent to you within say 48 hours, you'll have a good chance of keeping your sanity!

- **Power supply:** ensure the computer can be used on electricity mains supplies ranging from 100 to 240 volts at 50–60 Hertz.

- **Modem:** ideally, include a 56 Kbps modem or equivalent modem components built in that can also link in to a cellphone – even if you don't think cellphone compatibility is important now, the chances are it will be in a few months' time. If this is not possible, you can usually obtain a compatible equivalent plug-in card modem (PC-Card/PCMCIA). Also, ideally find a modem that includes a digital line guard protector in case you try to connect to an incompatible phone system.

- **Battery power:** include batteries that keep a working charge for as long as possible – ideally 4 hours or more. A well-thought out design nowadays can provide up to about 7–9 hours. Usually, lithium-ion batteries currently offer the longest charge times and battery life.

- **Phone connectors and adaptors:** before leaving for far off places, make sure you have a "universal connection kit" that includes the various phone connectors and adaptors you may need, so that, whatever country you're located in, you can physically connect your computer to the phone system. The number of different phone systems around the world is mind-boggling.

> **HOT TIP** If you live a highly mobile life and want to use the Internet regularly, get an Internet Service Provider that allows you to gain free access to your email accounts from the web. This approach ensures that wherever your are located, providing you can gain access the to the web – and that usually means a phone line connection – you can also use email.

Web mail

Please key in your BT Internet username and password.
You do not need to add '@btinternet.com' to your username.

Username [_____]@btinternet.com

Password [_____]

[Enter]

Thankfully, the US RJ11 phone connector is emerging as a world standard.

- **Networking**: finally, if your work involves connecting regularly to your company network (LAN), you'll probably want to include a network card or network capability in your list of desirable features.

The great thing about email is that once you have a web-based email address, unlike your mailing address, people can stay in contact with you wherever you're currently located – for a growing number of people in the next few years, an email address may become just about as important as a traditional postal address!

However, whenever you're on the move, usually you'll want to set your web mail program to "leave Mail on Server" and make sure that for each message you send to someone, you also send a copy to yourself using the CC (Carbon Copy) field in your mail program. Then, when you return home, you'll have a copy of all emails you sent while on the road.

> **HOT TIP** Consider getting a second stand-by email account set up and ready to use and use it from time to time to keep it "active" (open), to provide you with more options and "reaction" time in emergencies. For example, a free service like HotMail or YahooMail could be ideal. You can easily sign up for a HotMail account through Microsoft Outlook Express v5.x onwards – log on to the Internet, open the Tools menu, choose New Account Signup followed by Hotmail and follow the simple instructions.

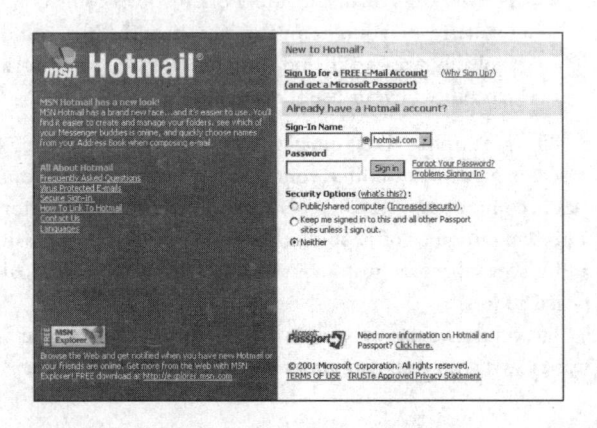

Preventing random phone line disconnections

If, while using the Internet abroad, you keep getting disconnected, here are few ideas to help prevent line disconnections or "dropout":

- Turn Call Waiting off on the line you're using. Call Waiting usually sends a series of beeps down the phone line and modems can misinterpret these beeps as a command to disconnect.

- The phone systems in some countries may send pulses down the phone line at regular intervals to calculate call times, for example: Germany, Spain and Switzerland. Therefore, unless you're using a modem that is compatible with the phone system of the country you're in, or you're not using a modem that can filter these pulses, you'll probably lose the connection. A third option is to install a filter between the modem and the phone socket. For more information, speak to your computer dealer.

- Try unplugging any other phones that share the same phone line – each additional phone on a phone line can reduce the overall current level.

Mobile phones

The Internet and mobile phones are natural partners as demonstrated in the latest WAP models that provide Internet access. Also, as the mobile networks expand and increase access speeds during the coming years, mobile phone screen sizes are expected to increase to provide a better "window" onto the Net.

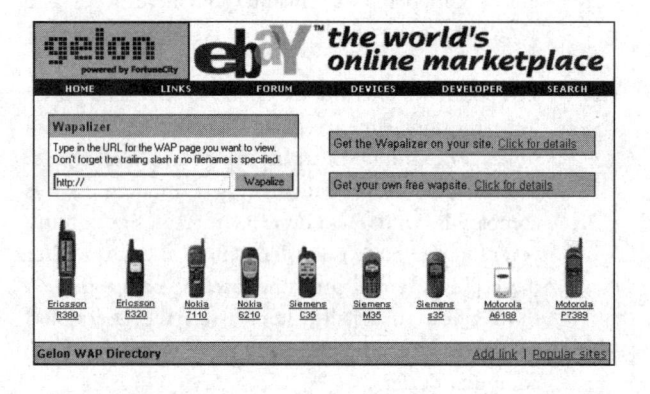

Eventually, built-in cameras too are expected to complete the video link – possibly leading to the first true global low-cost video wireless connection system. International videophone calls at low-cost Internet prices? Only time will tell but fierce global competition for business should benefit customers.

Unwired on foreign shores without a computer!

Sometimes when travelling abroad, through force of circumstances – or through personal choice – you may not have access to the Internet or email, but unexpectedly wish you had! So what are your options? A growing list of countries now includes WebTV access or equivalent, so you may find that you don't even need to venture out of your hotel room.

Also public places like airports, rail and bus stations, ferry terminals and shopping arcades or malls are set to include more Internet terminals or Net booths in addition to conventional telephones and fax machines. Other possible options might include Cybercafés – shops, bars and other public access areas that contain Internet access terminals from which you can rent Internet time and enjoy a beverage and light refreshments.

Working with fax while on the move

Yes you can send and receive faxes on the Internet too – using computers and mobile phones. Many Internet Service Providers and other companies now allow you set up a phone number from which any faxes sent to the number are converted to email message format and can therefore be sent to your email address. For example, my own ISP BT Internet provide this service. In the first instance, speak to your ISP – you may find a fax-to-email service is free for the asking.

Also, see Jfax at www.jfax.com – their service can also include converting voicemail messages to a small computer audio file format which can then be emailed to you as attachments.

For a currently free fax-to-email service, you can find more information at www.efax.com and www.plus.net/

13

Speeding up your Internet connection

Although many people use a modem to connect to the Internet, other faster options are usually available. In this section, we'll examine these topics to help you decide if the fast-track approach is for you.

For example, BT Internet offers their BT Home Highway service that essentially provides an extra telephone line purely for Internet access. Faster connections are also available with other ISDN- and ADSL-based services.

Do remember, though, that services which provide faster connections to the Internet than are currently available using the standard telephone system, usually have significantly higher running costs.

Free software tools to track your Net connection

If you're getting a continuously slow connection to the Internet, consider examining the VisualRoute utility at: www.visualroute.com/ or using some free tools to help identify where the problem lies. If results point to your Internet Service Provider, you can contact them armed with the evidence.

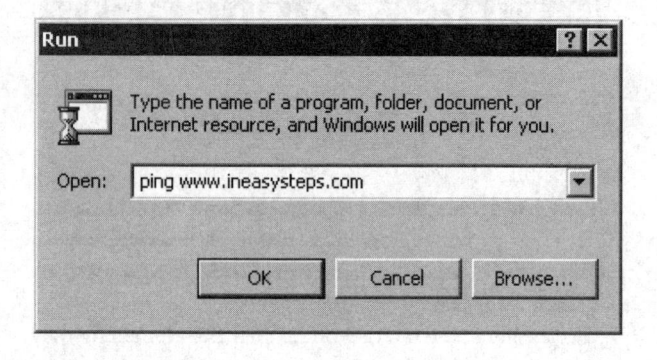

Ping is a software tool that is included with Microsoft Windows 98 onwards. Ping sends a beep to another computer somewhere on the Internet and measures how long it takes to reach its destination and return. Here's an example of how to use Ping in Windows 9x/Me/XP/NT/2000:

1. Go online.

2. Click the Windows start button.

3. Choose the Run command.

4. In the Run dialog box, type the word ping followed by a web address; for example: ping ineasysteps.com (or ping www.ineasysteps.com).

5. Copy and paste the results into a word-processed document or text editor and save. You can then present these to your Internet Service Provider to help them identify where the problem may lie.

```
Pinging websvr-1.tele.vi.net [212.78.64.33] with 32 bytes of data:
Reply from 212.78.64.33: bytes=32 time=521ms TTL=246
Reply from 212.78.64.33: bytes=32 time=420ms TTL=246
Reply from 212.78.64.33: bytes=32 time=331ms TTL=246
```

Trace Route (sometimes called Tracert or TracerRoute) is a utility that is included with Windows 95/98/Me/XP. Remember, information on the Internet hops from one main server to another to reach its destination. Trace Route traces the route and follows the number of hops taken from your Internet Service Provider to the web address – in our example, ineasysteps.com

If any delays or stoppages are found, you can identify where the delays are – for example, at your Internet Service Provider's computers – from the "time-out" indicators. With this new-found information, you can show your Internet Service Provider the results of your test – select all and copy and paste into a word processor document and save. Here's how to use it:

1. Repeat Steps 1, 2, and 3 as listed on page 247.

2. Type: tracert followed by the web location you want to trace into the box. For example: tracert ineasysteps.com (or tracert www.ineasysteps.com). If necessary, check your operating system Help file for the exact method.

Using your ISP's proxy server

Remember, web pages are stored on powerful computers permanently connected to the Internet called servers. Some Internet Service Providers make available a proxy server to help speed up access to the web. A proxy server is a system that includes a special storage area called a web cache that can help speed up access to the web by storing copies of certain websites situated on distant servers – which, therefore, are likely to take longer to display in your browser. Some Internet Service Providers even rely totally on use of a proxy server, so may form part of the set-up routine for an Internet Service Provider.

To use a proxy server, contact your Internet Service Provider and if available follow their instructions to install the correct web address for your browser to use. In Internet Explorer, you can install a proxy server web address, using the Internet Options command in the Tools menu, then click the Connections tab in the Internet Options dialog box and click the Settings button to see the proxy server box.

Avoiding Internet traffic jams

As the popularity of the Internet increases, so it becomes busier – especially the web. Just like on our roads and motorways, increased use of the Internet can sometimes result in Internet "traffic" jams! This can happen particularly on popular websites, when simply too many people are trying to access the same information for the networks to cope with properly.

When Internet traffic jams occur, users at those websites can experience delays. A web page may take much longer to display, or when you click on a link to another page you may not be immediately moved to the new page, and so on. In this event, sometimes the best remedy is to simply try again later.

ISDN & ISDN2

ISDN – or if you're feeling brave, Integrated Services Digital Network (ISDN) – is one option for people who want to have a faster access to the Net, or to an office network when working from home or on the road. In the UK alone, many companies provide ISDN services, including both British Telecom and Cable and Wireless. Typical ISDN connection speeds between a user and an ISP are 64 Kbps or 128 Kbps depending on how

> ### Welcome to ISDN
> ISDN uses digital signals as opposed to analogue (your normal phone line uses analogue). This means that it is ideal for carrying data and provides excellent quality speech lines.
>
> BT supplies two types of ISDN:
>
> ### ISDN 2e
> ISDN 2e is ideal for small businesses who need two or more normal telephone lines to handle their communications. Each ISDN 2e provides two channels of ISDN, each operating at 64kbps speed. You can bond the channels together to achieve 128Kbps speed. Often used for high speed internet access, for fast file transfer, or with an ISDN compatible phone system (PBX) for voice calls.
> ≡Read more
>
> ### ISDN 30
> ISDN 30 is ideal for medium to large businesses. It provides eight or more channels of ISDN, each working at 64Kbps speed. It is great for call centres, where clear lines and fast dialling are vital. It is often used in conjunction with Direct Dialling In (DDI), which allows individual extensions to have their own numbers, enabling your customers to talk to the right person straight away.
>
> ISDN 30 also supports many data applications, for example, providing connectivity at the central site for satellite offices linked in with ISDN 2e or Business Highway.
>
> You can easily add channels of ISDN 30 to an existing installation, so your communications can grow with your business.
> ≡Read more

your particular service is set up – up to 4 times the speed of a typical conventional modem speed of around 33 Kbps! And usually, a connection is made almost immediately!

Plus an ISDN line can handle two calls at the same time. So you can talk on the phone while sending computer data – however, you'll probably get two separate call charges under that kind of system. Even so, the pace of technological development has a habit of out-dating ideas of just a few years old. The advantages of ISDN and the more advanced ISDN2 are now being outweighed by developments in DSL, ADSL and cable technology as discussed in the following paragraphs. Nevertheless, to use ISDN, you'll need:

- A special modem also called a Terminal Adaptor or Terminal Modem.

- An ISDN telephone link: discuss this option with your ISP.

You'll also probably need to install key files to update your computer's operating system. You can discover more information about how to prepare Microsoft Windows for ISDN at: www.microsoft.com/windows/getisdn/ For Apple Mac computers, go to: www.apple.com/ Therefore, check your computer documentation or discuss the steps you need to take with your Internet Service Provider.

ADSL: just what the doctor ordered!

In recent years, one of the main challenges for telecommunications companies was to devise a system that could provide a fast Internet connection yet which could use existing telephone technology.

ADSL or more formally, Asymmetric Digital Subscriber Line, looks like it could provide an ideal solution! Essentially, ADSL can provide a very fast link to the Internet using the well-established conventional (copper wire) phone lines, so the need for any necessary upgrade or conversion work at telephone exchanges is minimised. Let's take a closer look at the main benefits of ADSL:

- Typically, a home-based user can receive information from an Internet Service Provider at an incredible rate of around 512 Kbps rising up to 2 Mbps and eventually 6–8 Mbps. Data coming in this direction is sometimes referred to as the "data-in" or downlink speed.

- Information can be sent ("data-out" or uplink) at about 64– 256 Kbps but is typically 128 Kbps! Compare that to a conventional 56 Kbps modem that most of us use today and which might typically connect at about 30– 45 Kbps – then you can appreciate what all the excitement is about! ADSL looks set to be the preferred connection method in many countries including Britain.

- Users do not have to share a phone link with other users, unlike cable. The overall speed of connection with ADSL is a combination of both the data in and data out values, leading to a much faster connection, with little upgrading to the phone superstructure being needed!

- ADSL also has an ace card: you can explore the Internet while talking on a conventional phone with both computer and phone connected to the same phone line.

Perhaps it comes as no surprise that ADSL promises some incredible benefits to Internet users and we suspect that many of the best Internet Service Providers in many countries – including Britain – will probably adopt the system sooner rather than later.

Where ADSL is new, currently prices tend to be higher but as the technology comes into the mainstream, prices usually drop, helping to provide a cheap, fast and reliable Internet infrastructure.

Currently, in Britain at least, ADSL looks like a much better option compared to say an ISDN-based Internet link. However, discuss options with your Internet Service Provider and phone company to arrive at the best choice in relation to your own particular circumstances. For more information about ADSL options from British Telecom, visit: www.btopenworld.com/

Using cable modems

A cable modem allows you to connect to the Internet using the same cable used to receive cable television programmes, providing that Internet access is supported by your cable provider – and most do. The big advantage is speed and low cost: cable modems can move information from an Internet Service Provider to a home-based modem hundreds of times faster than a conventional phone-based (copper wire) modem. Incredibly, cable modems speed can reach 8000–10,000 Kbps (8–10 Mbps) – if you're lucky. In practice, rates are often lower, but still in the Mbps range.

What speeds can I expect?

This has been the major advantage of cable modems and the force moving their development forward to end the www.wait. cable modems have been so fast (compared to analogue modems) that it exposes slow links in the net and slow ISP's backbones, the slowest part of the net is no longer form ISP to user.

TRANSFER RATE FOR A 10 MBYTE FILE

Modem speed	Type Transfer time
9.6 kb/s telephone modem	2.3 hours
14.4 kb/s telephone modem	1.5 hours
28.8 kb/s telephone modem	46 minutes
56 kb/s telephone modem	24 minutes
128 kb/s ISDN modem	10 minutes
1.54 Mb/s T-1 connection	52 seconds
4 Mb/s cable modem	20 seconds
10 Mb/s cable modem	8 seconds

Source: Cablelabs

Actual connection speed depends mainly on where you live and the number of other users currently sharing the connection. In some countries – like the USA – the ability of a cable modem to offer a fast, reliable connection to the Internet and television programmes has made cable a popular choice. Cable TV companies in the UK and other countries are now offering Internet access in addition to their standard cable TV subscriptions; a trend almost certainly set to continue.

Satellite connections

Companies that are providing television information through direct-broadcast satellites can also adapt their systems to provide fast Internet access. You'll need a special TV-type satellite dish to receive information (data in), while you send information

---

Beam™ is the super-fast affordable 'always-on' broadband internet connection for home users . . . surfers . . . downloaders . . .
everyone frustrated by home telephones and technology

The satellite link means you don't have to wait for modernisation down at your local telephone exchange, or for cable to be laid past your door.
Beam™ gives you home internet access at speeds of up to **10 times faster than a 56K modem**, propelling you into the world of interactive multi media, high-speed surfing, fast file downloads, and audio/video streaming.

A fully trained accredited technician will install the satellite modem, a satellite dish and driver software for you, to get you up and running in no time.

- Click **HERE** to to view the Home Users Frequently Asked Questions (FAQs)
- Click **HERE** to request more information and enter our **FREE prize draw**
- Click **HERE** for Home Users pricing

(data out) using land-based phone lines either through a Dial-up or leased line connection.

Typical transfer speeds from the satellite Internet Service Provider to a home-based modem (data in) are usually between 200 and 400 Kbps. However, transmitting information from your modem to your Internet Service Provider (data out) is typically at a much slower rate: 33.6 Kbps or a maximum of 56 Kbps using a modem. Nevertheless, overall speed is a combination of the two, so typical satellite connections speeds are very fast compared with a 56 Kbps modem.

Satellite connections are ideal for companies or organisations wanting a fast, "permanent" Internet connection or for individuals whose geographical layout means that using a conventional modem is simply not possible.

Using leased lines

Commercial users who want fast, permanent access to the Internet may opt to have a leased line installed. However, this option is expensive, really expensive! Leased lines are probably more suited to mid to larger-sized companies and organisations who do much business on the Internet.

14

Getting started with email

Just like the Pony Express, the telegraph, telephone and fax, email has changed – and still is changing – the world in which we live, work and play providing yet another reliable communications option – and the show has only just begun: video mail is just around the corner! However today, let's explore how to get up and running with email.

Introducing email

Electronic mail or email refers to the activity of sending and receiving electronic messages or documents across the Internet or a computer network. Most of these documents use plain text but you can also work with lots of different types of files and documents. Email is perhaps one of the oldest and most well

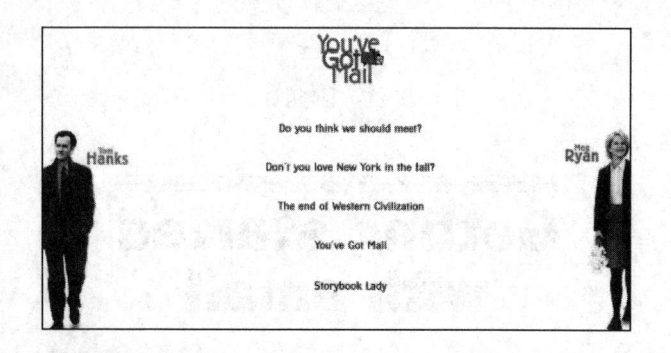

> **HOT TIP**
>
> The one big benefit is that email messages can take just seconds to travel anywhere across the globe for only a small cost outlay.

established "faces" of the Internet and, although still largely text-based, voice- and video-based email systems are set to dominate in the coming years. An email message travels at electronic speeds and should therefore take only seconds to arrive at its destination, wherever a recipient may live – providing all the "links in the chain" are in place and working normally. When you send an email, the message first needs to reach your Internet Service Provider's computer that deals with outgoing email and which examines the email address, to identify where to send the email first, then sends the email to the most appropriate computer for handling email sent to that particular address.

The next computer in the chain repeats this exercise and continues to route your email message to the following computer in the "chain." And so on across the Internet until your message reaches the Internet Service Provider (ISP) or the particular computer that provides the email "box" of your recipient. Remember, "box" for our purposes is not really a box, rather think of it as a special storage area on a computer reserved for email messages for a single person only.

Sometimes, the computers that handle and process email may stop working for a while (become overloaded) or work incorrectly in some way. However, these events that happen from time to time usually do not last for more than a few hours. Email is therefore considerably more reliable than conventional mail. Furthermore, many Courts of Law around the world now accept an email message as documentary proof or evidence of a communication taking place.

> To send and receive faxes and emails on a PC, your computer needs to have a compatible modem correctly installed (Internet ready). ISDN users need a special type of modem more popularly known as a Terminal Adaptor.

You can create an email document using software in a computer, mobile phone, WebTV, and a growing range of other electronic devices. Email is a great way to communicate with family, friends and work colleagues whether they live close to you or are located thousands of miles away in another country. Two key characteristics have helped email to thrive: it's simple to use and it offers a low cost way to communicate. So how do we use email? Once your email software is properly set up – we'll cover this important topic a little later – here's what you do:

1. Type your message and address it to someone else on the Internet – that is, someone who also has an email address (the Internet equivalent of a postal address).

2. Click the Send button to connect to the Internet, then sit back and watch the magic happen. Most email programs can send and receive email automatically during the same session.

Not used email before? No problem, when you really do start using it, you'll soon see the benefits and probably use the phone and fax less. Email is an informal, direct way of communicating so you can leave out any unnecessary words and just state your message plainly and simply.

As a bonus, you'll probably get things done quicker, and so have more free time – just don't become addicted to email. If, like me, you're always looking for ways to save time and get more done with less, email will help you do just that and regain some quality time in your life!

How do I work with email?

Currently, the most common tool for using email is a computer – desktop or portable – but that may change to mobile phones and television soon. You can send and receive email in two main ways:

- Using email software installed on your computer or other Internet access device. Popular examples include: Microsoft Outlook Express, Netscape Messenger, Pegasus and Eudora Pro.

- Through the use of email facilities already established on a website: this approach is popularly known as web mail.

> To ensure that both web- and discrete software-based methods of working with email are in place takes only a little extra work. Then you're guaranteed at least one other way to always have access your email box if for some unexpected reason, your usual method fails or is unavailable at any time.

Many people – especially those who travel or are away from their home or office often, use a combination of both methods above to ensure they can access their email system at any time and in almost any location.

Email benefits v. drawbacks

Email has a lot going for it; perhaps that's why it is now one of the most important ways to communicate around the world with millions of messages whizzing across the globe daily. Let's explore some reasons why the rapidly growing use of email is causing many changes to the way we communicate. Benefits include:

- **Email is fast:** it takes only seconds to send and receive an email and it operates 24 hours/day, 365 days/year.

- **A recipient does not have to be present** to receive an email.

- **Email is cheap** to use, much cheaper than phone or fax in which cost can vary depending on where you're calling or faxing to. Many Internet Service Providers (ISPs) now include free email accounts with their standard Internet access accounts. Often, your only cost, other than the time it takes to learn how to use email, may include only the cost of a local phone call irrespective of where an email is sent. New "free" Internet access deals promise to reduce the cost of email even further. In the UK, BT Internet for example offers free Internet Access through a freephone number from 6 pm – 8 am weekdays and from midnight Friday to midnight Sunday. Other organisations are also proposing various free Internet Access deals. However, do check the small print: hidden charges may still hit your wallet.

- The use of email **generally means less paper is used** saving some trees and helping reduce the amount of waste and resulting pollution! This has just got to be a great move, hasn't it? However, in practice, much depends on whether we print our email messages. With regular computer data backup routines in place, the need to have hard copies printed is often no longer a serious issue. So, why not pick out your imaginary tree in some precious part of the world and adopt it.

If you're in business, however, the use of computers has probably escalated the amount of printed material and the law in some countries requires that certain documents must still be kept in printed form.

- **An email is an original document** and many organisations – particularly some legal bodies – now recognise this fact. However, if this aspect is important to what you do, variations do exist so you may need to check what is valid with legal representatives in your country.

- To send and receive email, **you don't need to be concerned with stationery**, stamps, envelopes, mailing labels, DTP design or printing costs. A big saving for some!

- **Email allows you to concentrate on the content** of your message rather than spend time working with fonts, paper, logos, layout and design.

- **Duplication of text or web information is simple** with email. Like most software, Copy, Move and Paste commands are only a click away. Plus you can use the powerful **Carbon Copy (Cc) and Blind Carbon Copy (Bcc) commands**, to route a message to hundreds or even thousands of additional recipients.

However, to reduce the number of bulk emailing complaints, many Internet Service Providers now put limits on how many messages you can send at any one time.

- **Email is a superb way to communicate across different time zones** and so avoid the "red eye": email can be read when the addressee is ready. You can also attach a special "This message is important" marker to urgent emails to help ensure the addressee is alerted quickly.

- Compared to many other computer-based routines, **email is a simple, proven, well-established and reliable system.**

- "Smiley" characters are often used in plain text to put over **emotion, special meaning** or simply just to have fun. Smiley examples include:

    :-)   (smile)

    :-((frown)

    :-D   (laughing)

and so on. For more information on Smileys, see page 322.

- With email slang or the use of **abbreviations you can reduce the amount of typing required.** Of course this approach is only useful if all parties involved understand the slang. Common examples include: BTW (By The Way), HTH (Hope That Helps) and FYI (For Your Information). See also page 323.

- The **simplicity of email** helps develop quick, to-the-point communications saving time for all concerned.

- At the end of each message, you can automatically include an **email "signature"**– a few lines of text about you, your company, contact details, special offer, etc., without having to re-enter this information every time you send an email. You can often create several email signatures to use for a variety of different purposes and simply call the one you want when you want it.

- You can send email messages in **plain text** (no formatting, colours, and so on). Or if you want precise control about how an email looks, use different colours, etc. You can create an **HTML-based** email – HTML is essentially the language used to create web pages. Just make sure your recipient can also receive HTML email messages first though.

- A **permanent record** of what is being discussed can also be available with email, as opposed to phone or direct meeting communications.

- **No need for large filing cabinets** to store paper files that become a little more worn over time.

- Specific email records can be **searched** for quickly using powerful Search and Find commands.

- You can **add other types of files** to an email message as "attachments" – which can be made up of text, pictures, sounds, video files, database files, spreadsheet files and software programs.

- Email is an ideal way to communicate with someone who is usually busy, uses a phone often, or is on the road away from their office.

- You can literally **have fun with email!** Lots of folks play games, chess, etc., using email. Or if you want to send a special type of greetings card, the chances are the one you want is available to be sent by email. For example, if you celebrate Valentine's Day, maybe that special person might appreciate a smouldering email containing a web link that they simply click to fire up their web browser and see the **eCard** design you chose with perhaps a favourite tune playing in the background. Valentine's day may never be the same again!

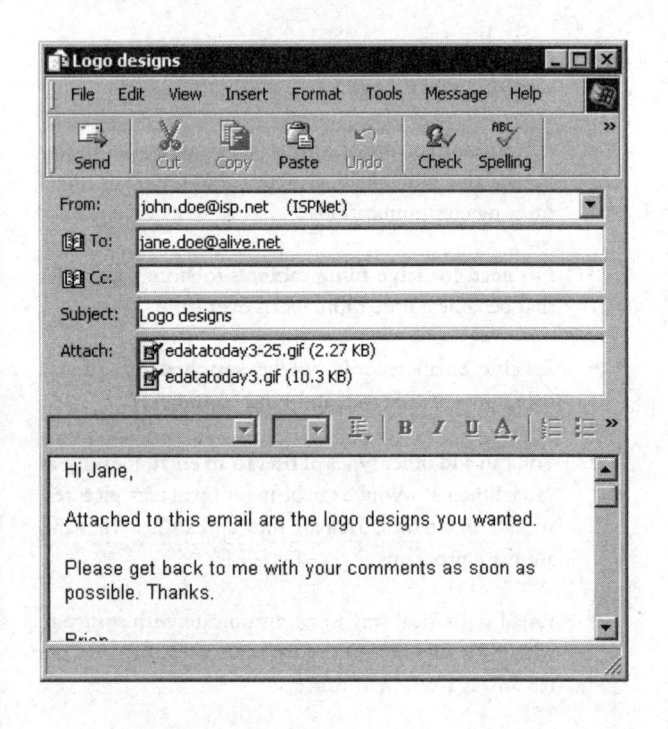

- A powerful feature of email is that you can send or **forward a single email message to multiple recipients with a single command!** However, as discussed elsewhere in this book, use multiple email tools with consideration and care – otherwise, you could get yourself into quite a lot of trouble. Bulk email refers to sending the same email to many recipients at once and can annoy people intensely – especially if they didn't ask for your message in the first place!

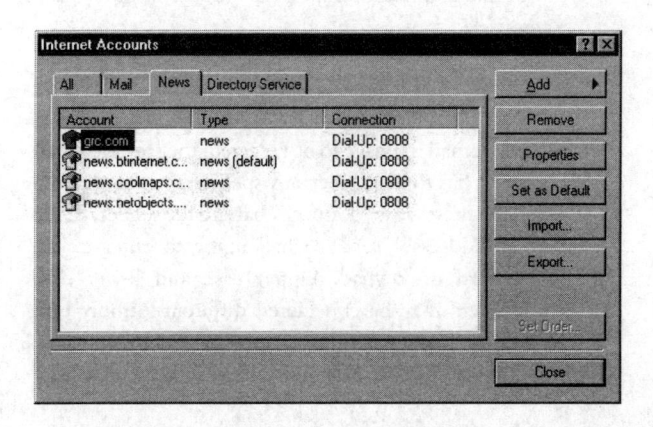

- You can use email to take part in **Internet discussion groups** and newsgroups covering the thousands of different topics available – or even start your own discussion group/newsgroup. However remember, subscribing to discussion groups or mailing lists is one of the quickest ways to suddenly start receiving a lot of email!

- Using email regularly can help you **compile better communications** and learn to type quicker.

- The beauty of text-based email is that **it's simple – and it works!**

- **Pure text-based email messages take up little storage space** in a computer's memory, and therefore don't make large demands. Plus, of course, you don't need filing cabinets, folders, paper, etc. – however, do get into the habit of backing up your computer data regularly.

Superb as email is, it has drawbacks:

- For an email message to be received, the specific **email address has to be correct:** any spelling or syntax errors and the message is "bounced" back to the sender. Some email addresses can be challenging to enter at the keyboard or keypad. Upper case and lower case characters may be considered different. Simply put, you need to know the exact email address before sending a message. However, often you can then store an email address in a special address book for easy retrieval next time.

- Email is **only useful if used regularly and all parties concerned know how to use their email systems.**

- Even though sending an email is fast, the speed advantage is only realised **if the person at the other end checks their email box often.**

- You **need access to a computer, mobile phone, WebTV or other Internet Access device** and know how to use them.

- Currently, most of us still **need to use a keyboard** to create an email message or understand the symbol systems that are used with a specific mobile phone.

- If you're completely new to email, like any new activity, it **takes time to learn** and get accustomed to new methods of communicating.

- To keep credibility when creating text-based emails means that users could benefit from **ensuring messages are clear, concise and accurate often demanding extra time input.**

- Arguably, **putting over emotion is difficult in an email and open to misinterpretation.** However, once the communicating parties become familiar with email, accepted methods and symbols have been developed which can help bridge the gap (see page 322 for more information about "Smileys").

- **The awesome power of email can trap the unwary.** Sending email to large amounts of people who have not asked for it – often referred to as bulk email spamming – is a sensitive issue to many. Most Internet Service Providers take a tough line with spammers – you can have your email and web accounts closed without notice and even receive a bill for their extra "clean up" time. Apologising to thousands of email subscribers is expensive in terms of time and resources.

- Email, like the Internet, **can become addictive** and so may reduce, not enhance, the quality of life for some people. As with any addiction, treatment is available and often the best guidelines are available online – the very place email and Internet addicts go.

- Although you can record messages and attach sound files to an email, arguably these systems have not yet gained wide use as several other factors need to be taken into account, and **computers at both ends must be**

compatible and set up to deal with these more complex types of files.

What do I need to use email?

Usually, the following components are needed to send and receive email:

- **Key electronic hardware:** computer, mobile phone, WebTV, one of the superb new Internet-compatible microwave ovens, and so on.

- **Phone line** or equivalent connection to the Internet.

- **An email account:** usually, with an Internet Service Provider.

- **Email software:** to send, receive and organise email messages.

Popular email programs include Microsoft **Outlook Express** – comes with Microsoft's **Internet Explorer web browser** and is currently free. Outlook Express also supports Microsoft's free Hotmail web-based email system, so you can literally get an email account within minutes – look for the command to set up a Hotmail account on the Tools menu (usually).

Others include **Eudora Pro** from Qualcomm: www.eudora.com and **Pegasus Mail:** www.pegasus.com **Netscape Messenger** is another fine email program that

> ## Eudora Products
>
> **Download Eudora 5.11**
>
> Eudora Products
> Eudora 5.1
>
> Free Download
> Buy Now
> Multi-user Licensing
>
> Updates & Upgrades
> Online Tutorials
> Technical Support
>
> PureVoice Technology
>
> ### Eudora 5.1 Email
> The best email program just got even better. Email traffic is on the rise. Eudora® is the best email program for people who get lots of email. If you're not one of those people now, you will be soon. So, take control of your email before it takes control of you. Eudora 5.1 is more than a way to send and receive messages - it's a powerful email management tool with features to increase your productivity and enhance your communications. Download the full-featured version of Eudora 5.1 now - it's free.
>
> Check here first if you are upgrading from a paid version of Eudora.
>
> MAIL SERVERS
>
> FREE MAIL SERVERS
>
> UTILITIES

comes free with Netscape Communicator/Navigator web browser – which you'll need to have installed first before you can use Messenger.

In fact, lots of different email programs and enhancements are available on the Internet. So if the list on page 273 don't fit your needs or if you're curious, why not perform a search. Even some of the latest refrigerators and microwave cookers allow you to send and receive email and more and more household electronic devices may well include some sort of email capability in the next few years.

So if you're in the mood to create a really spicy or exotic culinary masterpiece but can't quite remember the instructions to that superb meal you had last month at Roberto's, you can simply cheat: just tap in what you want to know on the fridge door and away you go!

How does email work?

In the editing window of your email software, remember, you enter the email address of the person you want to send your email to, type your message, then you might want to check it for spelling mistakes, etc., and click the **Send button** when ready.

Now depending on your email program and how it is configured, your email software may send your message immediately or move it to the **Outbox** for sending later when you're ready or when you next connect to the Internet. Once your email message is sent, it is usually stored in a special area on a powerful computer that is part of your recipient's Internet Service Provider network.

Alternatively, if the organisation to which you're sending your email has their own direct connection to the Internet, the relevant email is stored somewhere on their own dedicated PC, often also known as a **mail server, email server, mail client, mail host,** or other similar-sounding label. Each email message then gets rerouted to the correct person internally. On a mail server computer, the storage space for holding email messages is actually divided into numerous, smaller, separate areas each with a unique address and called an email box.

When a recipient decides they want to "open" their email box, they connect to the Internet (or company network) and choose the command to check or retrieve their email messages. A **user name and password** may need to be entered at this time to identify the authorised user unless the software has been previously set up to check email automatically.

Then any email messages present in the email "box" are sent to the computer authorised to retrieve it. Although we have examined the email process in some detail, in practice, checking for email usually takes only a few seconds. Furthermore, in most email systems currently you can send and receive email in two main formats:

- **Plain text:** includes no formatting, bold, italic, font styles, colours, etc, just plain text. The main benefit is that any recipient should be able to display your message without problems.

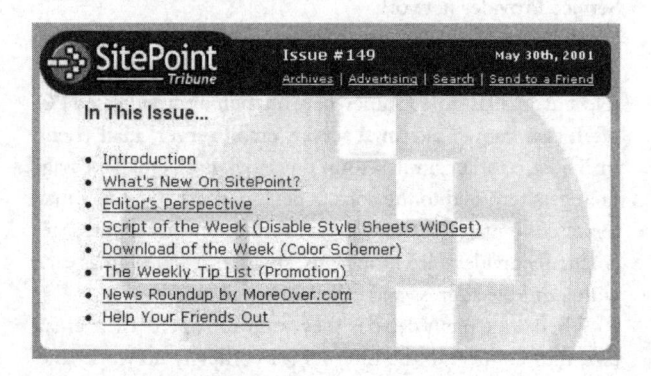

```
SitePoint                Issue #149              May 30th, 2001
    Tribune              Archives | Advertising | Search | Send to a Friend

In This Issue...

• Introduction
• What's New On SitePoint?
• Editor's Perspective
• Script of the Week (Disable Style Sheets WiDGet)
• Download of the Week (Color Schemer)
• The Weekly Tip List (Promotion)
• News Roundup by MoreOver.com
• Help Your Friends Out
```

- **HTML format:** here lots of design flexibility is built in, with similar options as available for web pages – text, hyperlinks, different backgrounds, pictures, different font styles and animations, etc.

If you use this much more colourful and possibly animated format to send email, make sure your recipient's email software can handle HTML-type messages. Even so, if an HTML message is sent to an address that is not set up to handle it, the message can still be read providing the recipient is using an HTML email-compatible program.

In this event, Outlook Express for example, ensures a recipient receives a plain text version of the message and the HTML version is included as an attachment. However, some email software might only send the HTML version and therefore would display as a mass of hard to read characters in a non-compatible email reader.

What's an email address?

For newcomers to email, it's not a street address in Cyberspace city; rather, an email address is a unique name so that only the email addressee can receive their email messages. Here are some imaginary and real email addresses:

- billgates@mycompany.com

- scully@xfiles.co.uk

- mulder@TheTruthIsOutThere.com

- president@whitehouse.gov

- primeminister@number10.gov

Currently, an email address is made up of two parts separated by an @ symbol to ensure they do not become mixed. Full stops are used to separate the various address components. Let's examine the structure of an email in detail:

- The first part of an email address is simply the name given to the addressee – not necessarily an individual's personal name, although that may be possible providing no one else in the same organisation or Internet Service Provider is using that name. Or you can use a shorthand version, a nickname, or simply something unique. However often, a "User Name" provided by an Internet Service Provider forms this first part of an email address, so you may not have a totally free choice. In the fun examples above, this part includes: "billgates", "scully", "mulder", "president" and "primeminster".

- Characters that follow the @ symbol and precede the full stop make up the address of the recipient's Internet Service Provider or a web domain name. For example, in the web address: www.ineasysteps.com, this part is "ineasysteps".

- At the end of an email address, the characters after the full stop usually denote the organisation type. The most popular (with their expanded meanings in brackets) for international uses include:

  - .com (commercial company)

  - .org (non-profit organisation)

  - .net (Internet-based company or organisation)

  - .edu (education establishment)

  - .gov (government)

  - .mil (military)

Country-specific addresses can also be used, if preferred, for example:

- .co.uk (UK-based company or organisation)

- .ltd.uk and .uk.com (examples of newer variations that emerging)

- .co.au (Australian-based company or organisation), and so on.

So using our previous example: "billgates@mycompany.com" translates to really mean: "Bill Gates at My Company.com."

Are there any characters I can't use?

Currently, not all characters available on your keyboard can be used in an email address. Some characters – like a forward slash (/), for example – will almost certainly have a special, reserved meaning in your computer's operating system. Full stops also have special meaning and as we have seen can only be used in a specific way in an email address. The full list of these "illegal" characters depends on computer operating systems (for example: Microsoft Windows, Apple MacOS, UNIX, Linux, etc).

However, most Internet connection standards allow you to use letters, both upper case and lower case, numbers, dashes and full stops as described in the previous paragraphs. Usually, using upper case or lowercase letters doesn't make any difference: both are considered the same. To discover your precise options, check with your Internet Service Provider. You can also learn more about what you can and can't use in an email address in your computer's email software or operating system software.

Autoresponders: tireless workers on the Net

Here's another type of email address: info@mysite.com It's an address that does not "point" to an individual, rather it uses the word info and suggests that when someone sends an email to that address, they're asking for some kind of information in return.

This information may be sent manually, however our relentless desire for instant results means that usually these types of email address are set up so that the desired information is automatically sent back to the sender, often within seconds using an autoresponder system – a kind of Internet fax-back tool.

One of the big benefits of using an autoresponder is that once it is set up, no one need be present to enable the

> **HOT TIP**
> Generic email addresses can also be used as autoresponders, like: info@companyname.com and report1@companyname.co.uk

autoresponder to work. For example, every time someone sends an email to the (imaginary) autoresponder info33@mysite.com, the autoresponder could automatically reply with an email message containing the desired information. The autoresponder message content need only be created once and stored on the web mail server computer as part of that particular autoresponder. You can set up autoresponders for all sorts of purposes, for example to provide:

- Basic information.

- Your latest newsletter.

- A report on a particular topic or theme.

- A Help file.

- A Frequently Asked Questions document.

Creating an email address

An email address must be unique to ensure that email intended for that address can be received. For best results and if you have a choice, try to make your email address short and easy to remember. The more complex an address is, the more likely people are to get it wrong, make typing mistakes and become frustrated – and if you're in business, this can have serious consequences.

For personal email addresses, obviously your name is probably the best option. However, many people have similar sounding names; so if someone else has already taken your preferred choice, consider perhaps adding numbers or dashes or providing some other variation. For example, imagine that your Internet Service Provider is called "Speedyjoe"; if john.smith@speedyjoe.com is not available, consider j.smith@speedyjoe.com or john.smith2@speedyjoe.com and so on. Or if you're in business, you might want to use job titles or service names like: publisher@mycompany.com, help@mycompany.com or special.offer@mycompany.com To set up a new email address, make a list of your preferred choices before going online. Experiment and try out different combinations.

CompuServe and AOL email addresses

Many CompuServe users still use numbers to make up their email address even though they can change these to more user-friendly nicknames. For example, I think you'll agree 13579,864 is arguably not as friendly as John_Doe@compuserve.com. CompuServe users can also exchange email using a comma instead of a full stop to separate the key components as shown in the above example. However, this approach does not work on the Internet.

To convert this kind of CompuServe email address for use on the Internet just replace the comma with a full stop and add @compuserve.com. Therefore, after we convert our example CompuServe email address above, it now becomes 13579.864@compuserve.com. AOL users can in a similar way convert their internal email address for use on the Internet by adding @aol.com to the end of their email name. For example: John_Doe@aol.com

Getting an email account

To use standard email, you'll need access to the Internet. For most people, this means using the services of an Internet Service Provider and, usually, a wide range of choices are available. An Internet Service Provider makes available at least one email box and some provide several – ideal if you have other family members. Other providers like BT Internet with their yearly Plan Unlimited package allow you to have an unlimited number of email boxes – a great option if you want to use different addresses for different purposes, for example:

- sales-smith@btinternet.com

- help-smith@btinternet.com

- and so on.

One of the main benefits of using the services of an Internet Service Provider is that, usually, the same configuration and settings used to enable your access to the Internet can also be used to make email services available to you. So, let's examine the two kinds of Internet email accounts that are available through Internet Service Providers:

- **Those that create their own standards and therefore use customised software:** examples in this category include: AOL and CompuServe (now part of AOL too). Usually, they provide their own software or customised versions of popular email and web software. A possible drawback with this approach is that sometimes communication with the "open" Internet can lead to problems or be unnecessarily complex. However, this approach is often popular with new Net users.

![AH Properties dialog screenshot]

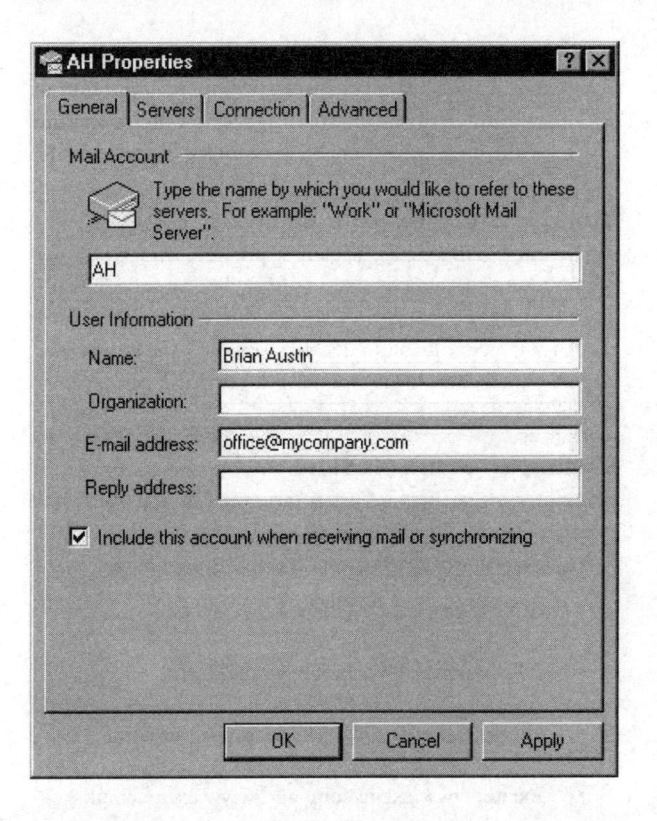

General tab showing:

Mail Account
Type the name by which you would like to refer to these servers. For example: "Work" or "Microsoft Mail Server".

AH

User Information
- Name: Brian Austin
- Organization:
- E-mail address: office@mycompany.com
- Reply address:

☑ Include this account when receiving mail or synchronizing

[OK] [Cancel] [Apply]

- **Providers that use open standards, protocols and software:** examples here include: HotMail, FreeServe and BT Internet. With this option, usually, you can use any standard email and web software to communicate with others on the Internet. Arguably, software available with "open" providers is easier to install and use.

Storage space for your emails

For storing your emails, usually a provider allocates a few megabytes of space on their mail server. For most people, this is more than enough; however, checking your email box(es) regularly is a good habit to develop to avoid losing any email. Regular email checking is especially important if you expect to receive emails with large attachments.

Finding an email provider

Computer magazines also often carry out surveys of the best Internet Service Providers and so include essential contact details. The table below lists some currently popular providers:

- **AOL (America OnLine):** www.aol.com/

- **BT Internet:** www.btopenworld.com/

- **CompuServe (CIX):** www.compuserve.com/

- **Excite:** www.excite.com/ and www.excite.co.uk

- **Freeserve:** www.freeserve.com/

- **HotMail:** (Microsoft): www.hotmail.com/

- **iName:** www.iname.com/

- **Tiscali:** www.tiscali.co.uk (now includes LineOne.net)

- **Yahoo:** www.yahoo.com or www.yahoo.co.uk/

Free email accounts

Many organisations now offer free email accounts. In combination with CD-ROMs that often accompany popular computer magazines, you can have all the software you need to get online quickly. Or if you already have access to the Internet, you can go online and easily sign up for a free email account.

Most free mainstream Internet Service Providers now provide some free web space and at least one free email account. For personal use and for most purposes, a free email address is ideal – hey, it's free and does the job. However for businesses, some caution is needed: credibility is at stake! How you appear online says a lot about you and your approach to business. An email address linked to a true website address arguably puts over a more professional image.

Billg@microsoft.com obviously means Bill is part of Microsoft.com, whereas john.smith@hotmail.com and jane.smith@compuserve.com immediately show that like many others, John Smith uses a free Microsoft Hotmail email box and Jane Smith uses a CompuServe email box. Convenient, easy and cost-effective to use? Yes absolutely! However a potential new customer might seriously question both John and Jane's business credibility with thoughts like: "If they have to use a free email box, or aren't even using their own domain name, maybe they're not as successful as they suggest." Ouch! A bad start before a new sale is even made.

Working with web email

Many free Internet Service Providers allow you to set up your email accounts on the web first, and then provide you with the know-how to have your email rerouted to your email software should you choose that option. In fact, you don't need to have dedicated email software installed on a computer to send and receive email! Equivalent 100% web-based options are available. Also many Internet Service Providers now provide free web mail accounts as part of their basic subscription package.

However, most people who pay for every minute while online currently prefer to access their email using dedicated email software like Outlook Express or Eudora Pro, to connect to the Internet, send and retrieve email then disconnect. Working with web-based email can arguably be more time consuming so may be more expensive for business users, but

> **HOT TIP** Web-based access is ideal if you're on the road or travel abroad often and most web email accounts also allow you to redirect mail to another email box if you prefer.

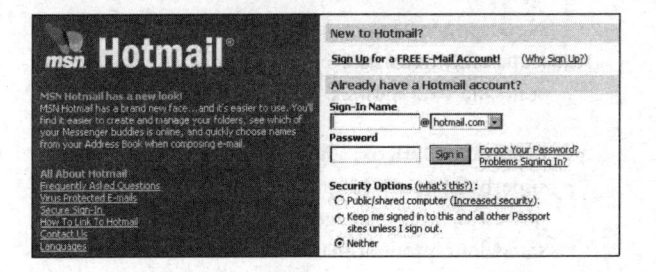

is usually much easier to work with while travelling away from your base and some would argue even essential.

Installing and setting up your email software

Working in partnership with your Internet Service Providers, email software allows you to create, edit, send, receive, view and manage all email messages with which you work. Lots of email programs are available, however some packages have become especially popular, including:

- **Microsoft Outlook Express:** probably by far the most popular email software in use today; also includes a fine basic newsgroup reader and currently comes free with Internet Explorer web browser. For details, visit: www.microsoft.com/

- **Netscape Messenger:** also includes a newsgroup reader; is currently free with Netscape Communicator Internet suite and web browser: www.netscape.com/

- **Microsoft Outlook:** a Microsoft "heavyweight" and a superb Personal Information Manager (PIM) and powerful email management program; available as a standalone product that is also part of the Microsoft Office suite: www.microsoft.com/office

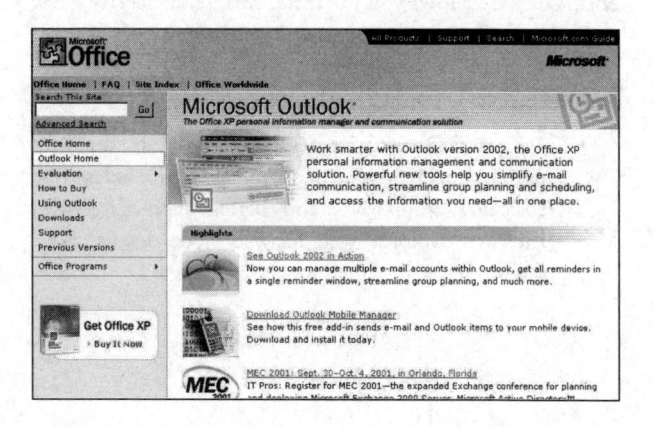

- **Eudora Pro:** from Qualcomm, this popular, powerful and well established email program is available for both the PC and the Apple Mac. Currently, a free version is available if you allow banner advertisements to display while you're using the software. If you don't like seeing the banner ads, a chargeable version is also available: www.eudora.com/

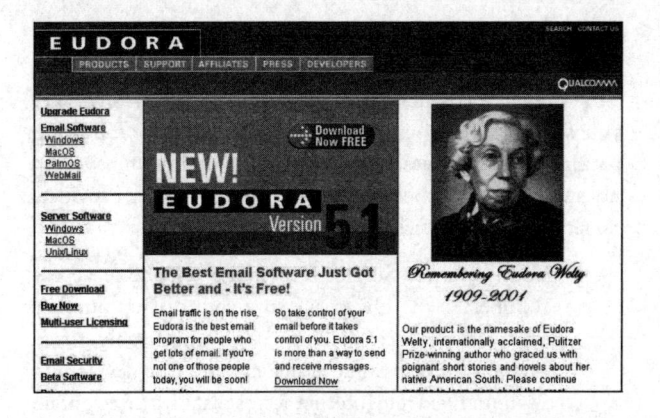

- **Pegasus Mail:** another powerful emailer that is currently free.

To use your new email account, you'll probably need to know several pieces of key information as described in the following paragraphs. Usually however, most of the information you need to get up and running quickly is provided by your Internet Service Provider. Furthermore, wizard-based installation software often available from good Internet Service Providers automatically covers much of what is listed in the

Getting started with email < 291

following paragraphs – so you may not even need to know the details to at least get up and running.

However, if you perform a manual installation at any time, you will need the specific information listed in the following paragraphs that applies to your account. Anything that you're not sure of you can check with your Internet Service Provider. So let's cover the basics:

- **Your Internet Service Provider's telephone access number:** in the UK, make sure your dial-up number uses either a local dialling code or preferably a free phone number. Some providers are now developing 24-hour fixed rate Internet access that uses a free phone number for dial-up.

- **User Name or Account Name:** often this is taken from the first part of your email address and so you may not have a choice. For example, in the following imaginary address: fox.mulder@TheyWontGetMe.com, the first part, "fox.mulder" or even just "fox" might form the User Name for this imaginary account.

- **A password:** this component is usually made up of letters/numbers and optionally some other special characters. The key point is, your password needs to be unique and known only to you or other trusted parties. While your email user name is public knowledge, your

> **BEWARE:** Anyone who knows your password could gain unauthorised access to your email box. Therefore keep this information private. Usually you can set up your software to "remember" a log-on password – a useful option to consider if other people do not have direct access to your computer.

password should be kept private. Within the set-up dialog boxes, a password should appear as a series of asterisks (★★★★★) for security reasons.

- **Your email address:** as agreed with your Internet Service Provider.

- **Return email address:** usually only needed if you want replies to be sent to an email address other than your default address. For example, if working from home, you may prefer to have any replies sent to your office or work-based email address.

- **Your Incoming Mail (POP3) address:** to recap, a protocol is nothing more than a set of rules. Post Office Protocol (POP) 3 ensures that all email addressed to you is stored and routed to your email box. If you're not using POP3, you can use IMAP below. Example: for BT Internet customers, currently, the POP3 address is: mail.btinternet.com

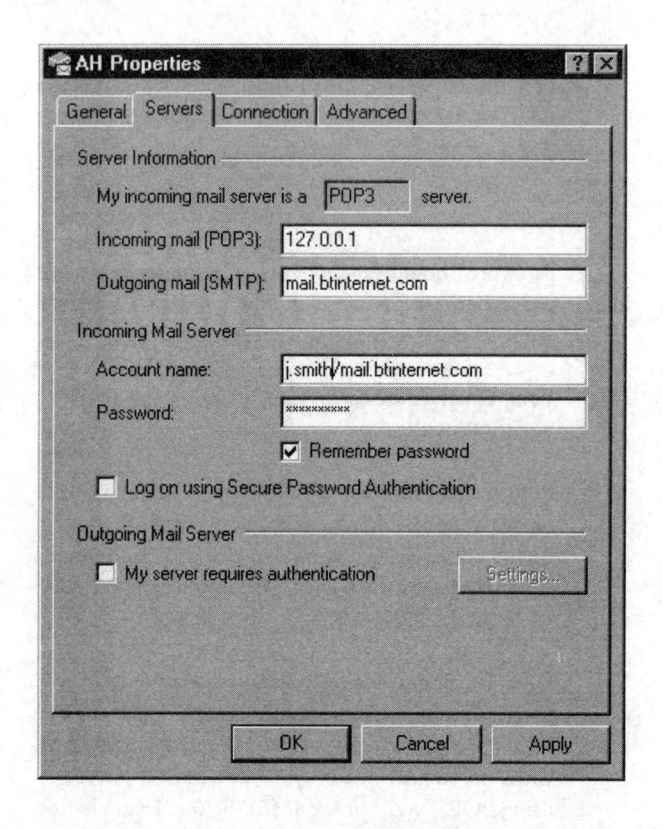

- **Your IMAP address (usually optional):** Internet Messaging Access Protocol (IMAP) is essentially a more sophisticated version of POP3 described in the previous paragraph. To establish whether you can use the advanced features of IMAP, check with your Internet Service Provider.

- **Your Outgoing Mail (SMTP) address:** Simple Mail Transfer Protocol (SMTP) handles all email messages you send to other people – hence "outgoing." Usually, you can use your own ISP's outgoing email server. Example: for BT Internet customers, currently, the SMTP address is : mail.btinternet.com – the same as the POP3 address. **Key point:** sometimes, POP3 and SMTP addresses may have different names: check with your Internet Service Provider.

- **And finally your name**.

Armed with the previous information, to start a new email account in Outlook Express, first choose the Accounts command from the Tools menu, followed by the Add Mail command in

> **HOT TIP** From my own experience with software and hard disk crashes that may occur from time to time (oh what joy!), even though you may think you don't need to keep a written record of the email settings like those above, do it anyway. You never know when you'll need it. But remember to keep your record in a secure safe place away from prying eyes.

Getting started with email < 295

the dialog box. Then to complete the set-up of your new account, simply answer the questions the wizard asks.

When you first install Netscape Communicator v4.6 which includes Netscape's email program, Netscape Messenger, the Mail & Newsgroups Setup Program starts. This wizard approach also asks for information similar to that listed earlier, so make sure you have the key information provided by your Internet Service Provider handy.

If you want to make changes later, in the Netscape Navigator web browser choose the Preferences command from the Edit menu, and in the dialog box, click on the Mail & Newsgroups category to gain access to the essential email settings.

A word about email security

"Normal" email is not a secure system: anyone with the correct equipment can tap into the entire contents of your email box,

Attachment Security Warning

WARNING!

The file may contain a virus that can be harmful to your computer. It is important to be VERY certain that this file is safe before you open it. You must save this file to disk before it can be opened.

Filename: frstqtr.zip
Type: ZIP file

[Save to Disk...] [Cancel]

peer into your PC while online and send you a virus hidden in an email message. And yes, there are bogies out there – or more precisely unscrupulous people who use email scanners in an attempt to discover key information. So what can you do to keep these people out?

If you're particularly concerned about your email privacy, take a look at encryption methods as discussed on page 341. But remember that even so-called unbreakable encryption systems may be "hackable" for someone with the right equipment and know-how.

However, for those of us who have no plans for world domination, or not to pay our taxes, or to do anything else that we know we shouldn't be doing, for most purposes, simple email is probably fine and works wonderfully well. Chapter 8, starting on page 173 also examines Internet security in a more general sense.

A peek at Microsoft Outlook Express

Outlook Express enables you to send and receive email messages on the Internet, and you can also set up multiple dial-up email accounts. So, for example, you can set up one account for John so he can work with his email; another account for Jane, so she can do the same, and another account for Jim, and so on.

In this way, providing each "account" holder has different email settings, user names and passwords, etc., each can work with only their own email messages without affecting others.

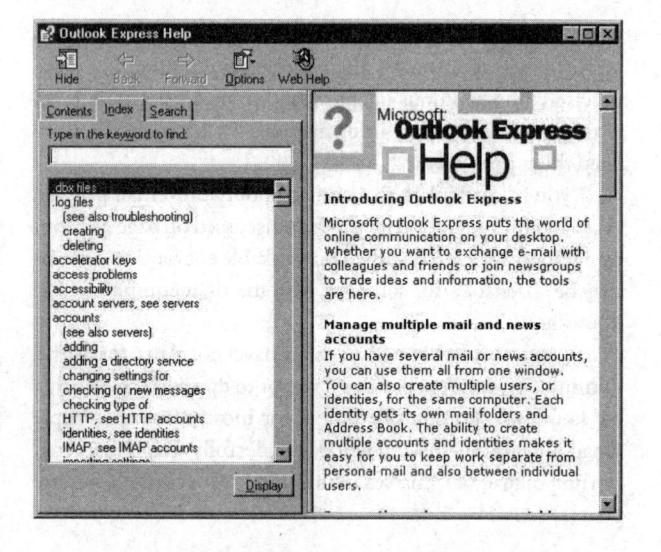

Also optionally, email messages can be adorned with images, animation and multimedia clips but more on this later.

Currently free of charge, Outlook Express is perhaps not surprisingly one of the most popular email programs available. The following paragraphs outline how to use the program. Most email programs have similar ways of operation and once you're familiar with a popular product like Outlook Express, if you choose to switch to another email program – say like Netscape Messenger or perhaps Eudora Pro – you'll probably be up and running sooner than you might think.

With Outlook Express correctly installed and set up, when you start the program, you'll probably see the main screen made up of at least 2 main panes. Towards the top of the screen, Outlook Express provides the essential drop-down menus, commands and convenient buttons to provide quick access to the most popular tasks. To see a brief tip about the purpose of a button, place the mouse pointer stationary on top of the button you want.

In the left column, you can see the various mail "boxes" you've created and are using, whether any waiting or unread email is present, and, at the bottom, a list of any newsgroups to which you subscribed. The main Outlook Express window provides quick and easy access to the most important activities, in which you can:

- Read and download mail.

- Compose a message.

- Use your email Address book.

- Work with newsgroups.

- Find people.

To read your mail, you simply click the small Read Mail text link or picture icon in the large pane or click the Inbox folder in the left pane. The Outlook Express main window, by default, then changes to a 3-pane arrangement. The left pane shows the list of folders available. If you select a folder in the left pane, for any email messages present in that folder, their message headers are shown listed in the top pane.

When you click a message header in the top pane, the lower pane displays the actual contents of the message. When you first install Outlook Express, you'll probably find one or two messages by default already installed in your Inbox. You can learn much simply by opening, closing, moving and copying these messages, but read them first: they may contain important new information.

Ideally, why not make a copy of one message and practice the various common commands and tasks on your message copy, rather than use the original. To get more familiar with your new email program, why not create a new message, send it to a colleague who is experienced with email and ask them to reply. And don't forget, many of the commands listed in the menus are available quickly through selecting an item, then clicking the right mouse button and choosing the command you want from the floating menu.

15

Sending and receiving email messages

The guidelines provided in this chapter assume that you already have an Internet connection and that you successfully installed and configured your email software as outlined in previous chapters. Now you're ready to really get to grips with email! In fact, email is simple to use; essentially, there are only four main email activities:

- **Receiving & downloading** email messages.

- **Creating** new email messages.

- **Sending** email messages.

- **Organising** the various email messages received.

The email header

When you send or receive an email message, some important information is recorded in an area of the email message called the email header. So where is the email header? In Outlook, if you double-click a particular email message in the top Outlook pane, a new, independent window opens showing the chosen email. The upper pane of this window contains the email header information. The most essential details are then made immediately visible, for example:

- **Who the message is from** (double-click to view full contact information).

- **Who the email is for** (double-click to view full contact information.)

- **Who else the message was sent to** (optional).

- The **time and date** when the email was sent.

- A **brief description** of what the email is about in the "Subject" line.

> When replying to an email, you can help save time for your recipient: consider deleting all unnecessary information from the original email and quote only the part that is relevant.

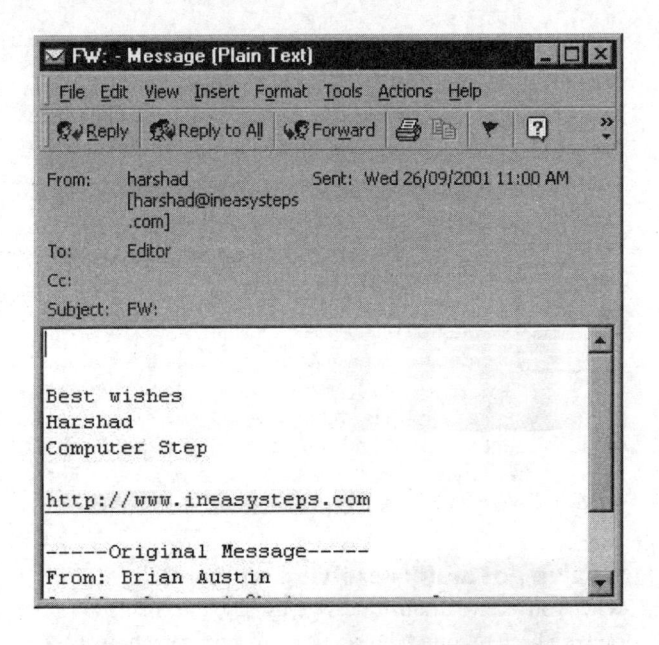

```
FW: - Message (Plain Text)                              _ □ ×
 File  Edit  View  Insert  Format  Tools  Actions  Help
 Reply   Reply to All   Forward                      ?   »

From:    harshad                 Sent: Wed 26/09/2001 11:00 AM
         [harshad@ineasysteps
         .com]
To:      Editor
Cc:
Subject: FW:


Best wishes
Harshad
Computer Step

http://www.ineasysteps.com

-----Original Message-----
From: Brian Austin
```

BEWARE

Check your email box regularly in order to possibly avoid losing email messages caused by an overflowing email box. Usually, once an email box is examined, the queued messages are downloaded to the caller's computer. This approach can ensure the amount of space reserved for an email account is never used up.

Sending and receiving email messages < 303

The "To" and "From" lines may contain nicknames that your email program may use. To view the true email addresses and optionally other contact information, simply double-click the line you want. To view full Internet header information in Outlook Express, choose the Properties command on the File menu.

> You don't need to have your computer, mobile phone or "whiz-bang" super microwave cooker switched on – and doing what they do best – in order to receive an email message! You can receive email messages any time (whether you're present or not while an email is being sent) once your email account is set up and running. Your Internet Service Provider stores your email messages until you're ready to receive them (within reason).

'You've got mail': receiving an email

When you receive an email message, usually your email software causes a beep to sound; however, if this arrangement irritates, check the options available – you can probably turn the beep off. Other "You've got mail" indicators include messages displayed on the screen and highlighted icons in your email program – so you can instantly identify new messages from those that have already been read.

Although an Internet Service Provider stores all your messages until you need them, do check your particular email box usage conditions with your provider: some only keep a limited number of messages for a finite time and if messages are not retrieved before the limit, they may be deleted.

> **BEWARE** Sometimes, it's easy to unintentionally select a message in the top pane, or when you're not really ready to read the message: selecting a message for only a few seconds is sometimes enough for Outlook Express to think you've read it. Remedy: simply don't change or move the current selection or click another message until you're ready to read the next message.

Reading your email messages

In order to know which messages are new and therefore unread, your email program has to identify each new message. In Outlook Express, new emails that you have just downloaded and have not read are shown in darker lettering (boldface). So at a glance, you know which messages are new and unexamined.

You can read mail in two main ways:

- To read a new email, in the top pane simply select the message you want and its contents appear in the lower preview pane. After a few seconds of previewing, the darker lettering style of the selected message in the top pane changes to a normal (lighter) colour to indicate this email has been examined.

- If you want more control and do not want to be distracted by other items on the screen, in the top pane simply double-click the message you want to read. Outlook Express then creates another independent window that you can maximise to fill the screen or adjust to the size you want.

> **HOT TIP**
>
> If you have to pay for every minute of Internet access, here's how you can save money. Set up your email software so that, once the program has sent and retrieved any email, your email program automatically disconnects from the Internet and hangs up the phone line. You can then read and organise your email messages without having to be concerned about excessive phone costs. When replying to an email message, you can queue your replies in the "Outbox" and, when ready, again send and receive in a single session.

At the top of the independent window, Outlook Express provides a toolbar that lets you easily work with your messages – in particular the 'Previous' and 'Next' buttons enable you to step through each message quickly and easily.

Also, the time you receive an email from someone new is the ideal time to consider adding that person to your Address Book. You can do this manually; however, you can usually set up your software so that anyone you reply to is automatically added to your Address book – a great timesaver!

Designing reader-friendly email messages

In Outlook Express, when creating an email or deciding what to put in it, you can import text from other locations and use the standard Cut, Copy and Paste commands; doing this saves time when you are moving information around. If you've got a lot to say, you can enter over 60,000 characters into one email message – not something I would recommend unless your recipient knows they're going to be receiving your condensed version of Tolstoy's War and Peace.

Although Outlook Express (and other great email programs) make a lot of power available at your fingertips, usually email programs leave the layout and formatting to the user. After all, as individuals most of us have our own way of doing things. However, it's easy to get carried away with all the superb features now available with most good email programs and this is something to watch carefully, especially if you want your message to be understood quickly by a large number of people. Therefore, let's look at some simple ways to help you create great emails every time.

1. Developing a compelling email writing style

Here's an obvious but often overlooked fact about email: as people (usually) cannot see you, they make judgements about you by what you write, how you write it and how it appears to them. With email, often your credibility is at stake. Also remember, the text-based nature of email means that a permanent record of what you've said may always be available – so don't say anything that you wouldn't mind your mother hearing or a judge sitting on the bench!

So let's look at some simple ways you can ensure your email creates a favourable impression, whether you're sending a simple message to a friend, family member, or perhaps sending a regular email newsletter to 10,000 keen subscribers eager for money-saving hints, tips and insights from your latest brain dump!

2. Which do I use: plain text- or HTML-based email?

Plain text format – sometimes referred to as ASCII (American Standard Code for Information Interchange) – offers a way to ensure that anyone who can receive email can read and see your email message properly. You can also send an email in HTML format – that is, using the same codes and tags that are used to create web pages – like the example shown on the facing page. Using HTML-formatted email, you can send exotic-looking email messages: formatted text, pictures, and so on. You can even create a web page newsletter in your favourite web design software, then use Copy and Paste to transfer a copy into your email program. For more information on how to create HTML (web) email messages, see page 340.

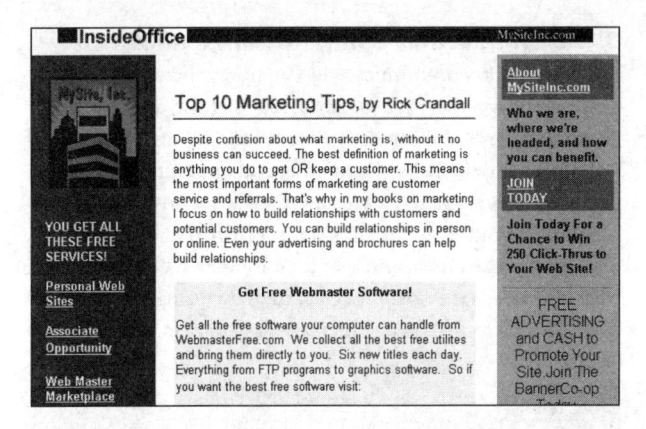

However, for your recipients to be able to view your email exactly as you intend, their email software must be compatible and be set up to properly detect HTML-based emails. Often you won't know which email programs your recipients are using, and therefore the capabilities of their software. If you send email in the wrong format, your recipients may only see a mass of jumbled characters usually as an email attachment. Therefore, unless you know otherwise, the safest course of action is to use simple plain text.

In Outlook Express, you can change the default format using the Tools > Options command pair and choose the Send format you want. In Netscape Messenger, open the Edit menu and choose Preferences and click on Mail & Newsgroups.

3. Keeping order: using left alignment

For those who communicate in languages that use a left-to-right and down-the-page sequence like English, to prevent any possible text misalignment at your recipient's end, if possible use only the default left justified text alignment. That is, the text you enter is aligned vertically at the left edge of the screen.

Try to avoid using indents, tabs, justified alignments and colours. Readers in countries that use other standard writing patterns can adapt this approach to their own language: the key point here is to make your message easy to read.

Word wrap ensures the text cursor is automatically moved to the following line when the end of the line is reached. Some email software defaults to 70 or even 80 characters – much too long, especially if you're reading from a larger screen.

4. Narrow columns = easier reading

Studies have shown that reading on a computer screen is generally acknowledged to be more tiring to the eye than, say, reading from paper. To make the job of understanding screen-based text easier and reduce eyestrain, consider narrowing the column width your readers have to read. An easy way to do this is to examine the program options in your email software and set or change the word wrap setting to about 60 characters or less.

5. Why short paragraphs make more sense

How about meeting a continuous 50-line paragraph just after breakfast on a rainy Monday morning! If you've got a lot to say, why not break your message into shorter paragraphs of up to about 5 or 8 lines maximum – and make someone's day! Most people hate to see long paragraphs of nothing but text – especially on a computer screen! If you're in business on the Net, your prospects and customers need to see and read your message if they're to respond to your call to action.

Although readers are often more tolerant with longer paper-based paragraphs, on a business-oriented web page or email especially, long paragraphs probably offer one of the quickest ways to lose money fast: few people feel like responding to your offer or reading about your latest incredible deal. Long spans of text often simply get scanned, skipped or not even read!

6. Keep it brief and get popular

Try to be concise and to the point in your emails. People who receive hundreds of emails each day welcome consideration given for their valuable time and carefully considered emails are, arguably, more likely to achieve their objective. Again, brevity is especially important for business-oriented emails where most people simply do not have the time to spend reading anything that is not relevant to the current theme or discussion topic.

7. Grammar reborn, ouch!

Technology drives us relentlessly towards a supposedly paperless society. Yet the widespread use of text-based email forces us to be more aware of and think about the words and sentences we use in our communications. Just when we thought that watching our grammar was a school-time activity that perhaps is not really relevant today, someone invents email!

Certainly when communicating about work and business, our sentences need to make sense; we still need to dot our I's and cross our T's – you never know who is going to be reading your email message. In personal emails however, we can loosen up, break the rules and have a lot more fun – and yes break the rules just because you can, if that's your bag!

8. Watch the file size

Why should the size of an email message make a difference? Some email software may reject or bounce messages that are larger than a specific file size. For most emails, file size is not really an important issue; for longer emails – newsletters (ezines) for example – file size does need to be considered. Early AOL email readers may not even deliver messages that are over 32 KB in file size. One way around this problem is to either split the message into several parts as needed, or consider using an email attachment approach. But again, check the limits on attachments.

Also, most users can set their email software to reject file attachments above a specific level, for example 100 KB, to help limit the amount of time online and save money. Therefore, if you plan to send a larger email message, consider sending a brief announcement email first to let your recipient know. This gives them time to change their settings (temporarily perhaps) or to contact you saving time and resources and avoiding confusion for all involved.

9. Focusing on your readers: email etiquette

Email is essentially just another form of communication; it reflects real life. People usually interact and work together better when a certain amount of politeness and consideration is involved. Email etiquette is simply just that: having consideration for other users.

Essential email address books

To send an email, you need to know your recipient's correct email address. However, although email addresses can sometimes seem confusing and difficult to remember, when you use an email address book, the task is much easier. When you send an email to a new contact the first time, you'll probably need to type the email address into the "To" box.

However, to avoid having to repeatedly type the same email address on subsequent occasions, you can copy or store email addresses in an address book using a nickname or the person's real name. Email address books usually come with email software or you can buy separate add-on utilities. To see the

Address book in Outlook Express for example, simply choose the Address Book command from the Tools menu. In Netscape Messenger, you can find the Address Book command in the Communicator menu.

> **HOT TIP**
> To reduce the possibility of making a typing mistake for an email address, use the correct pre-defined entries in your email address book whenever possible. Then you need only look for the recipient's name or nickname.

Microsoft Outlook includes a superb **Personal Information Manager (PIM)** address book. Whenever you want to enter a recipient's email address, you only need start entering the desired nickname or real name into the box, and leave the software to remember the entire precise and sometimes-tricky email address sequence.

The Address Book in Outlook Express by default attempts to use what you type into the recipient field. However, sometimes you may need to manually edit a record to create an entry. To open the Address Book in Outlook Express while creating an email, click any of the little book icons placed next to the "To:", "Cc:" and "Bcc:" labels. Select the email address you want and use the buttons provided to copy it into the relevant recipient field.

> **DON'T FORGET:** Check an email address carefully. Even a single typing mistake can result in producing a "valid" email address, but which nevertheless may be the wrong recipient.

In the Address Book dialog box, you can also enter a "New Contact" and easily edit the contents of an existing contact using the Properties button. In Netscape Messenger, just click the New Card button in the Address Book dialog box and enter details about a new contact. You can quickly add an email address to your Address Book in Outlook Express: right-click the email address you want and choose the Add to Address Book command. In Netscape Messenger, you can use the Add Sender to Address Book command from the Message menu.

> **HOT TIP:** To help reduce the number of incorrect email addresses in your Address book or to avoid sending multiple identical messages to the same destination, regularly check for duplicate email addresses and delete those not needed.

> **HOT TIP:** Gradually keep adding entries to your email address book. The extra time needed in the early stages pays off later when you want to seek an address quickly.

Finding an email address

You can guarantee it will happen just when you're really busy and you haven't got the time to spend searching: you can't find that email address you need. But if it's unavoidable, and you're prepared to spend 15 minutes trying, how do you rectify this? Before looking for complex answers, try the obvious: friends, colleagues and acquaintances. Failing that, here are several other ideas to consider:

- Check any previous paper communications like letterheads, business cards, etc.

- Has this person had any contact with a website? If so, log on and go to that website. If you can't find the address you want, consider sending an email to an appropriate contact at the website.

- Try several Internet search services like: WhoWhere at www.whowhere.com/ and Big Foot at www.bigfoot.com/ and so on.

- Try to develop a habit of adding contact details to your email or other software address book to avoid the same problem later.

Creating a new email message

To create a new email message or reply to an existing message, remember you don't need to be online. You can create each email then transfer it to the Outbox in Outlook Express, or the Unsent Messages folder in Netscape Messenger, ready for sending later when you go online.

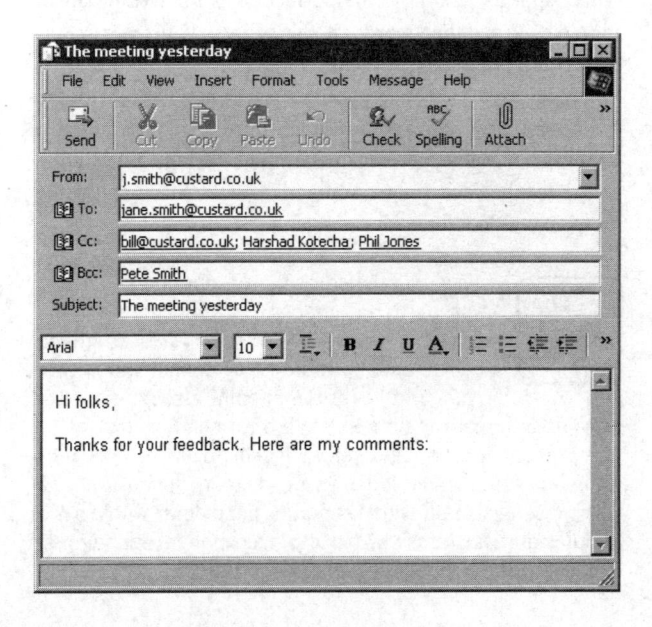

Usually, the command for starting a new message can be found on the File menu. In Outlook Express, simply choose the File > New Mail Message commands or click the New Mail button on the main toolbar. On other versions of email software, look for the equivalent commands and buttons like, "Compose Message" or "New Mail Message", and so on. A blank new mail window should then display with the mouse cursor placed in the "To" box.

In the "To" box, enter the email address of your recipient. Outlook Express then underlines the email address if the syntax appears to follow the correct rules for writing email addresses – in other words, if the address you enter seems correct to your email program.

In Netscape Messenger, you can start a new email with the New Msg button, enter your recipient details and your message. If you're not online, you can queue email messages for sending later: click the Send Later command from the File menu of the message window for each message.

> For your first email, why not send yourself a brief message? This checks that your computer and email system are set up to correctly send and receive email. Before going online, set up your email not to automatically disconnect after sending and receiving email. Then after sending your email message, stay online and keep checking every few seconds until you have received your own message. You should receive your message ideally within seconds, but at least within a few minutes at most. After which you can disconnect and re-enter your preferred connect/disconnect settings.

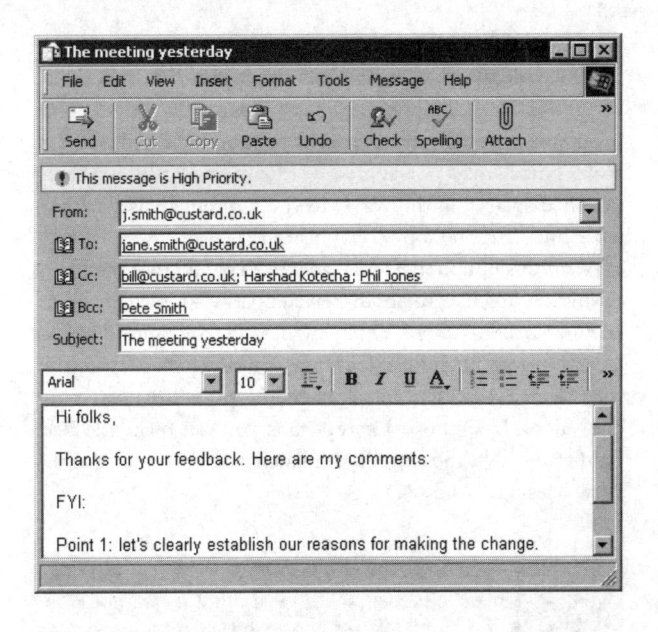

Doubling up with Carbon Copy (Cc) and Blind Carbon Copy (Bcc)

If you want to send an email to more than one person at the same time, you can enter additional email addresses into the "Cc:" (Carbon Copy) box. For more than one Cc recipient, place a comma, or sometimes a semicolon (;) between each additional email address: check your email program documentation for the exact separator to use.

If you use Carbon Copy, each recipient on the list can see the email address of every other recipient on the list. Sometimes, Cc: is not the most appropriate way to send a message. Some recipients, especially if they're sensitive about receiving a lot of spam email, may not appreciate their email address being openly displayed in this way. However, a remedy is available: use Blind Carbon Copy (Bcc) instead.

With this option, the email addresses of all other members of this mailing list are not displayed openly – hence the name "Blind Carbon Copy." Often by default, the Blind Carbon Copy box may not be visible at first: you may have to switch on the command in your email program Option's dialog box or equivalent. In Outlook Express v5.x, you can make the Bcc: field visible by choosing All Headers in the View menu of the New Message window.

> **HOT TIP**
>
> If you have to pay for every minute while online, you can usually save money by setting your email software to not send all email messages immediately after you create them. Rather, you'll probably prefer to send each email message to the Outbox or equivalent, for sending later in a single batch when you go online. At which time, you'll click the Send and Receive command or button to send any emails you have ready and download any emails queued up to be received by you, then disconnect from the Internet.

The email Subject box

The final component in the email header is the Subject box. Enter a short description in the Subject box, ideally using fewer than about 7 words outlining what your email message is about. The Subject is what your recipients usually see displayed in heavy lettering style until they read the message – a few seconds after which the "normal" lettering style usually applies to show that the message has been read.

> To avoid wasting further time later, before sending your email message, do this. Consider getting into the habit of spending a few seconds double-checking the email address and making sure the email is completely free of errors.

Did you really mean to shout?

A continuous sequence of capital letters in an email message is considered to be the equivalent of shouting and is also generally harder to read. Capital letters force the reader to slow their rate of reading. Therefore, use capitals with care rather than simply to emphasise a point: your recipient may think you mean something very different to what you're trying to say.

Misunderstandings can easily arise possibly leading to problems that really have no basis – a definite no-no if you're trying to persuade or sell an idea or product. Upper and lower case letters – like this paragraph – provide the easiest and fastest way to read an email message. However, capitals are ideal for headings and short sequences of text that have a clear meaning to which you want to give special attention.

> In most email programs, you can easily identify if an email message sent to you is a reply: just look for 'Re:' in the Subject box.

> You can easily identify a forwarded email message: look for 'Fw:' or 'Fwd:' at the start of the Subject box.

Adding emotion with a Smiley

In a plain text email message, the options for putting over emotion or feeling are limited. However, you can use combinations of special characters to create Smileys – sometimes called emoticons. You can imagine how Smileys get their name: look at the list of popular Smileys below by tilting your head sideways to see the rough outline of eyes, nose and mouth.

Smiley	Emotion
:'-(	Crying
:-(	Frowning
:-I	Indifferent
:-D	Laughing
:-)	Smiling

:-0	Surprised
;-)	Winking

Saving time with abbreviations

Email abbreviations are a great way to type less, provided of course they make sense to all involved. Here are a few to get you started:

Abbreviation	Meaning
B4	Before
BTW	By the way
CUL	See you later
FAQ	Frequently asked questions
FOAF	Friend of a friend
FOC	Free of charge
FWIW	For what it's worth
FYA	For your amusement
FYI	For your information
FYIO	For your eyes only
HTH	Hope this helps
IME	In my experience
IMHO	In my humble opinion
IMO	In my opinion
IOW	In other words
KISS	Keep it simple stupid
L8R	Later
LOL	Laughing out loud

MOTAS	Member of the appropriate sex
MOTOS	Member of the opposite sex
MOTSS	Member of the same sex
NRN	No reply necessary
OBTW	Oh, by the way
OTT	Over the top
ROTFL	Rolling on the floor laughing
RSN	Real soon now
RUOK	Are you OK?
SO	Significant other
TIA	Thanks in advance
TTFN	Cheerio
TVM	Thank you very much
WRT	With respect to

The above are just a few of the hundreds of abbreviations used in email and Internet Chat communications, so if typing is not your bag, there's one answer.

Sending an email message

To create and send an email, here's what you'll need to do in sequence:

1. Enter the **recipient's email address**.

2. In the **Subject box**, enter a word or phrase describing what the email is about.

HOT TIP: Perhaps the best way to create a lengthy email list is to copy and paste the list into a plain word processor window – say Windows Notepad or equivalent – then simply enter or arrange each email address with the separator character between them. Finally, save the file as a plain text file (.txt). Your email list is then ready for copying and pasting whenever required.

3. Type your **email message** (or for multimedia-based software: speak your message).

4. **Check** entered details: have automatic spell-checking turned on.

5. Click the **Send** button.

Once you click the Send button, depending on how your email program is set up, two possible results can occur:

- Your email software may **immediately** dial your Internet Service Provider and send the message, or…

- Your message is moved to the **Outbox** in Outlook Express or Unsent Messages in Netscape Messenger – both provide a temporary holding area **ready for sending later** when you dial up your Internet Service Provider to send and receive your email.

Although Outlook Express provides a "Check Names" or "Check Addresses" command if an email address is invalid, your Internet Service Provider usually returns or "bounces" the faulty email back to you with an error message identifying where the problem may lie.

Usually by default, most current email software is set up to ensure you can Send and Receive email during the same session. Outlook for example, provides the "Send and Receive" button on the main toolbar allowing quick and easy email processing although you can fine-tune your choices.

Usually, once an email is sent from the Outbox or Unsent Messages folder, the software either places a copy of the sent email in the Sent folder or marks an email in a special way to identify sent email messages from other emails.

Here's probably one of the quickest ways to have your email (and optionally website) account closed without warning. Send an email to a large number of recipients without getting written evidence of their permission to receive emails from you.

Marking an email message as urgent

If you need the recipient of your email to respond quickly, you can mark the email as urgent. Microsoft Outlook and Outlook Express provide a command/button that allows you to indicate that an email is of "High importance". Then when your recipient receives a high priority email, an attention-getting marker – for example, an exclamation mark (!) – is included with the email Subject.

Replying to an email

To reply to an email, select the message you want, then click the Reply button or choose the Reply command from the Message menu. Then usually your email software copies your original message – including its original header information – into a new message window and places the prefix "Re:" – short for Reply – in the Subject line box.

You're now ready to enter your reply information and optionally edit or delete unnecessary information in the original email. People who use email regularly can receive many messages every day so when replying, your recipient will probably thank you for including only the relevant part of the original message. We refer to this as Quoting. Also by deleting the parts that are not relevant when replying, your message is shortened and so gets sent faster and helps keep the Internet less cluttered for everyone to benefit – resulting in faster, better connections.

You might ask, how can we ensure that the part we are quoting does not get mixed with our reply? Simple. Fortunately most good email programs provide an easy way to identify an original message when you hit the Reply button: often the "Greater Than" (>) character may be automatically placed at the start of every line of the original message.

Other email software may use text indents or even colour coding in the same way so that you and your recipients can identify all the parts of the original message from the new message. Often you can change the default character or indicator that email software uses through the Tools > Options command and look for the Send or Reply options in Outlook Express, or Edit > Preferences command in Netscape Messenger. Now all you need do is reply to the parts you want and delete the irrelevant parts of the original message – usually, simply highlight all the text you don't want and press the Delete key.

Forwarding an email

Sometimes, you may want to send a copy of an email message that you receive, to friends or colleagues for comment or feedback, or you may want to add your own comments first before sending. Most email software refers to this as Forwarding. Essentially, Forwarding is the online equivalent of sending a memo. Forwarding an email is simple; here's what you do. While viewing the email you want to forward, choose the

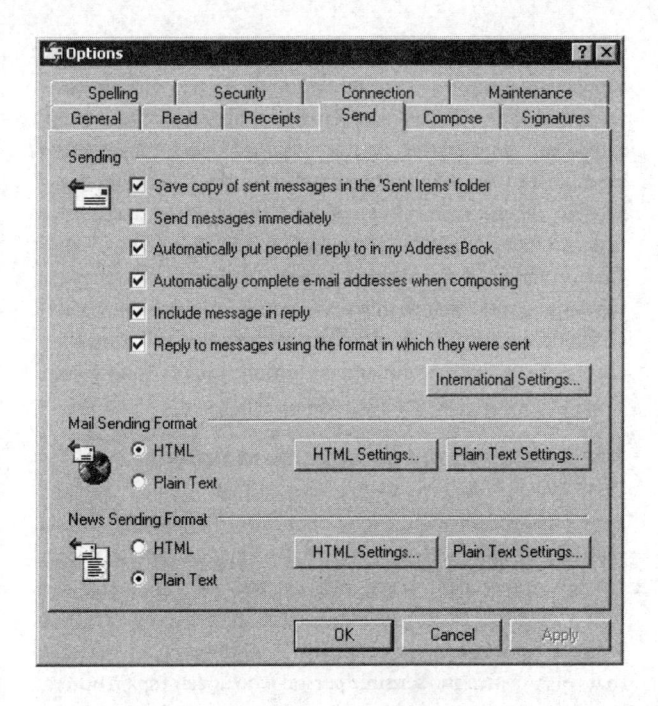

Forward command or click the Forward (email) button. Then usually, your email software places the prefix "Fw:" or something similar in the Subject Line box. Next, in the "To:" box, enter the email address of the person to whom you want to forward the email.

Also, you can choose to forward an email message as an attachment to another message. Here's how: select the message and choose the Forward as Attachment command usually found on the Message menu – or you can right-click the message and choose the command from the floating menu.

If you want to send a copy of the email to others at the same time, include their addresses in the Carbon Copy (Cc) or Blind Carbon Copy (Bcc) boxes as covered earlier in this chapter. Optionally make any changes, add comments and delete parts of the message you don't want to forward and finish by choosing the Send command or button. Finally follow your usual procedure for actually sending emails.

Sending an email to several recipients

Earlier in this chapter, we mentioned that you can send the same email message to several people or many people. If you send an email newsletter, essentially that's all you're doing. However, in recent years, Internet Service Providers – in reflecting the views of many subscribers – have become sensitive to the issue of Spam – or bulk emailing. However, let's assume that you're a nice and sensible person who doesn't spam others. You simply want to send your newsletter to 600 people who have asked to receive it.

The obvious option would be to first open a copy of the message you want to send and enter one email address from your list into the "To:" box. Then Copy and Paste, the remaining several hundred others into the Blind Carbon Copy (Bcc) field. To do this, you would first have to make sure all the email addresses were valid and correct, then separate each one with a comma or semicolon (;) or whatever separator your email documentation instructs. When ready, simply choose the Send command. But wait!

Most Internet Service Providers put a limit on the number of email addresses you can put into the Blind Carbon Copy (Bcc) field – usually 50 or thereabouts. Any more, and they may assume that you're bulk emailing. Often, the simplest answer is to use a purpose-designed email list service. Providing you're not spamming anyone, you should have few problems with a genuine list.

Your Internet Service Provider may even provide a list service – often called a listserver – free with your email or web hosting account, so check with them before seeking an outside list solution. Some good quality free independent listservers are now available and if you want tight control, you can opt for a paid listserver service, but shop around, check out and compare what's on offer.

Re-sending an email message

If you sent your email message but, for some mysterious reason, your recipient hasn't received it, you'll want to resend the message. If you're using Microsoft Outlook, in the left pane, simply click the Sent messages folder, select the message you want to resend in the right pane, and just choose the Resend command. If a direct Resend command is not available, you can copy the message contents window in the Sent items folder and paste into a new message window. But remember, you'll probably have to delete the header details in the original message and any other unnecessary characters, re-enter the recipient's email address and Subject box details and click Send to finish.

Attaching a file to an email message

Sometimes, you may want to send more than just a plain text file or a HTML-based document. Attachments are the answer. An email attachment is simply any document or computer file that is "attached" to an email message. For example, you might want to send a Microsoft Word document perhaps containing additional charts and pictures. Or even a computer program. However, sometimes the simplest solution is to copy and paste a document as plain text into an email window avoiding the need to attach the document.

If both you and your recipient are using a modern email program, then the business of sending and receiving attachments will probably go smoothly. For an attachment to be sent successfully, both parties must be using the same encoding standard. When you install your email program, the software chooses a common default standard, so the chances are you'll never need to change this. However, options include: MIME, Uuencode and Binhex. So although rare nowadays, if you come across problems, check that you're both using the same encoding format or consider both switching to using an easier automatic up-to-date email program like Outlook Express, Netscape Messenger, Eudora, Pegasus or Microsoft Outlook.

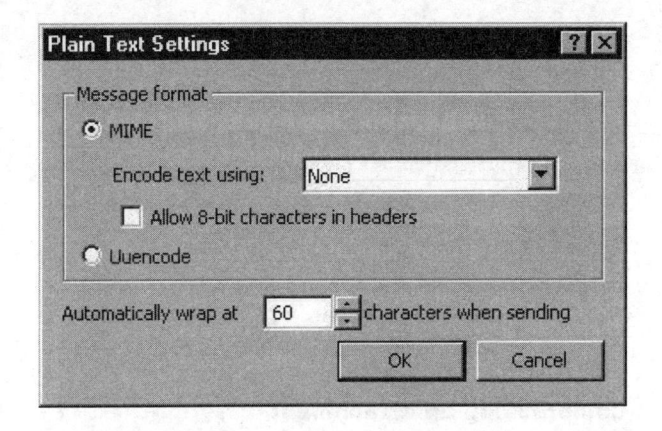

To attach a file to an email message, with your email message window open choose the Attach File or Send Attachments command, button, or its equivalent option in your email program. For example, Microsoft Outlook Express provides the Attach File button on the main toolbar in the message window. Your email software then usually displays a dialog box to allow you to choose the file you want to attach.

Microsoft Outlook identifies an attached file using a paperclip symbol. If you want to attach more than one file, usually all you need do is repeat the procedure. If you pay for every minute while online and if the file you want to attach is large in file size, to reduce the time spent online, consider compressing the file as examined in the following paragraphs. Also, do remember that the larger the file size, the longer the overall email transfer time and the more likely the possibility of transfer problems.

> To quickly and easily add an email attachment to a message, you can probably use drag and drop to simply drag a document/attachment icon into the current message window. You can check your computer documentation to find out if your computer supports drag and drop.

Compressing an attachment

A file compressor program is designed to squash a file to a smaller file size where possible. Some file types already exist naturally in a compressed form and so may not compress much further, like Adobe Acrobat files for example, so usually these are probably best left in their native state.

So why bother compressing files? Well, here are several reasons. Transferring large files at their normal file size over the Internet is still not 100% reliable and may take a long time. If you pay for every second while online and can reduce the time needed to send a file by say 75% simply by compressing the file, you're going to save time and money.

Also, when sending or receiving larger, uncompressed files, hang-ups, dropped phone lines, and so forth may occur during the transfer, so the task of sending the entire message with the attachment will have to be repeated. After several hours of doing this when you really don't have the time, you can almost feel your hair falling out! So reducing the file size using a file compressor helps minimise these kinds of problems.

Thirdly, to prevent email boxes becoming jammed with spammed messages and unauthorised attachments, some users change the settings in their email software to limit the size of any file attachments that are automatically accepted when checking their email. A popular setting is 100–200 kilobytes. If you try to send a 250 KB file to someone who has set the upper limit to 200 KB, the email message will be rejected and you'll probably receive an appropriate but sometimes vague error message. Now if that same attachment were compressed to say 50 KB, it should transfer without problem – and do so more quickly.

One of the most popular file compressors today is **WinZip**, which I use regularly and consider this little program absolutely essential when working with the Internet. WinZip is shareware – that is, you get to try it first and if you decide to keep it, register and pay the small fee for your copy. For more information, go to: www.winzip.com/ Also remember, to decompress a compressed file, usually you must have the same type of software used to compress the file. Likewise, if you send a compressed file, your recipient must have the same type of software to decompress the attachment at their end.

HOT TIP

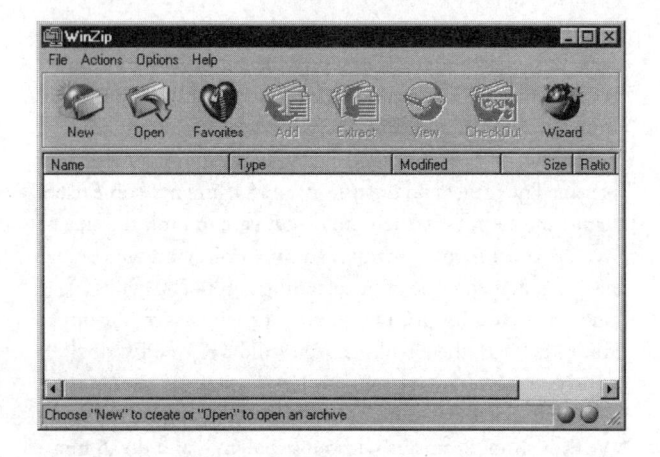

Before sending an email that contains a large attachment, consider sending a brief message to the recipient stating that you're about to send a large email and check if that is acceptable. For users who have to pay for every minute while online, downloading a large 'unannounced' email can be annoying and costly for the recipient – especially if they did not want or ask for the information or attachment in the first place.

About you: using email signatures

An email signature is a few lines of text describing who your are, what you do and perhaps a brief phrase promoting a website (yours or someone else's), special offer or product or service. Here's an example business-oriented signature:

/_/_/_/_/_/_/_/_/_/_/_/_/_/
Brian Austin MISTC
brian@mycompany.com
Author, publisher, Web designer, Webmaster
http://www.mycompany.com
Fantastic NEW August promotion!
FREE Offers - only while stocks last!
/_/_/_/_/_/_/_/_/_/_/_/_/_/

Consider including mailing address, phone and fax numbers in an email signature if this information is especially important for you.

Sometimes, having several different email signature files to serve different purposes, can be useful, save time and avoid unnecessary repetitive typing. For example, you could define one for private/personal use, two or three for business – one for Sales, one for Support, etc. – and additional ones perhaps for other members of your family or work colleagues.

When creating email signatures for personal and not business use, you can have a lot more fun, creating patterns, faces and all sorts of Smiley-type symbols. To create an email signature in Outlook Express, choose the Tools > Options commands, then click the Signatures tab. In Netscape Messenger, choose Edit > Preferences and click the Identity tab under the Mail & Newsgroups category.

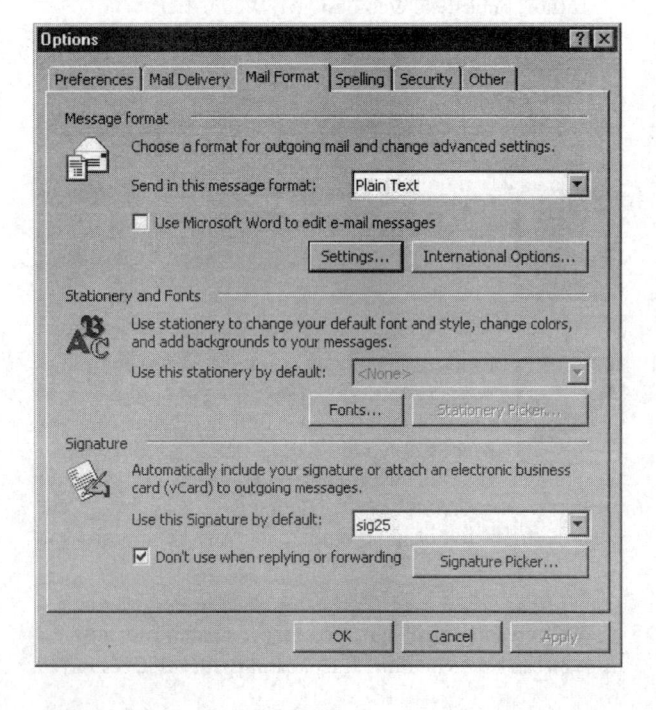

Make an impact with a vCard

A vCard is a sort of online business card – a collection of details about you that you provide and make available, so that recipients can, if they choose, easily copy your details into their email address book.

To create a vCard in Outlook Express v5.0x, first choose the Tools > Options command pair. Then in the Options dialog box click the Compose tab. You can then create your vCard under the Business Cards category.

Enter as many details as you wish to be made available. vCards made in Outlook Express have a .vcf filename extension. To create a vCard in Netscape Messenger, start by choosing Edit > Preferences. Then in the dialog box, click the Mail & Newsgroups Category, followed by Identity. Click the Edit Card button to start creating your vCard.

Dealing with email bouncers

If you send an email to an address that is incorrect or which does not exist, the sent message is usually returned to you as a "bounced" message. Check the email address again – remember, an email address has a certain structure. For example, all current email addresses must include an "@" character. For more information, see: "What's an email address?" on page 277.

Only a single-character typing mistake is enough to cause a message to bounce. If the email address you chose is "old", remember the person to whom you're sending the message may have cancelled that address or perhaps has a new address, so perhaps re-check your records.

Sending and receiving HTML email messages

Although most of this chapter focuses on sending email messages in plain text format simply because that is a universal worldwide standard, remember that you can also send emails in HTML or web page format.

The advantage is you can add colours, text formatting, pictures, animations and so on to an email, in fact most of what goes into a web page can be included. Like web pages though, the more you put in, the longer a message takes to download, so just keep to the essentials unless your recipients know what to expect.

To create and send email in HTML format, first make sure that HTML is turned on in your email software. In Outlook Express v5.x, choose Tools > Options then click the Send tab and edit the settings to make HTML format live. In Netscape Communicator/Messenger v4.6x, choose Edit > Preferences then click Formatting under the Mail & Newsgroups category and choose HTML formatting.

Setting up secure email

Although most current generation email programs like Outlook Express and Netscape Messenger are reasonably secure, when working with sensitive or valuable information, you might prefer better security. So let's examine the options.

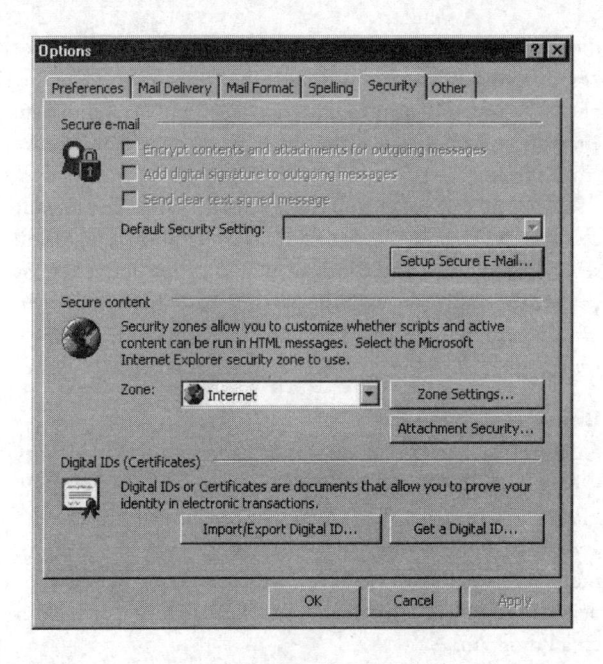

Keep them guessing with PGP encryption

The best systems use encryption so that only the genuinely intended recipient who has the correct software key built into their email program can read the information. PGP – short for "Pretty Good Privacy" – is, despite the rather amusing name, one such system that uses what are called public and private encryption keys that work together to create a more secure email system.

Here's how it works. You freely send the public key to your contacts. When your contact wants to send information to you securely, they encrypt the information using the public key. As you are the only party with the private key, only you can open the encrypted message. For more information, refer to: www.pgpi.org/ and www.research.umbc.edu/pgp/

Using a digital ID

A digital ID is another option that helps verify an email identity – however, remember this system is not as secure as PGP. Here's how it works. First you need a certificate from a secure and trusted third party like Verisign (www.verisign.com); more information is available at their website. When your personal certificate is installed, you'll need to turn it on in your email program.

In Outlook Express, choose the Options command from the Tools menu, then click the Security tab and enter your settings. In Netscape Messenger, choose the Security command from the Help menu and follow onscreen prompts or see the Online Help. You then have two options:

- Include your digital ID with every email you send – but all recipients must also install your digital certificate.

- Or you can use normal mail for most operations and turn on digital ID-based email for specific recipients – and again those recipients receiving your ID-based email must install your digital certificate in order to read email from you.

When you send email with a secure digital ID, compatible email software from those recipients who have also installed your digital ID recognises that these secure emails can come only from you.

Converting a fax to email

Lots of Internet Service Providers and other companies on the Net now provide various additional services, like for example: fax-to-email and voicemail-to-email. Therefore, you may no longer need a separate fax machine and so make savings in electronic hardware and maintenance costs, electricity and fax paper. Web-based fax and voicemail services may also be particularly valuable to anyone who wants to stay in touch while travelling.

eFax at www.efax.com is just one of the many companies that provides a free service to convert faxes and voicemail to email messages. Some ISPs may include these additional fax and voicemail services free of charge with your email account – so if you think this might be for you, check what's on offer from your own Internet Service Provider before looking further afield.

Printing your email messages

It's got to be straightforward, hasn't it? To print an email, surely we just, well… print it! Yes, that's true – usually. Often, however, you can set up various print options. For example in the superb Microsoft Outlook, you can:

- Use Print Preview – where you can see a representation of what your printed page will look like when printed successfully.

- Choose Table Style or Memo Style.

- Print each new item on a separate page.

- Print attachments along with your email message.

- Change your default printer.

- And so on.

Other email programs usually offer various printing options. Although limiting the amount of printing is a noble aim, for businesses who have to keep hard copy records of email invoices, receipts, etc., printing paper copies is, of course, essential.

16

Managing your email messages

Many people nowadays use email daily to communicate with friends and work colleagues. The more you use email, the larger your email "collection" may become – unless you consider ways to manage your email messages. Plus, most email users eventually start receiving irrelevant email messages or "Spam." So let's look at ways to filter, organize and manage email.

Dealing with the garbage

Most of us get it! When you hear the mail hit the floor, you race to beat the dog before he does what some consider all good dogs should do: chew up the latest offering of junk mail. On the Internet, arguably, the practice of sending uninvited email usually in an attempt to sell a product or service is even more

> # CAUCE
> **Coalition Against Unsolicited Commercial Email**
>
> Take back your mailbox
>
> - Home
> - Join CAUCE
> - Latest News
> - About the Problem
> - Pending Legislation
> - How YOU Can Help
> - FAQ
> - Info For Congress
> - Info For Media
> - Who is CAUCE?
> - Other Resources
> - Spam Incidents
> - True Tales of Spam
> - Contact Us
>
> ## Welcome to CAUCE!
>
> *Latest News:* Washington State Supreme Court Upholds Constitutionality of state anti-spam law, overturns lower-court rulings.
>
> Did you get spam from datamrp.com?
>
> **Recycle your Spam!** to find out how.
>
> CAUCE, The Coalition Against Unsolicited Commercial Email is an *ad hoc all volunteer organization*, created by Netizens to advocate for a legislative solution to the problem of UCE (a/k/a "spam").
>
> CAUCE Welcomes our New Affiliates to the Fight Against Spam!

of a problem than conventional junk mail – and it's a problem that is probably getting worse for most Internet users.

Uninvited junk email, otherwise known as "Spam"; Unsolicited Commercial Email (UCE) or various other unmentionable terms dreamed up by real dedicated Spam haters. Few other topics on the Internet bring out such strong opinions both from those who send it and from those who receive it! Of course, there are always two sides to every argument and different people we've spoken to have different views on this sometimes emotive topic.

Some say that we tolerate it coming through our letterboxes, so why not tolerate it online as well? Others vehemently hate Spam and would shrink in horror and plot your downfall if you should even mention the previous sentence as an option! Whatever your views on receiving junk email, if you don't want it, you can get pro-active and do something about it. If you're a real spam hater, here are some basic guidelines to help kill the beast:

- The most important first rule is to **have more than one email address and keep your most important email address as private as possible** – use with only trusted parties who know your views on spam.

- **Use your second, less important email address for more public online activities,** like mailing lists and newsgroups. You could even use a web mail account, rather than have email sent through your email program. Many web email providers have strict rules in an attempt to protect their users from email spam. When you examine your web mail, you can easily delete any spam that gets through the net. At least then, you're in control.

- When you visit websites, **check out their privacy statement** and particularly their commitment to protect your email address and avoid interacting with websites that you think don't come up to the mark.

- Most good email software allows you to **filter junk email**, add any emails that come from selected sources to your "junk email list." Then, the next time an email arrives from that address you won't even need to see it – the little critter is sent straight to your computer's equivalent of the Internet garbage dump.

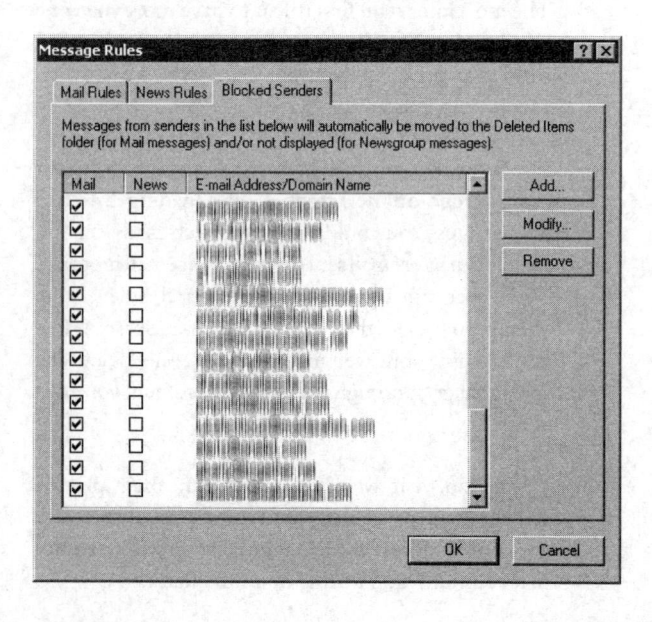

However remember, even with email filtering turned on, you still have to receive the email in the first place for the software to evaluate whether it should be filtered. The bottom line is most people can't effectively stop receiving all junk email – yet: the variables are just too complex for current generation software to handle.

> **BEWARE** With email filtering turned on, it's possible that you may receive email from a source of which you approve, but because of the way you may have set up your filter or the way the filter works, wanted emails may get deleted before you ever see them! The key point here is, you need to understand the junk email and filtering options available in your email software and decide what level of filtering you want to use or even whether filtering is really necessary.

If junk email becomes a particularly annoying problem to you, nevertheless, consider automatic filtering options carefully before activating them – especially if you're in business. A new customer or client may simply be testing you or your company's response timing. Not acknowledging a communication from a

> **HOT TIP** One option to consider is to quickly scan emails as you receive them and optionally add any junk emails to your junk list, or simply delete unwanted emails immediately – this is the approach I take and it is an acceptable compromise.

Managing your email messages < 349

new prospective client is not an ideal way to foster new business. Answering a routine simple email enquiry may be the first step in gaining an order equivalent to your entire year's normal work: you just never know!

> **HOT TIP**
>
> Here's another way to limit or at least control junk email. However, this method does include the rather drastic step of first cancelling your current email address. Next, get two more addresses. Keep one of your new email addresses for serious communications and therefore only provide this to trusted parties. Then use your other email address for contributing to public forums like newsgroups, mailing lists, etc. – and if the amount of spam all gets too much a few months or a year later, simply cancel this address and start the cycle again with a new address. Drastic, I know, but it works!

How to keep spammers guessing!

If you particularly dislike receiving Spam emails, consider carefully whether you should vent your frustration on every Spam email that arrives. Even if "Unsubscribe instructions" to "prevent further emails being sent to you" are provided, unless you know this is a trusted and honourable source, my advice is to simply ignore the message and just delete the email manually, rather than replying. So why not just reply?

The problem is, if you do reply with an unsubscribe instruction, these people may decide to simply ignore your request anyway and if they do not have any genuine respect for your choices, they then know for sure that your email address is (1) valid and (2) that it's a "live" address – that is, someone is responding regularly.

Unscrupulous parties can then add your email address to the tens of thousands of others who may also have chosen to unsubscribe in disgust. These email "harvesters" can then sell this "live" emailing list to other parties, for another round of email spam! You then receive another batch of unwanted email. And so the cycle repeats. The best and safest advice we can provide here therefore is to simply delete any unwanted emails that you did not originally ask to receive.

Organising your email messages

As the number of email messages increases, if you don't delete or back up the ones you don't need, the efficiency of your email program may start to suffer. However, many people want or need to keep some or all copies of emails they receive.

> If you have just "answered" your email box, you can easily identify new unread emails from those you have already examined, simply by clicking on the "Date" or "Received" option or by grouping your emails in the current folder using the Date or Received column. Sorting by date order is usually the best standard option for most people.

The absolutely simplest way to handle email is to keep everything in a single folder. For most people, however, this approach is simply not practical: for example, you might want to separate emails you receive from your boss from those sent by Aunt Sally – just in case you accidentally send the wrong reply to the wrong person: not a great way to make a good impression on either party. Therefore consider the following guidelines to help create a more logical and easier email set up:

1. Creating new folders
Simply create folders with different names and organise them into a logical structure that makes sense to you. All good email software allows you to create different folder structures in this way. Other key organisation options include the ability to archive and compress older email messages and simply delete those no longer required.

2. Grouping and sorting messages
In Outlook Express, with the 3-panes visible in the main window (left: folders; top: files; bottom: contents of the selected file), you can also easily change the way Outlook Express sorts your items. Here's how. Notice in the top pane each column has a heading; simply click the column heading you want to sort the list of items by that column. So for example, if you wanted to group all emails received from Jane Jones, simply click the "From" column heading, then scroll down the list to the Js to find all Jane Jones' emails. To sort in reverse order, click the

Folder List

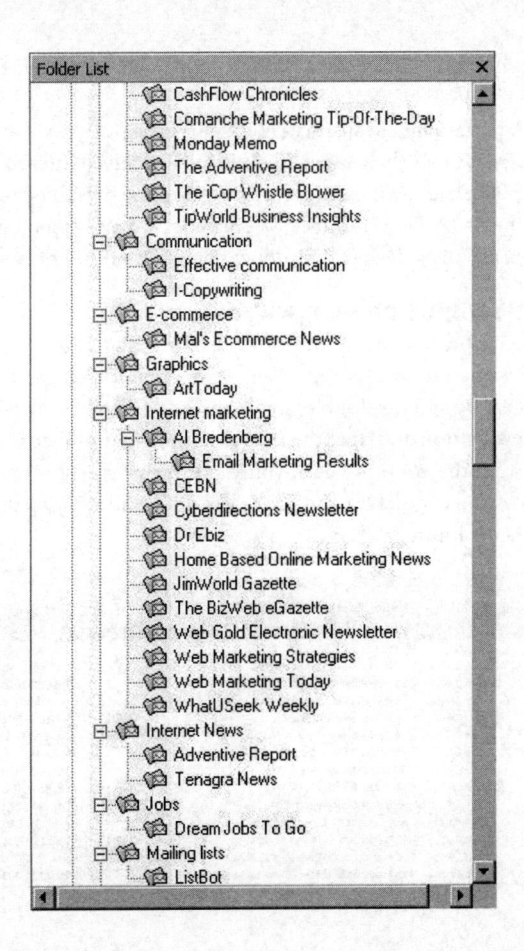

- CashFlow Chronicles
- Comanche Marketing Tip-Of-The-Day
- Monday Memo
- The Adventive Report
- The iCop Whistle Blower
- TipWorld Business Insights
- Communication
  - Effective communication
  - I-Copywriting
- E-commerce
  - Mal's Ecommerce News
- Graphics
  - ArtToday
- Internet marketing
  - Al Bredenberg
    - Email Marketing Results
  - CEBN
  - Cyberdirections Newsletter
  - Dr Ebiz
  - Home Based Online Marketing News
  - JimWorld Gazette
  - The BizWeb eGazette
  - Web Gold Electronic Newsletter
  - Web Marketing Strategies
  - Web Marketing Today
  - WhatUSeek Weekly
- Internet News
  - Adventive Report
  - Tenagra News
- Jobs
  - Dream Jobs To Go
- Mailing lists
  - ListBot

column you chose once again – in our example, the "From" column.

After replying to an email message, you can arrange for any messages older than a specific time to be archived, or you can simply delete the message to help control the overall quantity of emails. A large number of emails can make some email software unstable and slow down operation of the software.

3. Changing column widths

Place your mouse pointer on a dividing line between two adjacent column headings. When the pointer changes to an opposite-pointing double arrow, press and hold down the mouse button and drag the mouse left or right to increase or decrease the column width you want to change. This option allows you to quickly see more or less of the information detail in that column.

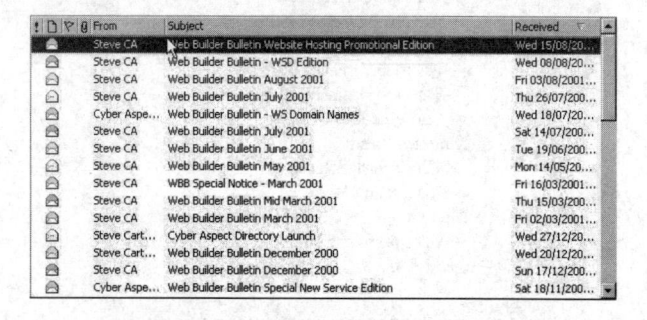

Rerouting messages automatically

Most email programs can be set up to automatically go online at regular intervals to send and receive email messages and then disconnect from the Internet. You can combine and enhance this approach with creating folders for specific email messages and rules that automatically route messages to the correct folders as soon as they're received: a great timesaving feature.

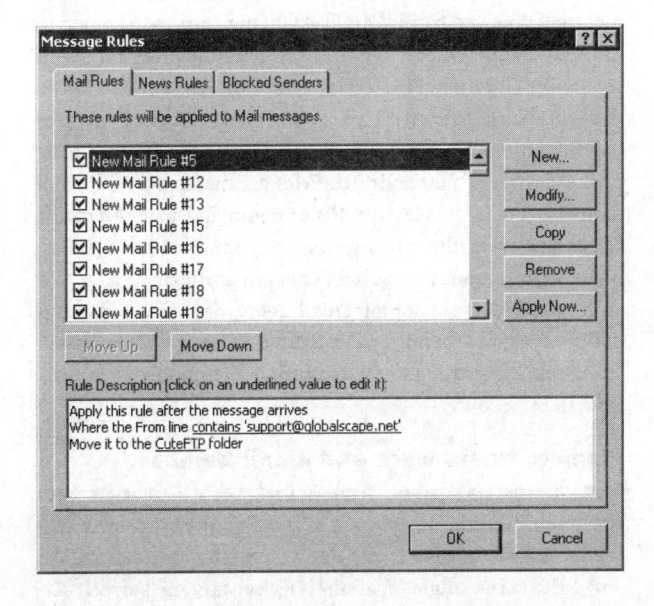

Message Rules	? ×

Mail Rules | News Rules | Blocked Senders |

These rules will be applied to Mail messages.

- ☑ New Mail Rule #5
- ☑ New Mail Rule #12
- ☑ New Mail Rule #13
- ☑ New Mail Rule #15
- ☑ New Mail Rule #16
- ☑ New Mail Rule #17
- ☑ New Mail Rule #18
- ☑ New Mail Rule #19

[New...] [Modify...] [Copy] [Remove] [Apply Now...]

[Move Up] [Move Down]

Rule Description (click on an underlined value to edit it):

Apply this rule after the message arrives
Where the From line contains 'support@globalscape.net'
Move it to the CuteFTP folder

[OK] [Cancel]

Managing your email messages < 355

Automatic rerouting works by examining specific parts of an email message and comparing those parts with some reference text you provide. For example, the program might look at the sender's email address, the subject box, characters in the body text, and so on, and if any matches the reference text the program sends the email message to the folder set up for that particular rule.

For example, you can create a rule that ensures any email messages received from: john@skydiving.com are rerouted to the "Skydiving" folder. Or all messages containing the word sequence: "Internet Tips Today ezine" can be sent to a folder that you name Internet Tips Today ezine. Outlook Express handles automatic rerouting of email using the "Create Rule From Message" command on the Message menu in combination with the Tools > Message Rules command pair. Netscape Messenger uses the Message Filters command on the Edit menu to automatically redirect email in a similar way.

If you receive a lot of email every day, this feature is definitely worth spending a little time to learn how to set up. It's the quickest way I know of cutting 30 minutes organising time to 30 seconds.

Flames, flame wars and email bombs

Slang terms and jargon have always been associated with computers and the Internet and, as we've already seen, email too has a few unusual terms that you might come across. An email flame is a single email message sent to one person designed to insult or annoy the recipient. When the recipient replies in the same manner, a flame "war" can start, with abusive emails travelling back and forth. Often, these events can also occur in public forums like newsgroups.

Sometimes, you may find that you're getting drawn into a heated Internet discussion, so what do you do? Obviously say your piece but if things start getting out of control, my advice is to simply never respond to an email flame – ever! As a reader of this book, you're an intelligent person. Just do the Internet equivalent of walking away; simply delete a flame and forget about it.

If you really don't want to hear from that person, most good email programs include commands that allow you to automatically send emails from a specific source straight to the email junk bin every time you check your email, so you won't even need to see another email from that source again – unless they use another email address. For instructions on how to make this option active, check your email program's Help documentation.

Listen to your email virtually anywhere

Here's an Internet gem! Using services like BT's SpeechMail or equivalent, you can listen to your emails over the phone line any time anywhere across the globe! Also, Genie and many other similar Internet Service Providers and other companies are now providing services that allow a PC user to send basic text messages direct to a mobile phone and surf the Internet with a new generation **WAP** mobile phone that contains a kind of mini web browser. To discover more:

- **Openwave:** www.openwave.com/

- **WAP Forum:** www.wapforum.com/

- Visit your own Internet Service Provider's website.

In this way, you can find other companies who provide these exciting new services and discover more about what's on offer now and what's just around the corner.

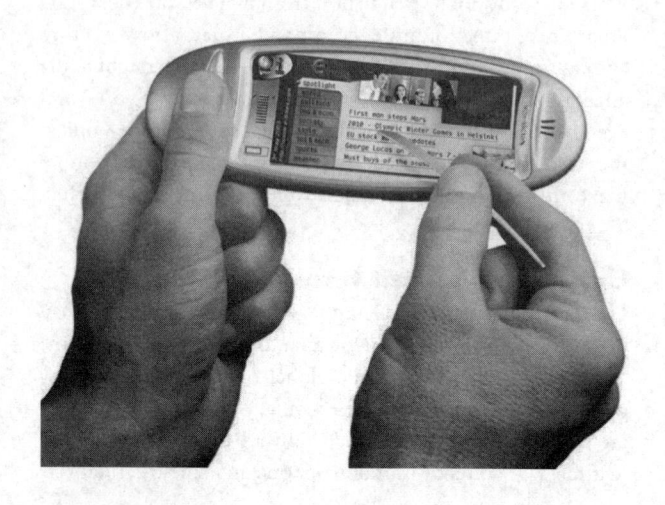

17

Playing online games

Playing games on the Internet is a compelling experience – especially if you're playing against live opponents and not just another computer program. Your opponents could be located anywhere across the globe and some take on their tasks with almost religious devotion and fervour. Online gaming can also be a great way to meet new friends on the web – perhaps most of whom you might never meet otherwise. So if Internet games are for you, let's take a closer look at what's available and how to take part.

What you need to play online games

Computer muscle: most current games are designed for 3D. These often make high demands from computer hardware; the electronic video chips on 3D cards must be fast and powerful if they're to cope with the often high tension and speed of Internet games. To play 3D games, you'll need to have a 3D video card or capability built into your computer. Also, most games have a minimum specification for the main electronic chip – the Central Processing Unit (CPU) – and the amount of memory (RAM) installed. The faster the CPU and the more memory your computer has installed, usually the faster and more stable a game will run. Therefore, first make sure that you have the necessary computer hardware before getting on board.

Up to 2 players: for two players to participate in a computer game, both computers need to be connected together. If you're not connected to the Internet, you can use a special connector called a null modem cable and install each end into the serial port connectors of each machine. On the Internet, you can do the equivalent except you don't use null modem cables, rather modems or ISDN terminal adaptors can make the connection for you.

Three or more players: options here include using a Local Area Network (LAN) in which several computers are connected together in the same building. Each computer will need the relevant network cards or electronic networking chips installed, the cabling (although wireless networks are now available) to physically join the computers and the network software that allows each computer to "talk" to the other members on the network.

However, if you want more bodies to come to the party, why not go on the Internet – the ultimate computer network? Now things can really start getting interesting, challenging and yes, sometimes frustrating. I mention frustration because, as all regular Internet users know, delays and information "dropouts" can sometimes occur, so sometimes a command may need to be repeated – just hope that this doesn't occur at a crucial moment.

Downloading game software: some popular current games are quite large in file size, so rather than download them over the Internet, you're often better checking out the demo versions that often accompany computer and Internet magazines from your newsagent. And remember, you can check out online sources to discover what others are saying about specific games. See also: www.netgamer.net/

> **HOT TIP**
>
> If you're physically located close to the server on which the game is hosted, you'll probably enjoy faster game response times and therefore enjoy a built-in gaming advantage. Also, if you play only with other participants from the same Internet Service Provider, overall game "quality" may be much better with shorter delays and fewer dropouts, compared to playing on the "open" Internet.

> **PC PLAYSTATION NINTENDO DREAMCAST**
>
> www.yac.com: Free Communication Upgrade
> Get your phone calls, voice mail and faxes wherever you are, whenever you want? [OK] [Cancel]
>
> Sunday 28 May **TOP STORIES**
>
> ### Old Has-Beens Sneak Into E3
> ■ News
> Hasbro's Line-up to feature classic cameo's from *Pac-Man* and friends
>
> ### Hooked on Classics
> ■ News
> They don't make games like they used to, do they? Aha, but they do. They make them exactly like they used to and bung them up on the Web where you can play them for free. Midway, that is
>
> ### Midway's Nintendo E3 Line-up
> ■ News
> Yet more E3 tomfoolery for the N64
>
> ### They're Taking Us For A Ride!
> ■ News
> EA are bringing *Theme Park World* to the PlayStation2
>
> ### Quake III Mission Pack confirmed
> ■ News
> We tried to think of a witty headline for this, possibly rhyming with *Team Arena*, but all we could come up with was an obscure reference to The Man With The Stick*
>
> ### Strawberries And Cream From Sega
> ■ News

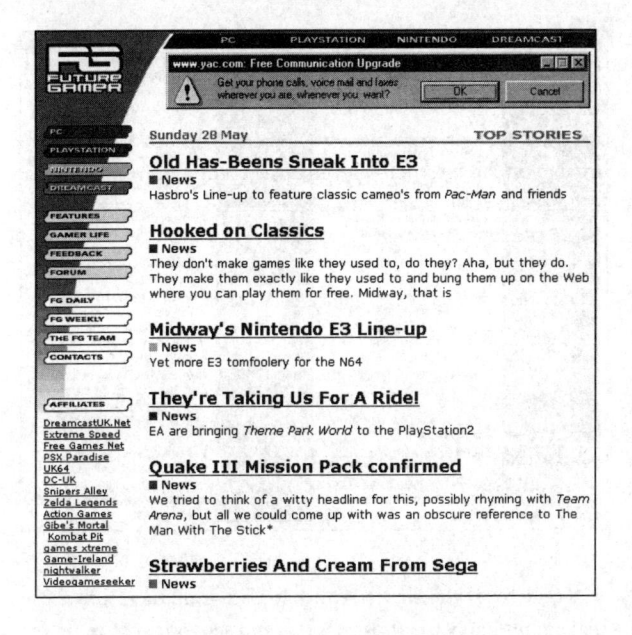

Getting started

With some online games, you can jump straight in as soon as you connect, while for others you'll need to hold back in a waiting area until a space comes up or the game you want becomes available. Some of the more recent games even allow you to talk to your opponents while playing – some interesting and colourful conversations can take place.

Playing online games < 363

MULTIPLAYER ZONE

Quake is the original and, some say, still the best 3D FPS. Multiplayer games such as Capture the Flag began life here.

Quake II continued the Id tradition of fast-paced multiplayer action, and captured the imagination of the community.

Quake III: Arena - super-fast, good-looking and inheritor of the legions of Quake I and II fans. Lots of good stuff here!

Half-Life - the greatest single player FPS ever made. Once you're tired of single-player, though, you'll find plenty here to keep you going.

Counter-Strike is based on the Half-Life engine - but it's practically a game in its own right. One-shot kills and team play make it a must.

Soldier of Fortune, a great single-player game and gory to boot. When you're bored of that, however, there's plenty of MP fun to be had.

Unreal Tournament's multiple game styles made it a smash hit. Now fans have created an array of new games to play with it.

Unreal looks like it could have been released yesterday - funnily enough, some new maps and utilities were!

Alien vs. Predator brings you the terror of facing lethal killing machines in space. Remember, on a server, no one can hear you scream.

Deus Ex is one of the finest action adventure games on PC is now multiplayer. Delve inside and get maps, mods and utilities.

Duke Nukem 3D: Hail to the king, baby! Check out the maps for this classic and charismatic shooter from 3D Realms.

Daikatana, if you bought it, you're probably looking for something to make it more interesting. We've got all you need right here.

To discover the closest games to you – and therefore those that are probably the most stable – and set your system up for automated connections, you can install some purpose-designed software. For more information, see: www.gamesdomain.com (current popular examples are shown in the above illustration), www.gamespy.com and www.kali.net

Playing in teams

By combing the computing power and ingenuity of multiple participants – who may be located anywhere on the Internet –

an online game can take on an entirely new look and feel. Power, emotion, intensity are three words that can help describe these experiences. Most new computer games designed for two or more participants can also be played on the Internet. Three of the most popular team games include Quake Team Fortress, Ultima Online and Unreal Tournament. See also: www.owo.com/

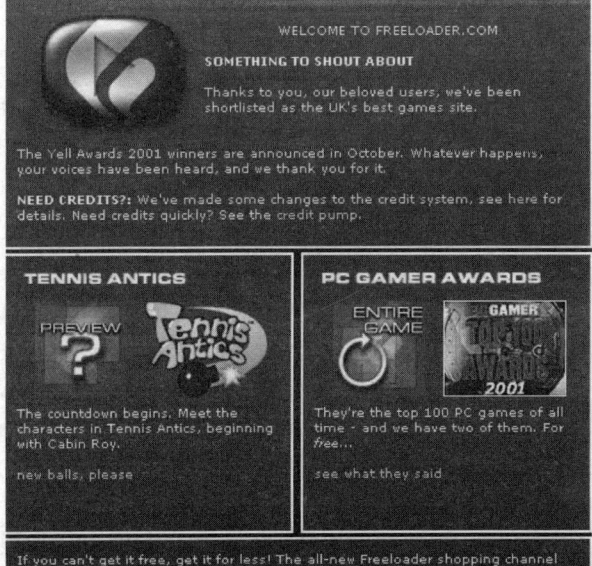

WELCOME TO FREELOADER.COM

SOMETHING TO SHOUT ABOUT

Thanks to you, our beloved users, we've been shortlisted as the UK's best games site.

The Yell Awards 2001 winners are announced in October. Whatever happens, your voices have been heard, and we thank you for it.

NEED CREDITS?: We've made some changes to the credit system, see here for details. Need credits quickly? See the credit pump.

TENNIS ANTICS

The countdown begins. Meet the characters in Tennis Antics, beginning with Cabin Roy.

new balls, please

PC GAMER AWARDS

ENTIRE GAME

They're the top 100 PC games of all time - and we have two of them. For free...

see what they said

If you can't get it free, get it for less! The all-new Freeloader shopping channel allows you to take your pick of products from the best on-line retailers using a single shopping basket. Check it out now!

Finding online games

Current popular online games include: Commanche3, Age of Empires, Quake, TombRaider and Chessmaster to name but a few. To get started and discover what's currently available, consider visiting the following websites:

- **WirePlay:** www.wireplay.com (UK & Australia)

- **FreeLoader:** www.freeloader.com

- **MSN:** www.zone.com

- **Gamespot:** www.gamespot.com

- **GamesDomain:** www.gamesdomain.com

- **Happy Puppy:** www.happypuppy.com

Good luck, have fun and try not to become addicted!

18

Internet newsgroups

Newsgroups and mailing lists have much in common: both are great for meeting new friends, creating profitable business relations and generally interacting with lots of different people from around the world. However, mailing lists and newsgroups do have striking differences. Let's examine those differences by taking a close look at newsgroups.

A cautionary note: computer virus warnings

Message files downloaded from newsgroups are one of the most common ways to spread computer viruses. Therefore, before participating in a newsgroup, make sure you have an up-to-date antivirus program working in the background. Don't ever trust anyone from a newsgroup who says a file or message is virus-free: if you decide to download it, always check it yourself using your antivirus program.

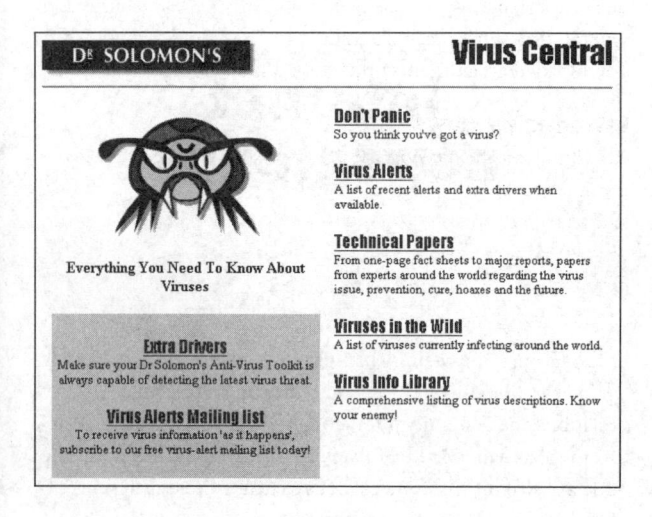

Dr SOLOMON'S

Virus Central

Don't Panic
So you think you've got a virus?

Virus Alerts
A list of recent alerts and extra drivers when available.

Technical Papers
From one-page fact sheets to major reports, papers from experts around the world regarding the virus issue, prevention, cure, hoaxes and the future.

Everything You Need To Know About Viruses

Viruses in the Wild
A list of viruses currently infecting around the world.

Extra Drivers
Make sure your Dr Solomon's Anti-Virus Toolkit is always capable of detecting the latest virus threat.

Virus Info Library
A comprehensive listing of virus descriptions. Know your enemy!

Virus Alerts Mailing list
To receive virus information 'as it happens', subscribe to our free virus-alert mailing list today!

Even when a virus is present in a file, remember that antivirus software may still not detect the virus if it is a new strain or your antivirus records have not been updated to cover that particular virus. Therefore, do keep your antivirus software tables up-to-date: as a heavy Internet user, I update mine once every 2 weeks – sometimes more often. The safest option is to make a rule not to download any attachments from newsgroups, period. Plus make regular backups of your computer data.

Sorry to spoil your fun but I needed to say that! From my own experiences, I've had a lot of fun in newsgroups and several times my antivirus software has detected infected downloaded attachments and zapped them promptly.

Introducing newsgroups

Also known as discussion groups, newsgroups are a branch of the Internet where you can meet Internet users with interests similar to your own. You can discuss issues, solve problems and upload and download files but unlike Internet Chat (page 398), newsgroups are not "live."

Thousands of newsgroups are available on the Internet covering thousands of different topics including: cooking, travel, employment, humour, current events, music, films, sports, religion, the environment, and television to name but a few. Currently, over 60,000 newsgroups exist with more being added daily! Newsville.com provides a good idea of the range of newsgroups currently available.

A newsgroup can have many thousands of messages stored, however when you first connect usually only a few hundred may be displayed by default. If more messages are available, you can simply click a button to have your newsreader download another batch. By default, Microsoft Outlook, for example, downloads 300 messages each time, but you can change that amount if you wish in the "Options" dialog box.

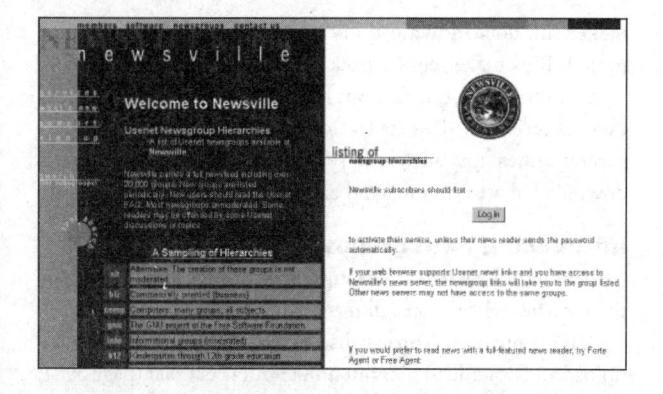

Usually, an Internet Service Provider provides a newsgroup server to handle all newsgroups they provide. The term newsgroup server is a collective name for all their computers that handle only newsgroup information. If you want a newsgroup that your Internet Service Provider does not already include, check their acceptable user guidelines and if you think the subject of that newsgroup does not break their rules, simply ask if they will add the newsgroup you want to their list.

Top level newsgroup categories

All individual newsgroups are grouped under several "top level" categories. In fact, in a newsgroup name, the characters before the first full stop show to which "top-level" category a newsgroup belongs.

For example, the newsgroup: comp.sys.laptops shows that this newsgroup is about computers – portable computers to be exact as the ending characters suggest. The table below shows some of the most popular top-level categories:

Category	Covers
alt	Alternative topics to the other main groups.
biz	Business-related newsgroups.
comp	Computers.
news	News and newsgroup discussion.
rec	Recreation-related topics.
sci	Science.
soc	Social topics.
uk	UK-specific newsgroups.

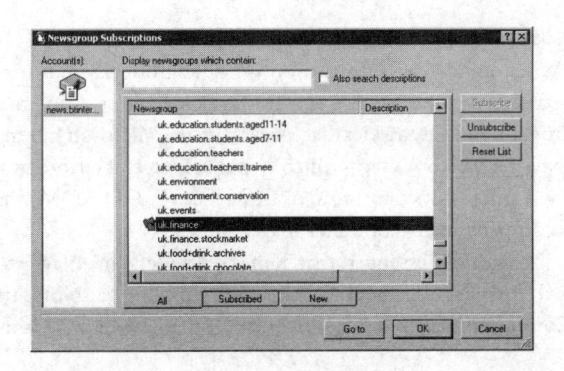

Newsgroup names

A newsgroup name is made up of two or more words separated by full stops. The first word describes the theme – as shown above. The words that follow gradually focus on more specific parts of the theme of that particular newsgroup.

You can usually work out what a newsgroup covers by its description. For example: "uk.jobs.wanted" discusses employment wanted in the UK. Or "alt.chinese.fengshui" discusses the ancient Chinese art of designing living and working spaces and what implications – if any – that has for you. "alt.cardgames.magic" discusses magic tricks with card games and is found in the alt(ernative) category.

Other popular categories include: aus(tralia), misc(ellaneous) and talk (hot discussions). When first starting out, you can use alt.test to practice posting to newsgroups to avoid irritating other more experienced users.

Newsreader software overview

To send and read information on newsgroups, you'll need newsreader software. Microsoft Outlook Express is an email program and newsreader that comes with the Microsoft Internet Explorer web browser – which is available free of charge from www.microsoft.com/ or often from the free CD-ROMs that accompany many computer magazines.

Netscape Messenger, that comes with Netscape Navigator web browser as part of the free of charge Netscape Communicator suite, also includes a fine newsreader. Other popular newsreaders include Free Agent and Agent from Forte and MicroPlanet Gravity.

Configuring your newsreader

The guidelines provided in this section relate mainly to Outlook Express and Netscape Messenger – both of these free programs include excellent newsreaders. If you choose another newsreader, relate the steps here to help configure your copy.

To recap, most Internet Service Providers have what is known as a news server – computers on which newsgroups are stored and which are made available to customers. Now, when you first install Outlook Express, you'll need to enter the address of your Internet Service Provider's news server. For example, BT Internet customers use: news.btinternet.com

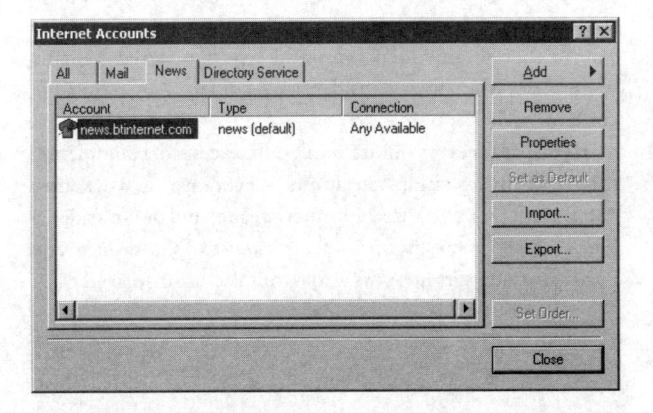

If you ever want to add an additional news server, or just perform this step directly, in Outlook Express first choose the Accounts command from the Tools menu. Next click the Add News button and follow the instructions from the wizard to complete the news server installation.

In Netscape Messenger, open the Edit menu and choose the Preferences command. Then under the Mail & Newsgroups category, choose Newsgroup Servers and click the Add button to include the news server name that your Internet Service Provider has given you (example: news.btinternet.com).

During your newsreader set-up, the first time you connect to your news server, usually you'll be asked if you want to download a list of available newsgroups. This operation can take some time and essentially depends on the size of the newsgroup file being downloaded, the speed of your Internet connection and the power of your computer. Also some Internet Service providers censor the type of material available to remove what they consider may contain "objectionable content", others do not.

If you pay for every minute while online, consider completing this task during cheap-rate hours – evenings or weekends. After you have configured your newsreader and downloaded a list of available newsgroups, you can choose to subscribe to any individual newsgroups you want from the list displayed.

screenshot content

members software newsgroups contact us

newsville

services
what's new
support
sign up

search
(for newsgroups)

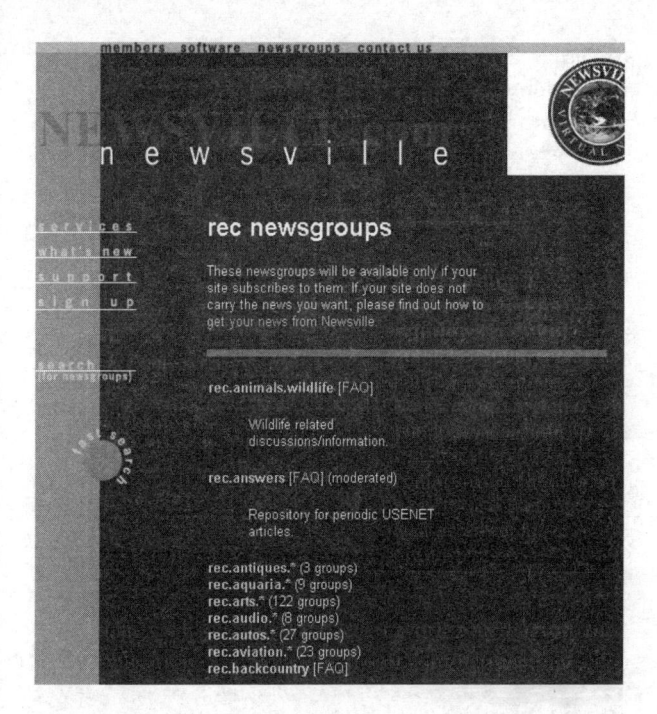

rec newsgroups

These newsgroups will be available only if your site subscribes to them. If your site does not carry the news you want, please find out how to get your news from Newsville.

rec.animals.wildlife [FAQ]

    Wildlife related discussions/information.

rec.answers [FAQ] (moderated)

    Repository for periodic USENET articles.

rec.antiques.* (3 groups)
rec.aquaria.* (9 groups)
rec.arts.* (122 groups)
rec.audio.* (8 groups)
rec.autos.* (27 groups)
rec.aviation.* (23 groups)
rec.backcountry [FAQ]

Protecting your email address in newsgroups

Just like mailing lists, contributing to newsgroups can cause you to start receiving a lot of irrelevant email messages – usually from people and organisations trying to sell something to you.

You can reduce this effect by not using your most important email address – instead, use another spare and preferably web-based email address that you keep especially for newsgroups, mailing lists and other more public Internet communications.

Alternatively, you can change your email address slightly to help block or confuse automatic email harvesters – these are software tools often used by spammers that regularly scan newsgroups trying to collect email addresses. Here's one way to help beat email harvesters. Suppose my real email address is brian@mysite.com I can change this to brian@NOSPAMmysite.com

As NOSPAMmysite.com is a domain that really does not exist, any uninvited email messages sent to that domain name would usually get bounced back to the sender – with an error message. Using this technique, you would probably have to include a line of text with your changed email address that says something like: "please remove the NOSPAM part when replying", so that genuine people know what to do in order to contact you.

> Newsgroups are open to anyone who wants to subscribe, so when you join a newsgroup and participate, other Internet users know and a permanent record is available at your Internet Service Provider.

> **BEWARE**: Don't say anything on a newsgroup, mailing list, Internet Chat or WebCam-based system that you're not prepared to repeat in a court of law. The key point is: be careful what you say. Avoid making slanderous or libellous statements.

Moderated and unmoderated newsgroups

Like mailing lists, individual newsgroups can be moderated or unmoderated. A moderated newsgroup may have the word added at the end of a newsgroup name, for example: rec.arts.sf.tv.babylon5.moderated.

A moderated newsgroup has volunteers (usually) who monitor email messages sent to the newsgroup and decide if the message is relevant, acceptable and has not broken the rules of the newsgroup. If a message is about a topic already covered, the moderator may refer the sender to the newsgroup archives where information about their chosen topic is covered.

If the message is accepted however, the moderator makes the message available to all members on the newsgroup. In an unmoderated newsgroup, all messages sent to the newsgroup are made freely available to all participants of the newsgroup as they come in. In some unmoderated newsgroups, strong opinions and personal clashes can result in the language becoming "colourful" to say the least.

HOT TIP If you see a message that you find offensive and just have to tell this person what you think, consider sending an email direct to the sender rather than voicing your anger to the entire newsgroup. Sending personal attacks to a newsgroup or list is called flaming, and is generally frowned upon. Flaming may not help you get answers to your questions, solve your problem or endear you to the list.

HOT TIP If you subscribe to several newsgroups, make sure you post the right message to the correct newsgroup to avoid embarrassing comments.

Discovering what's available in newsgroups

Usenet – shortened from Users Network – is a description covering all the powerful computers on the Internet that enable all the newsgroups to operate.

Although Usenet currently has over 60,000 newsgroups, your ISP usually determines the exact type and nature of available newsgroups. So if a newsgroup you want is not available on their list, simply ask if they can provide it. They naturally try to meet the needs of customers so may make your desired newsgroup available to you, but this may not always be possible.

Some newsgroups are deliberately omitted from an Internet Service Provider's list on moral or censorship grounds – no

> # CriticaPath.
>
> ## Welcome to Supernews®
>
> Supernews offers Usenet outsourcing services to ISPs and individual Usenet access to consumers. We were recently acquired by Critical Path, the dominant global provider of business-to-business Internet messaging and collaboration solutions.
>
> Supernews' Personal Accounts provide individuals interested in Usenet access with the most complete source of Usenet available. Our Spam Guard technology leads the industry in eliminating unwanted advertising and spam, leaving subscribers with rich, relevant discussion content.
>
> Supernews' Usenet outsourcing services allow ISPs to free themselves from the equipment, maintenance and administration headaches that come with providing Usenet access to their customers. They can also improve the quality of Internet discussions they offer their users at a lower cost.
>
> **Personal Usenet Accounts**
>
> o 30 day **RISK-FREE** Trial
>   click here
>
> o **New to Usenet?**
>   click here
>
> **ISP & Corporate Info**
>
> o Outsourcing Services for ISP's and Corporations
>   click here
>
> **News Server Statistics**

Internet Service Provider wants to be branded pornography-friendly or linked to any extreme political views – at least openly. Essentially, for business reasons, most Internet Service Providers prefer to reflect what it considers is the general public's view on sensitive issues. However, some providers prefer to let their customers dictate what they make available – within reason, so some negotiation may be possible.

However, if your Internet Service Provider does not include what you're looking for, check other providers or consider using publicly accessible news servers. To gain access to the content of a publicly accessible news server, you don't usually need an account. Take a look at:

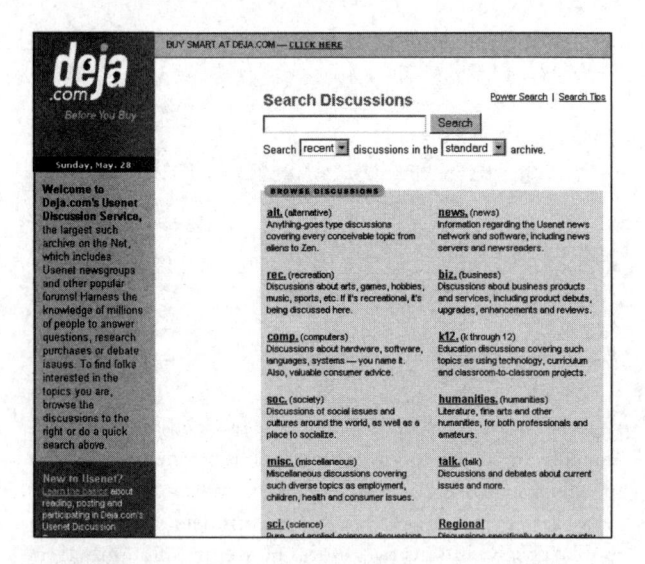

HOT TIP If you participate in any particularly popular or busy newsgroups and want to follow closely what is happening, check back at least every couple of days. Why? Busy newsgroups fill up the space available more quickly; the providers may then delete older messages every 3 days or thereabouts to make room for new threads (a single discussion theme) and new topics.

- www.remarq.com/

- www.freenews.net/ and www.freenews.com/

- www.newsvillle.com/

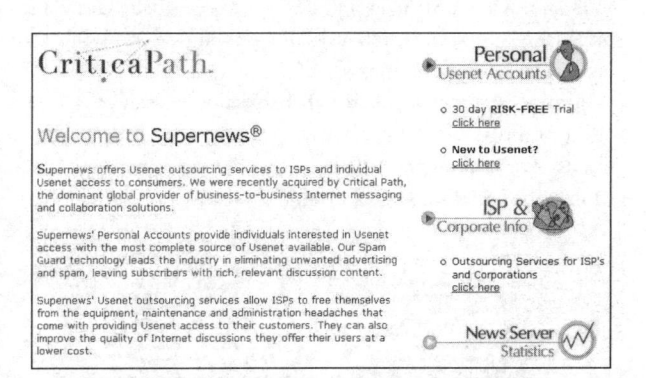

CriticaPath

Welcome to Supernews®

Supernews offers Usenet outsourcing services to ISPs and individual Usenet access to consumers. We were recently acquired by Critical Path, the dominant global provider of business-to-business Internet messaging and collaboration solutions.

Supernews' Personal Accounts provide individuals interested in Usenet access with the most complete source of Usenet available. Our Spam Guard technology leads the industry in eliminating unwanted advertising and spam, leaving subscribers with rich, relevant discussion content.

Supernews' Usenet outsourcing services allow ISPs to free themselves from the equipment, maintenance and administration headaches that come with providing Usenet access to their customers. They can also improve the quality of Internet discussions they offer their users at a lower cost.

Personal Usenet Accounts
- 30 day **RISK-FREE** Trial
  click here
- **New to Usenet?**
  click here

ISP & Corporate Info
- Outsourcing Services for ISP's and Corporations
  click here

News Server Statistics

New newsgroups are being created every day and some newsgroups simply close down through disuse. Therefore, to start with, try subscribing to the following newsgroup to see the current range of newsgroups available: news.lists or examine and post to newsgroups without using a dedicated newsreader. Instead, you can use the web's largest and most popular newsgroup directory Deja.com at: www.deja.com/ On Deja.com's Home/Index page, click the link for "Usenet", and you can gain access to a surprisingly wide range of newsgroups.

Subscribing and unsubscribing to a newsgroup

To participate in a newsgroup – even just to discover what is being said without contributing directly – you'll need to join or subscribe to the newsgroup you want – using a real email address, not a NOSPAM version as listed previously. Use your NOSPAM version when actually posting or replying to individual newsgroup messages.

Joining a newsgroup is free of charge and you can subscribe or unsubscribe whenever you want. Although each newsreader has its own unique procedure for subscribing to newsgroups, subscription methods of different newsreaders are similar. To subscribe to a newsgroup in Outlook Express, first click on the news server name in the left pane, then click the Newsgroups button on the main toolbar at the top of the Outlook Express window.

You can also find the Newsgroups command in the Tools menu, or by right-clicking the desired news server name and choosing the command from the floating menu. In the dialog box that appears, click the newsgroup you want from the list and click the Subscribe button. Outlook Express then inserts a small marker next to each newsgroup to which you subscribe.

To download messages, select the subscribed newsgroup name you want and click the GoTo button. If you're not already online, Outlook Express prompts you to connect to the Internet and the first batch of message headers starts to download once your software connects to the news server.

For newcomers to newsgroups, an ideal way to try out posting a message is to subscribe to the alt.test newsgroup and practice sending test messages. Sending test messages to other newsgroups is often frowned upon by other members who may ask you to stop.

When you subscribe to an individual newsgroup, usually the first 300–500 message headers are automatically downloaded to your newsreader. Then once the batch has finished downloading, to read a specific message you'll need to select the message header, the content of that particular message is then displayed usually in the lower larger pane. You can read, reply and sort messages as described in the following sections.

In Outlook Express, to unsubscribe first right-click to select the newsgroup you want in the left-side pane, then choose the Unsubscribe command from the floating menu. In Netscape Messenger, you can subscribe using the Subscribe command in the File menu. In the dialog box, navigate to find the newsgroup name you want, select it, then choose the Subscribe button and click OK to finish. Then click the newsgroup name in the left pane to start downloading messages. You can also unsubscribe from a newsgroup using the Subscribe dialog box: select the name you want and click the Unsubscribe button followed by OK.

A newsgroup's money-saving strategy

Once you have subscribed to any newsgroup, if you have to pay for every second while online, you can save money by first reading only those messages that interest you. Then disconnect – those messages will still be present in your newsreader. Comment or reply to any message you want, then reconnect to the Internet and send your messages before disconnecting again. Later – say perhaps every couple of days – you can reconnect to the Internet and view any comments or replies to your messages and those of others. Repeat the sequence as necessary.

In this way, you make use of off-peak telephone rates and avoid having to spend a lengthy period online. Of course, if you have free or low-cost access to the Internet, then staying online while participating in newsgroups offers the easiest method to use as you can react while information is fresh in your mind.

The Frequently Asked Questions file

Many newsgroups have a Frequently Asked Questions (FAQ) file, which is useful for new members to read before posting and may indeed answer your question. If you don't see the FAQ on display, email the newsgroup moderator or, as a last resort, email to the newsgroup.

If you're new to newsgroups, before immediately posting a message, consider viewing and reading some of the current postings to get a better idea of what is acceptable. Taking a little time to familiarise yourself with newsgroup ways is worthwhile to avoid asking the kind of questions that regular participants hear repeatedly – and some are less tolerant to newcomers.

To get the best from newsgroups and avoid potential intolerance or unpleasantness, taking a little time to learn newsgroup netiquette can help you solve your problem quicker and is much appreciated by other members.

Reading newsgroup messages and contributing

A newsgroup message is simply an email a contributor provides to the group – also known as posting to the group. People can contribute opinions, ideas, software, images, sound and video clips. Although a short message is usually preferable – it takes less time to read – a message can often be much longer.

You can simply browse through the newsgroup message "headers" – a line of text describing what the message is about – and read only those messages that interest you. Message headers can include the subject, email address of the contributor, date sent and an indicator of any file attachments, and sometimes the message file size.

If you see a header line that interests you, click the message header and the main message text appears in another usually larger pane. Just like any other computer file, you can also save or print interesting newsgroup messages. If you're replying or commenting on an existing topic, your message is added to the other messages on that same topic and becomes a "thread" in that series, so keep to the topic in the thread, or start a new thread yourself and post it for discussion. Most good newsreaders – the software that allows you to send and read newsgroup messages – let you sort and arrange messages by thread to make tracking the progress of a specific discussion topic easier.

Posting to a newsgroup

Remember, people from around the world post to newsgroups and so in different cultures similar words may have very different meanings. Therefore, try to make sure your message is simple, clear and concise with no chance of being misinterpreted and spell-check it before posting. Before posting to a newsgroup, spend a little time watching how others post – also known as "lurking." Read some posts and observe how

> **HOT TIP** — Keep messages short and to the point and be sure you understand the kind of newsgroup to which you're contributing. For example, sending the entire script of Shakespeare's Hamlet to a newsgroup and then asking: "Is this dude great or what?" could result in some colourful replies!

Doug,

I reckon the one to visit is Poland Street in the West End
(http://www.thenosebag.net/map.asp?RestaurantID=1719&Postcode=W1V3DF)

The Kaiten thingy (the conveyor belt) is quite good fun, though there are some bits and pieces that are a rare find and may have to be ordered specifically. You sometimes need to be a bit quick of the mark to make the most of the beer robot (where can I get one of those?)

The best recommendation that I can give is that we took a couple of friends there, who'll return - not bad as one of them doesn't like fish (though we didn't know that at the time).

--
Regards

Simon

---

others reply; which parts of the original message they include, etc.

To post a message in Outlook Express or Netscape Messenger, first click to select the newsgroup name you want in the left pane, then click the New Post or New Message button on the main toolbar. Or you can use the New Message command in the Message menu.

The newsgroup to which you're sending the post is shown in the upper box. If you want to post the same message to several different newsgroups, after the first entered newsgroup name type a comma and a space, then enter the remaining newsgroup names likewise. In the Subject box, enter a brief description of what your message is about. Try to provide a specific rather than general brief description so that users have a clear idea of what the topic is about. Click the Send button to finish. After posting a message or reply to a newsgroup, your message soon appears with all the others in the newsgroup. However, if later you decide that you want to scrap the message you sent, you can use the Message Cancel command if available in your newsreader – but remember this option does not guarantee that every instance of your message will be removed and may take some time to implement.

In Outlook Express first select the message header then choose the Cancel Message command in the Message menu. In Netscape Messenger, the equivalent message cancel command is available on the floating menu when you right-click the message header you want to cancel.

Newsgroup spamming

Don't post the same message to several (or more) unrelated newsgroups or you may be accused of newsgroup spamming. Often, newsgroup users can become very annoyed at blatant commercial self-promotion of a product or service in a post – especially if that post does not in any way contribute to the current theme or topic. Some newsgroups, however, will tolerate commercialised postings. Check the rules in the FAQ for the newsgroup you want before posting commercial emails.

Many Internet Service Providers now take spamming very seriously and in some situations may close your email, newsgroup and web access account, sometimes immediately and without notice. In extreme cases in which an ISP has had to handle hundreds or even thousands of email complaints, they may even send you an invoice for the time spent in getting their system back to normal! So consider carefully.

Replying to newsgroup messages

Once a message has fully downloaded, the Reply button is made available for you to use. To reply first click the message header you want, then choose the desired Reply command or button. Usually, you can reply directly to the sender, the entire newsgroup, or to all in a single action. Whichever Reply command you choose, a new window opens addressed to whoever you chose and containing the original message usually below the flashing text cursor prompting you to enter your reply, after which you click the Send button.

When replying to a post, you can save time for everyone concerned by only including (quoting) the part of the post that is relevant to what you're saying. Quoting only the relevant parts makes the task of possibly reading many posts so much easier, as all irrelevant parts are deleted before being posted. Reply to a post when you have something worthwhile to contribute. If you want to thank a member for their help, consider emailing this person directly rather than posting a heartfelt "thank you" to the entire newsgroup.

Downloading and uploading images, programs and audio/video clips

Sometimes, newsgroup messages may include attached images, programs, sound clips, video clips, and so on. However, do remember copyright laws may apply. If unsure, ask and if still unsure, simply don't download an attachment. Newsgroup names that include attachments are usually easily identified: look for the word "binaries" in the newsgroup name. For example: alt.binaries.pictures.cartoons

Good newsreaders like those found in Outlook Express and Agent or Free Agent contain the necessary components to encode and decode information that is sent or received as an attachment. Larger images, sound and video clips can be huge in file size, so are often broken down into smaller chunks. To view one of these images or to play a full sound or video clip, you'll first need to download all the individual chunks that make up the file. Usually, each chunk is given a number reference along with the name, for example if someone makes available a large photographic image of Niagara Falls from their last holiday, it might be split into 6 parts: niagara_falls1of6.jpg, niagara_falls2of6.jpg, and so on.

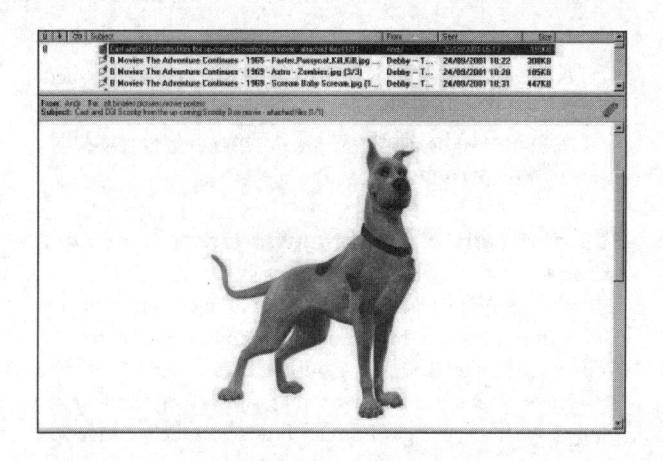

In Outlook Express, after you have downloaded all the chunks, you can select every chunk that makes up the entire sequence and choose the Combine and Decode command from the Message menu. Then if necessary, use the Move Up and Move Down buttons in the dialog box to arrange the sequence in numerical order and click OK. Finish by choosing the Save Attachments command and finding a location on your computer to save the file. Then move to the relevant location in your computer and double-click the file, then if it's:

- an image, your default graphics program for viewing those kinds of images (.jpg in our example above) starts up with the picture displayed.

- a video or sound clip, the full sequence should start playing – providing you have the correct player installed. The Windows Media Player can interpret several common video formats. Or you may need special video player software.

Automatically blocking unwanted newsgroup emails

Sometimes, you may not want to read messages from a specific contributor or want to ignore a specific message thread. Newsreaders like those in Outlook Express and Netscape Messenger provide commands that allow you to block or ignore a specific message or thread. First select the message you want to stop, then look for the Block Sender command on the Message menu in Internet Explorer or the Ignore thread command in Netscape Messenger.

Dealing with flames

The Internet is made up of contributors from many different cultures, sexes and viewpoints – some mild and some extreme. Sometimes, someone can say something – often without meaning to suggest what someone else might think they mean – while contributing to a message thread and so "push someone else's buttons". Before the originator can draw breath, explain what they really meant or apologise, they're receiving a barrage of personal abuse.

This sometimes-animated event is known as a flame. Other members may then join in on the rapidly degrading debate, on one side or the other, some trying to control tempers while others just add more abusive insults to the chaos. Soon, the original discussion topic is all but forgotten in a sea of high emotions and vitriolic hate – resulting in a flame war.

Most reasonable Internet users won't want to get involved in these events. So what do you do if you're drawn into a flame war when you would rather be spending your time on more useful activities? Consider the following guidelines:

- Before contributing, get some foreknowledge: lurk a while and try to see how others use the group.

- When contributing to a newsgroup, don't use all CAPITAL LETTERS – unless you mean to shout. The tone of capital letters may be misinterpreted.

- Watch the jargon: keep your message simple; make sure people can understand what you're saying so misunderstandings don't develop in the first place. Many flames start from ignorance or misinterpretation.

- Some newsgroup members enjoy starting an argument or handing out abuse. Avoid starting or getting involved in any kind of abuse or insult in the first place. Everything that you say in a newsgroup is on public record and you never quite know how long it'll stay that way.

- If you insult someone without meaning to, stay calm, just apologise and leave the topic. If they still persist with abuse, don't respond. Use the commands in your email and newsreader to block their postings.

- Make sure you're posting to the right newsgroup – some regular members become irritated with inappropriate postings and are intensely interested in the theme 'thread' and nothing else.

- If you're new to a newsgroup, check the Frequently Asked Questions (FAQ) file often made available so you know what's acceptable and what's not.

- Business contributors often use newsgroups to promote their products and services usually through their email signature file attached to every response. Try to keep this kind of promotion low-key; demonstrate that you care more about genuinely contributing than short-term gain. Consider creating a completely separate signature file just for use in newsgroups.

- If you openly try to promote a business product in a non-commercial newsgroup, expect big trouble. Therefore, keep open commercial postings to commercial newsgroups like biz.comp.services, biz.misc and biz.general.

19

Talking and viewing on the Internet

At the heart of the Internet is the strong need for humans to communicate. Although email, newsgroups and (to a certain extent) the web each have their individual benefits, often you cannot get an instant response. But other tools like Internet telephony, video conferencing, WebCams, and online Chat have emerged to provide live Internet communications.

Internet phones

You can currently make telephone calls using the Internet in two main ways:

1. With this first option, users at both ends needs a computer, modem, microphone headset, sound capability and access to the Internet plus special Internet phone software installed and set up. If your sound card/sound chips allow both sending and receiving at the same time (duplex transmission), then you can hold a normal telephone-like conversation. Otherwise, you'll each have to speak in turn: could be boring – unless you're a CB radio fan or already have had a taste of "walkie-talkie-speak", in which case you'll probably find the entire show a lot of fun.

   Here's an overview of how the above system works. First, your recipient needs to have the same software installed. Then, once you know the Internet address of the person you want, you simply enter this email address into your Internet phone software, dial the address and wait to see if your recipient is available to respond.

2. The second option is to dial their number using a normal phone device that has been modified to route calls through Internet Service Providers rather than the normal phone network.

Internet phone headsets containing a microphone and at least one speaker can be bought from good local computer stores. With either approach, you can usually make international calls for the cost either at local phone call rate per minute, or if you have low-cost or free Internet access, the cost is minimal.

Once your Internet connection is set up, you only have your Internet Service Provider costs to pay – the same costs as you pay for say browsing the web or using email! So with this system, whether your call is to Kidderminster, Khartoum or Kathmandu, the cost is the same. So what's the catch? Currently, the person you want to call must have an Internet address and using this system is often not as easy or reliable as an established phone network – yet! See also:

- The superb **PalTalk** service: talk to anyone around the world without having to call long distance rates: www.paltalk.com/

- **MediaRing** (software currently free) at: www.mediaring.com/

- And **Microsoft NetMeeting** as described below.

Conferencing with Microsoft NetMeeting

NetMeeting is a superb Internet telephony, video-conferencing and collaboration tool. NetMeeting also comes free with Internet Explorer web browser suite. With NetMeeting you can talk with another person live on the Internet using Multimedia

> **New to NetMeeting?**
> **Calling from Home?**
> **Running a Business?**
> **Web Author or Developer?**
>
> Download
>
> **Netmeeting 3 now included in Windows® 2000!**
> Windows 2000, available in February, contains NetMeeting version 3. The Windows real-time collaboration and conferencing client is an easy to use Web phone as well as a tool for corporate productivity.

Chat, exchange files and even work together on the same publication. See: www.microsoft.com/netmeeting/

Internet Chat overview

Internet Chat offers a way to instantly communicate with people from around the world. As the cost of Internet access continues to fall and more people gain access to the Net, Internet Chat too has become popular. However, in contrast to newsgroups or email, remember, Internet Chat is always "live." Chat is available in two main forms:

- **Text-based** using a keyboard.

- **Multimedia** Chat is possible when both communicators have video and sound components installed and set up in their PCs or other Internet connection devices.

With Chat, usually you won't have to pay any long distance phone charges – check with your Internet Service Provider. For most people, the only cost is a local phone call or the standard connection charges through an Internet Service Provider.

You can use Internet Chat to discuss ideas live and ask questions of family, friends and work colleagues or with anyone around the globe that also has Internet Chat installed and set up. Microsoft Chat is one popular Chat program that comes free as part of the Internet Explorer web browser suite. Other popular Chat areas or "Conference Rooms" are present in MSN (UK section), CompuServe, AOL and Excite.

Text-based Chat

To use text-based Chat, you'll need a Chat program installed and set up to communicate with a single person or – more usually – several. Internet Chat can involve interacting with lots of people that "enter the Chat room", also known as a

"Channel" or Chat "forum." When your Chat program is "active", whatever you type immediately appears on the display monitor screens of all the people taking part in that particular Chat session.

Chat nicknames and maintaining your privacy

Many of those who take part in Chat sessions often prefer to use nicknames rather than reveal their true identity. A nickname must of course be unique so that no two members can use the same name or nickname. Also, don't reveal your real name, address or telephone number and consider using a common web-based email provider, for example: www.hotmail.com/

---

ichat ROOMS

Virtual chat rooms, moderated virtual events and online training all under your brand. Deliver a rich interactive experience and draw users to your Internet community.

ichat ROOMS allows real-time discussions between participants in a customizable environment. Increase customer traffic, build user loyalty and generate revenue on your community site, all with ichat ROOMS.

The ichat ROOMS Java Interface is easy to use and easy to customize.

Using ichat ROOMS, you create a community destination that not only attracts people to your site, but it keeps them while they participate in the ongoing discussions. ichat ROOMS is scalable- thousands of participants are possible in multiple rooms or in one giant event!

rather than your "main" email address. This approach should limit the chance of anyone pestering or harassing you at other times.

If you do eventually decide to meet someone you originally met in a Chat room, meet in a public place and let trusted friends know what you're doing and the when and where of your meeting, until you're sure this new friend can be trusted. Kids, don't even consider it! Talk to your parents or guardian.

Netspeak Dictionary

There are over than 500 emoticons and abbreviations that are used in online chat programs. NetSpeak Dictionary is a detailed compilation of every one of them, all sorted for easy reference.

Our Review:
For all those newbie chatters out there, this is for you. Sick of people blabbering strange combinations of letters at you? Tired of being thoroughly outclassed with smiley faces? Well, with the netspeak dictionary, all of your problems are solved. It contains over 500 different references to emoticons (icons used to express feelings). Have fun!

Licence: Shareware - Unlimited	**Version:** 3.0	
OS: Windows 95/98	**Date:** 1999/10/07	
Developer: 3D Dan Design	**Size:** 2.35 MB	Free download

Yippee Ratings Breakdown (5 is best):
Installation: 4.00 **Interface:** 4.00 **Functionality:** 4.00
Documentation: 4.00

Internet Relay Chat (IRC)

Internet Rely Chat (IRC) provides Chat "rooms" or Chat Channels that focus on specific topics. Hundreds of subject areas are available; examples include: cooking, watercolour painting, tennis or beer.

IRC is also an ideal tool for distance learning: a tutor can interact with students wherever they may be located – although time differences around the world need to be considered. To use Internet Relay Chat, you'll need an IRC program. For more information, visit: www.mirc.co.uk

Chat commands

To take part in Internet Rely Chat, you'll need to learn some basic Chat commands. Although lots of different commands exist, most are logical and easy to learn. However, unless you're a real Chat enthusiast, you probably only need learn the basics.

All Chat commands start with a slash (/) and are followed by the command itself. Text without a slash preceding it is interpreted simply as text. Here's an example of a Chat command: /JOIN. The /JOIN command shows that you would like to join the current Chat "room". When entering commands, you can type in capital letters or lower case letters. To discover the kinds of Chat topics available, with your Chat Program active enter the following command: /LIST. To help get you started, here are some of the most popular commands.

Command	What the command means
/AWAY	Tells others you've moved away from your PC and plan to return

	later, so replies may take some time.
/CLEAR	Clears the Chat window.
/HELP	Displays a list of all the commands available.
/JOIN	I want to join this Channel.
/IGNORE	Some contributors may be rude or worse. Lets you filter out or remove contributions from your Chat window that a specific person makes.
/KICK [nickname]	Delete this nickname from this channel.
/LEAVE	I'm leaving this Channel.
/ME	Lets you tell other contributors that you are performing a task. For example: "/ME checking those figures" (without the quotes), would appear in each of the other members' Chat windows as: "Brian Austin is checking those figures."
/MSG	Allows you to send a private message to only one participant in the Chat session.
/SIGNOFF or /BYE	Signals that you're leaving the Chat session.

/TOPIC [new topic]	Change the current topic.
/WHO	Tells you who is participating in this Chat session.
/WHOIS	Provides more information about a participant.

Using web-based Chat

To take part in web-based Chat, you don't need special Chat software, only a web browser. To enter a Web Chat "room",

WHAT CAN ichat® DO FOR YOU?

ichat® collaborative solutions help increase productivity, efficiency and profitability by improving the way you communicate with your customers, employees and community.

● FREE TRIAL!   ● Learn More!

🖻 Get Boards 4.1 Today!   🖻 ROOMS 5.0.4 is Now Available!

With ichat®, your public and private sites become vibrant - making use of **interactive chat**, **instant messaging** and **group discussion areas** to enhance communication with your customers, employees, business partners and community members. And when you improve communication, you increase your productivity, effectiveness, efficiency and profitability.

Whether you are working to improve internal enterprise requirements, support customer relationships or build stronger common interest communities, ichat® has designed dynamic solutions that will provide your organization with the solid collaboration tools it needs to succeed. Let us help you create an interactive ichat® environment that seamlessly blends with your current inter, extra or intranet. Click here to learn more.

Why ichat®?
As a leader in the communication and collaboration industry, ichat® holds such **high-profile accounts** as Ford Motor Company, Beliefnet.com, WebMD, Sony Corporation and iVillage.com. Over ten million individuals have downloaded ichat's award-winning software. Learn more about us here.

you just click the relevant link on a web page to open up another usually smaller window.

However, often the response time of web Chat may not be as fast as Internet Relay Chat. Sometimes, you may need to wait a few seconds for the Chat window to appear and to refresh regularly. See also Chat options available at:

- www.wbs.net/

- www.100hot.com/

- www.aol.co.uk/ or www.aol.com/

- www.compuserve.co.uk/

- www.uk.msn.com/

Although communicating by typing live messages using a keyboard is the oldest and most well established Chat method, with the fast-paced development of the web, multimedia-based Chat – using live WebCams and sound – is also growing in popularity and will probably dominate Internet Chat in a few years.

One-to-one communication with instant messaging

An instant messaging system enables you to communicate in private with another person live on the Internet. Several

406 > Talking and viewing on the Internet

messaging systems are now available. Some especially popular instant messaging programs include:

- America Online's **Instant Messenger (AIM)** with Netscape: www.netscape.com/chat

- The popular **ICQ** available at: www.icq.com/

- **Netscape instant messaging:** www.netscape.com/

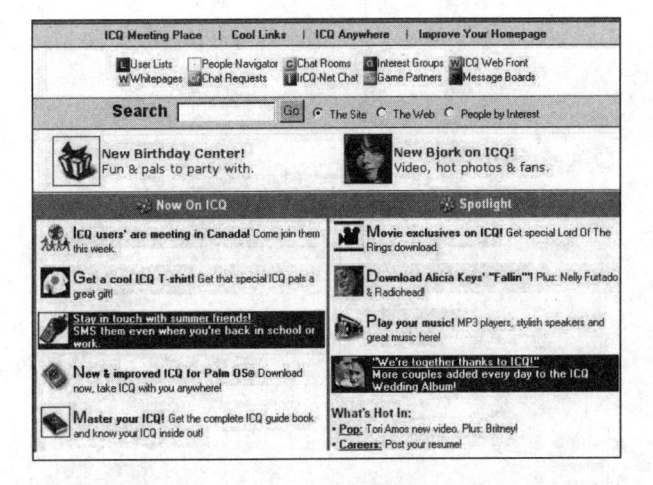

Internet Relay Chat and online games

Perhaps not surprisingly, many of the popular Internet Relay Chat Channels are dominated by computer and online games. You can play or compete with other Chat participants or the purpose-built automated programs or Chat bots. For more information, see:

- www.mpog.com/

- games.yahoo.com/

For further information, see "Playing online games" on page 359.

20
Downloading and uploading

The Internet is chock full of information files and software that are often available, free of charge, on a try-before-you-buy basis, or you can read the blurb and, if you like what you see, pay the fee online to gain access to the essential information you'll need to download the product.

So where are the goodies and how do you get them when you find them? The key to downloading information and software from the Internet is through the use of a technology called File Transfer Protocol (FTP). Don't be intimidated by the name – it simply refers to what's involved in sending and receiving files to and from other computers on the Internet. And to use FTP, you don't need to know the details of how

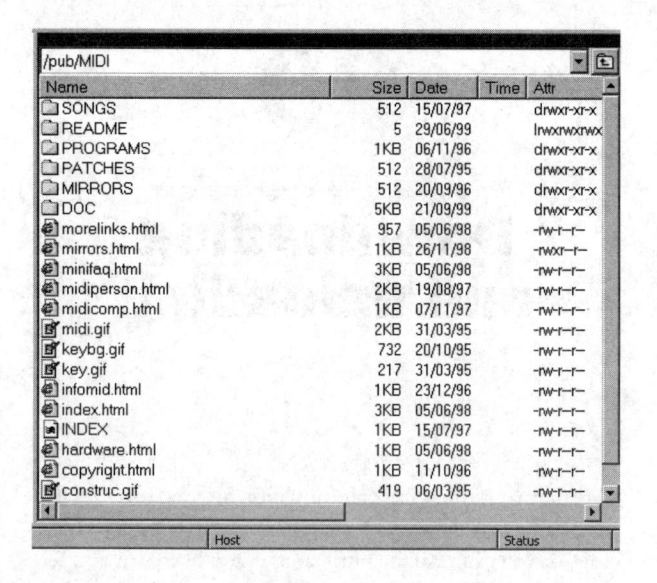

/pub/MIDI					
Name	Size	Date	Time	Attr	
SONGS	512	15/07/97		drwxr-xr-x	
README	5	29/06/99		lrwxrwxrwx	
PROGRAMS	1KB	06/11/96		drwxr-xr-x	
PATCHES	512	28/07/95		drwxr-xr-x	
MIRRORS	512	20/09/96		drwxr-xr-x	
DOC	5KB	21/09/99		drwxr-xr-x	
morelinks.html	957	05/06/98		-rw-r--r--	
mirrors.html	1KB	26/11/98		-rwxr--r--	
minifaq.html	3KB	05/06/98		-rw-r--r--	
midiperson.html	2KB	19/08/97		-rw-r--r--	
midicomp.html	1KB	07/11/97		-rw-r--r--	
midi.gif	2KB	31/03/95		-rw-r--r--	
keybg.gif	732	20/10/93		-rw-r--r--	
key.gif	217	31/03/95		-rw-r--r--	
infomid.html	1KB	23/12/96		-rw-r--r--	
index.html	3KB	05/06/98		-rw-r--r--	
INDEX	1KB	15/07/97		-rw-r--r--	
hardware.html	1KB	05/06/98		-rw-r--r--	
copyright.html	1KB	11/10/96		-rw-r--r--	
construc.gif	419	06/03/95		-rw-r--r--	

| Host | | Status |

FTP works, just what you need to do to grab or send files – and that is what we cover in this book.

Introducing File Transfer Protocol (FTP)

File Transfer Protocol lets you examine files that are stored on computers around the world and copy those files to your own computer if you wish. However remember, you can only view and copy those files that have been made available to you.

Often, large files are also stored in compressed form and therefore must be decompressed after downloading before you can use them. Providers of some exceptionally busy FTP sites may generously make mirror FTP sites available. A mirror site provides the same information at different locations – possibly one near you.

Therefore, if the "main" FTP site is busy and you're having trouble connecting, you could try other mirror sites if they're available. Using FTP, you can also upload your own files to any other computer that is set up for you to do this. For example, lots of people use an FTP program to help manage their websites.

You can upload your web files, make changes to the files already uploaded, and download or delete files that you no longer want stored on the computer containing your website. See also about publishing a website on page 439. First though, let's examine what an FTP site is and how to access it, and find and copy selected files.

> Before connecting with any FTP sites – or the Internet – you should install suitable antivirus software and make regular backups of your computer's files. Computer viruses can be found anywhere on the Internet and may be hidden in files at FTP sites. For information about computer viruses and the action you can take to protect yourself online generally, see page 173.

What is an FTP site?

Files that you may get authorisation to view and copy are stored on computers at an FTP site. Individuals, companies, schools, colleges, universities and governments have established many thousands of FTP sites around the world.

An easy way to picture an FTP website is to imagine it as a large office building containing hundreds or thousands of filing cabinets. In each filing cabinet, there may be several drawers each containing many categories of files. Each category may itself contain many individual files.

Private and anonymous FTP

Some FTP sites provide private access but most offer public access. Private FTP sites usually ask you for a password to gain access. An example of a private FTP site could include an international company that provides access to essential company files for employees around the world and support materials for customers in different countries.

Some private FTP sites may restrict access or charge for access to some files. Anonymous or public FTP sites allow anyone to access their files free of charge without having to enter a password – a user simply logs in as "anonymous". More later.

What's available from FTP sites

All kinds of files and documents can be stored at an FTP site. Often FTP sites provide key documents in the "top" level or "entry" folder or directory that shows what is stored at the site; look for files with names like "index" or "readme" to discover what's available at that location.

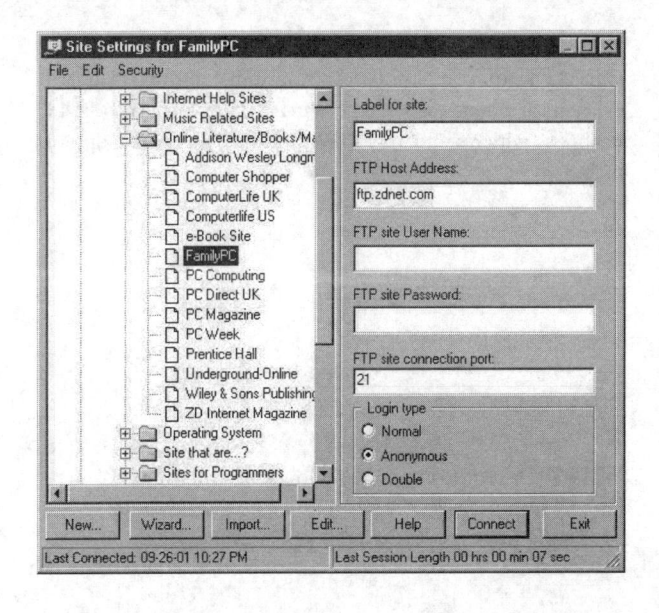

Also, files for different types of computers may be stored in different parts of an FTP site for good reason. For example, files for IBM-compatible PCs will probably not work on Apple Macintosh computers and so files for different "platforms" need to stored in separate locations on the same site. Key point:

you need to make sure that the files you download are of the correct type for your computer. As various computer standards exist, often when you connect to an FTP site you may be asked to choose which standard you want. Usually, available options include:

- DOS.

- PC/Windows.

- Apple Mac.

- UNIX.

> **BEWARE**
> If you download and try to run program files for the wrong standard, you may damage the operating system of your computer.

> **HOT TIP**
> The procedure of uploading or downloading files using FTP software is often made much easier using simple drag-and-drop commands if they're available on your computer or other Internet access device.

Therefore, if necessary, choose the correct standard before downloading any files or information.

An enormous range of file types is often available from FTP sites. A useful source containing links to thousands of FTP sites on the Internet is available from Filez at: www.filez.com/

You can download books, magazine articles, electronic magazines, images, computer games, shareware programs, word processors, spreadsheets and databases, speeches, music clips, simple sounds and movie and animation clips, to name but a few. Most files at an FTP site come under one of the following five categories. You can identify the types of files available by their filename extensions. The five main file categories including some of the most popular file formats are show below:

- **Text:** filename extensions include: .txt, .doc, .htm, .html, .wpd, .msg and .asc

- **Pictures:** filename extensions include: .bmp, .jpg, .gif, .tif, .eps, and .pict

- **Programs:** filename extensions include: .exe, .com and .bat

- **Sound clips:** filename extensions include: .ra, .wav, .au, .mid and .snd. Remember, you'll need a sound card/motherboard sound chips and speakers to hear sound clips.

- **Video clips:** look for file endings like: .rm, .mpg, .avi, .mov and .qt. To see and hear video clips, you'll need the appropriate video player software – most now are available on free download – for the file you're viewing and a sound card/sound chips to hear any sound component.

Every file has a unique name and follows the standard computer naming system of a name followed by a full stop followed by an extension – which often determines the type of file. For example:

- report.txt is a text file.

- kathmandu23.gif – GIF is an image file type that is usually quick to download and often used in web pages.

Any computer system that contains hundreds, thousands, tens of thousands or even millions of files, needs to be highly organized if we are to gain relatively easy access to only the information we want and not get lost in a mass of irrelevant information. FTP files therefore, are usually stored in a highly organised manner. An FTP site also uses folders and sub-folders within which all the relevant files are (usually) stored in the most logical locations.

Can I use these files free of charge?

Most files from FTP sites are available to use free of charge for non-commercial purposes. But do check the conditions of use available at the FTP site first. Often, a Frequently Asked Questions (FAQ) text document may be available so certainly examining this should be one of your first tasks.

Copyright usually stays with the author or owner of the file; check if necessary. Ignoring copyright – certainly in relation to the web – can seriously damage your wealth if you're caught, so why take the risk? Always get written/emailed permission before use if unsure to avoid some nasty surprises later. Software programs are usually made available in five main ways:

- **Public domain:** suggests a program or file that is free for anyone to use and for which the originator has surrendered the copyright. Therefore usually you can modify, update, redistribute or do whatever you want with public domain software.

- **Freeware:** usually means that the program can be used free of charge but the owner still maintains some or all of the copyright. Before editing or distributing freeware, check what restrictions are in force with the owner.

- **Shareware:** you can try the program for a limited period after which if you wish to continue using the software, you must pay the licence fee for your copy. Usually, copyright stays with the owner and you cannot change the software but may be able to distribute copies. Read the documentation that comes with the software.

- **Chargeable licence:** you pay for the software before buying it, and this includes a licence to use your copy

> You can download information in text or binary mode. When downloading a file, in most instances your FTP program should be set to binary mode or automatically know which mode to use. Usually, the binary option is set for you, but if a downloaded file appears faulty, certainly double-check this option.

> **HOT TIP** If you download many FTP files, first create a folder structure on your computer that makes sense to you. Then download the various programs and files to their most appropriate folders or directories, rather than store them in one folder. Otherwise, when you expand compressed files, you can never be sure which uncompressed file belongs to which program or archive.

of the software. The owner keeps copyright and usually you can't change the software and need permission to distribute copies. Most commercially developed software is sold under chargeable licence conditions.

- **Beta software:** as a company develops a software product, when the product development is almost complete, sometimes they may make a limited number of copies available – to try out – often for free, on condition that you report back to them about any problems you come across while using the software. Often, beta software is essentially fully working – at least to meet the needs of most people, so can provide a superb opportunity to use a product.

However, don't rely on beta software for doing important tasks: it may be unstable, could muddle your computer's file system or even damage some files. Usually, no guarantees are available for beta software and you'll probably have to agree not to hold the software provider responsible for any damage if you choose to use a beta copy. The risk is all yours. You'll probably come across strange quirks, bugs, unusual program crashes, but hey, if the software is free...

Working with compressed files

A large file or program, if left in its native format, can take a long time to download from an FTP site or anywhere else on the Internet and occupies a set amount of storage space. Large files therefore are usually compressed using special software to reduce their file size. A smaller file takes up less storage space and therefore can be downloaded quicker whatever the speed of your Internet connection.

However, compressed files need to be uncompressed once they reach their destination before use and some may uncompress automatically on first use, while others need to be manually uncompressed. Popular file compressors include WinZip (www.winzip.com/) for the PC, and Stuffit Expander (www.aladdinsys.com/) for Apple Macs. You can easily identify if a file is compressed: look at the filename extension. Popular compressed formats include: .zip, .arc, .tar, .z, .arj, .hqz, .gz and .sit.

> To find a particular variety of compression/decompression software, check the "INDEX" or "README" files in the introductory areas of FTP sites. Or the compression/decompression software you want may be provided on some CD-ROMs that accompany popular computer magazines.

Single compressed file archives

A single software program may contain many different individual files. To make the process of transferring software across the Internet easier and more reliable, many software providers compress all the relevant program files in a special way to create a single all-in-one file called an archive.

One great benefit from using an archive is that you only need to download the archive file and often simply click or double-click it to automatically start installing the file on your computer. Many popular IBM-compatible PC archive files use the .zip, .exe, or .lzh filename extensions.

StuffIt Deluxe™
The complete compression solution.™

UPGRADE   BUY IT NOW

Current Version: 6.0.1
Min. System Requirements:
- PowerPC or better
- Mac OS® 8.1+, Mac OS X
- 15 MB RAM
Suggested Retail: $79.95

International Versions

Send files faster, access anything on the Web!

Tired of waiting for large email attachments and downloads? Frustrated with files that you can't open? You need StuffIt Deluxe! Award-winning, industry-standard StuffIt Deluxe compresses your files up to 95% smaller than their original size, so they transmit faster. Plus, StuffIt Deluxe opens just about any file you download off the Web or receive in your email. And, as the worldwide compression standard, your StuffIt files can be accessed by any Mac or PC user, anywhere, hassle-free!

Save time. Save money.
StuffIt's smaller files save you time. Whether you're expanding a download or sending a file to a friend, you get it done in record time. When time is money, StuffIt delivers.

So for example, imagine that you're downloading a freeware interactive Calendar program that sits on your Windows desktop. After downloading calendar.zip, you simply move to the relevant folder and double-click on calendar.zip – which then automatically decompresses the various installation files to a temporary folder. You can then double-click the "setup.exe" file to complete the installation of your Calendar.

> **HOT TIP**
>
> If you're getting low on hard drive space, some websites provide free space on their servers to which you can upload some files. For example, see: http://www.freedrive.com However, never upload any files containing private or sensitive information.

Configuring your FTP program

To set up your standalone FTP program, follow the installation instructions that come with your FTP software. Often, during the installation, an FTP program may automatically install and configure settings for some existing free access (anonymous) FTP sites for you. Take a little time to examine these settings, then you can gain a better understanding of the kind of information you'll need when visiting the FTP sites you want.

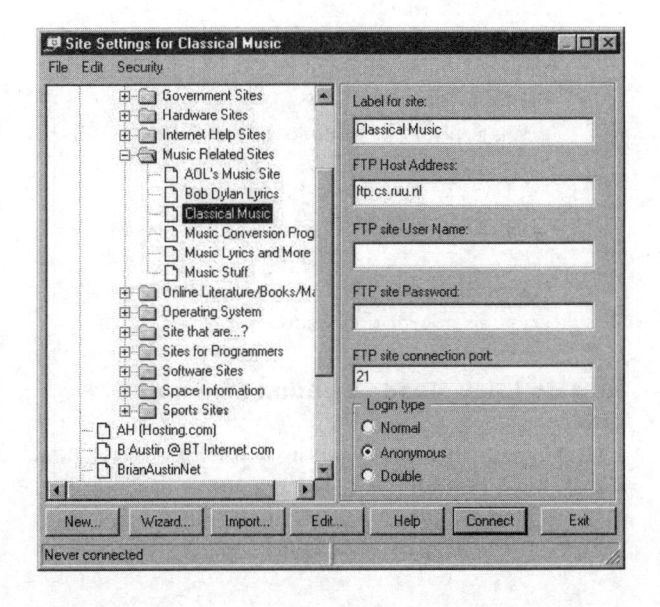

Usually however, to gain access to any new FTP site, three settings especially are important to ensure that your computer connects to the FTP computer:

- **FTP domain name:** example formats include: ftp.companyname.com or for uploading web pages to a web host, some accept: www.companyname.com However, the FTP name may be longer, for example, look at this imaginary FTP address: ftp.mysite.com/files/pc/pdf/net-tips.zip

    From the above address, we know that the compressed file "net-tips.zip"can be found in a folder called "pdf" that is a sub-folder of a folders "files" and "pc" on the "mysite.com" FTP server.

- **User name:** if the FTP site has private access.

- **Password:** again if your FTP site has restricted access, keep this information secure.

How do I download something from an FTP site?

FTP programs that come built in as part of a successfully installed web browser don't need any further configuration. You simply visit the web page containing the file you want, click the link and the file download automatically starts.

Follow the onscreen prompts and dialog boxes usually appear asking if you want to open or save the file. For now, choose the Save option – you can open it later – and decide where on your computer you want to store the file you're downloading. The download window then appears and shows the progress of the download.

BEWARE: If you're downloading a file to the location of a file with the same name, your FTP program erases the original file and replaces it with the new one – and you may not get a warning that the original file is being wiped. Use a different file name if unsure.

The most popular way to download files from the Internet is to use a separate FTP program, which must be correctly installed and configured before use for the FTP site you want to connect to as covered in Configuring your FTP program on page 422. The main window of most standalone FTP programs

HOT TIP: While downloading files from FTP sites or the Internet, you can complete other tasks with your computer – like surfing the web or working on a document. Usually when a file has completed downloading to your computer, your FTP software shows a message on the screen or it may sound a beep to let you know this task is complete.

is usually much like that of Windows Explorer and may be split into multiple panes.

One pane may show the location on your computer where you want to store or upload files. Another pane may show the folder or directory structure of the FTP computer to which you're connected. A third pane may be available to show the progress of files as they are uploading or downloading between your computer and the FTP computer. Usually, you can move from folder to folder in the destination and target panes.

Once a download has started, most good standalone FTP programs also provide a regularly updated estimate of how long the download is expected to take. So if some time is needed, at

> Once connected to an FTP site, if you stop using your FTP program, after a specific time delay most FTP servers will disconnect you (not from the Internet, just from their server). When ready, simply choose the command to reconnect.

> Try to avoid using your web browser to download large files. Instead use a standalone FTP program that supports resume downloads. Then, if your Internet connection is temporarily broken for any reason, you can reconnect at the earliest opportunity and continue the download from that last point reached. CuteFTP – the author's favourite – for example, can resume downloads, as does FTP Explorer.

least you can work on other tasks and re-check the download progress occasionally.

Also install a program like GoZilla (currently free of charge from www.gozilla.com) – which can handle downloads for you. One of the most important benefits of GoZilla and similar FTP programs is that if you temporarily lose your Internet connection, after you reconnect again you can resume the broken download from the last point reached, providing the server you're downloading from allows resumed downloads. Superb – GoZilla can save your sanity if you're downloading a

> In order for resume downloads to work, the FTP program installed on your computer and the relevant FTP server must both support resume downloads. If either doesn't, then unfortunately, you'll have to try the download again. When downloading large files from FTP sites that do not support resume downloads, whenever possible try to consider other options if available – CD-ROMs, DVDs, Zip & Jaz disks and even floppy disks.

file that takes several hours or more. The following paragraphs also include information about a few popular programs.

Previously, we introduced the idea of compressed and archived files. Remember, to use one of these files you may have to manually uncompress or "unpack" a downloaded compressed archive file before you can use it. Therefore, if the file you want to download is compressed, you'll also need the correct decompression software installed and set up. Often, FTP sites also provide copies of popular decompression programs free of charge. Popular compression/decompression programs include: WinZip and PKZip for IBM-compatible PCs and StuffIt Expander for Apple Macintosh computers.

Busy FTP sites

Each FTP site allows only a specific number of users to connect at any one time. If you try to connect but keep receiving an error message, perhaps the user limit has already been reached; try again later. Some FTP sites are extra busy during business working hours, so again maybe try connecting in the evening or at weekends.

If you cannot connect to any FTP site, then double-check your FTP set-up – log-on web addresses, user names and passwords particularly have to be correct for the FTP site you're using and we all know how easy it is to type an incorrect character in a password. However, usually you'll only need to enter your correct password the first time you connect to the particular FTP site. Each individual password along with other key information is usually stored in the relevant FTP profile you create on your computer.

Uploading files with FTP

Instead of accepting or downloading files, you can also send or upload files to another computer on the Internet. A popular example is if you publish your brand new "ritzy-glitzy" website.

When you're ready, either directly through your web design software or using a dedicated FTP program, you can transfer all the relevant web files from your computer to the web server on which your website will be stored.

Some FTP programs may provide a Wizard to help you set up the connection to the FTP location. Alternatively, you can enter the information yourself manually – you'll only need do this once as the FTP program should store the settings you choose.

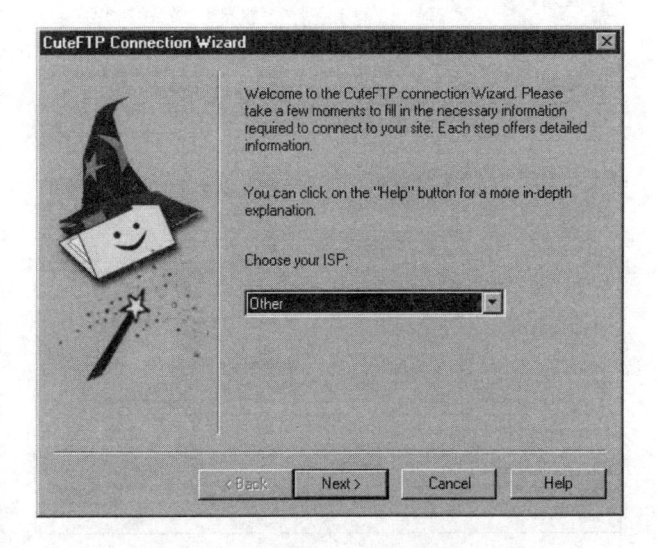

```
CuteFTP Connection Wizard

    Welcome to the CuteFTP connection Wizard. Please
    take a few moments to fill in the necessary information
    required to connect to your site. Each step offers detailed
    information.

    You can click on the "Help" button for a more in-depth
    explanation.

    Choose your ISP:

    [Other            ▼]

    < Back    Next >    Cancel    Help
```

Downloading and uploading < 429

The process is much the same as when downloading files. Here's what to do:

- You'll need a web or ftp address using the format: ftp.domainname.com, for example: ftp.mysite.com or even the standard format www.mysite.com may be

---

Get the Most Out of the Internet with CuteFTP!

CuteFTP is absolutely the easiest way to transfer files across the Internet. Its built-in Connection Wizard will walk you through connecting to an FTP site in seconds and its user-friendly interface will have you transferring files in no time, even if you are a beginner. Whether publishing a Web page, downloading the latest digital images, software and music or transferring high-volume files between branch offices, CuteFTP provides the tools you need to make your life on the Net more enjoyable and productive. Download your free trial of CuteFTP today!

CuteFTP 4.2 .... $39.95   Add to Cart   Download Free Trial

New Features in Version 4.2

Features

Quick and Easy Setup and Administration
Don't know how to setup an FTP site? No problem! In a few short steps, the built-in Wizard will walk you through the process of connecting to a site without having to know the technical details.

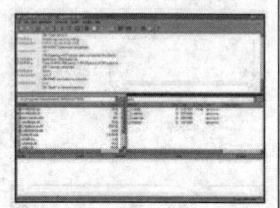

Simple Drag'n'Drop File Transfers
CuteFTP's user-friendly, Windows interface will have you transfering files in no time. Its dual-pane interface makes it easy to transfer files from your local PC to remote computers simply by dragging and dropping files from one side of your computer screen to the other.

Includes CuteHTML LE
This version of CuteFTP includes CuteHTML LE, a powerful, text-based HTML editor that allows you to easily create compelling Web sites with full control over your code.

acceptable with some web hosts. Check this information with your web host or Internet Service Provider.

- Next you'll probably need a User name.

- A password.

- And a location where to upload the files.

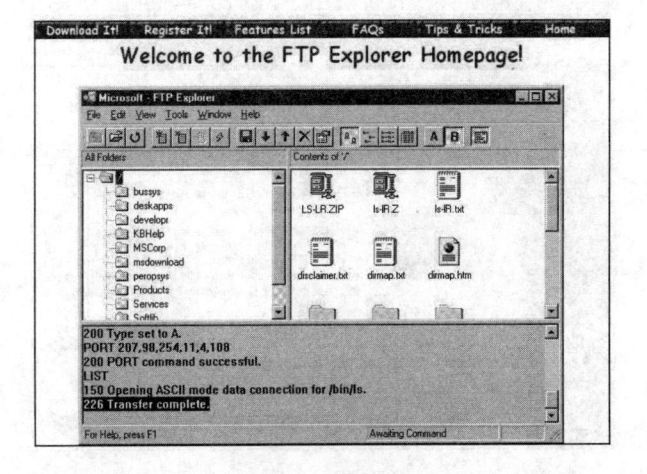

If you're publishing a website, all this information is provided by your web hosting company. If you're uploading some files to an FTP server, you'll probably need to know some or all of the information above. Again, check what you need to provide with whoever is receiving the files you're sending.

However, don't send important data, programs or sensitive information using conventional FTP and always keep backup copies of what you're sending, just in case your files get lost somewhere on the Internet. Once computer files go beyond your computer, you lose a certain amount of control and these free providers usually cannot accept responsibility for any loss.

Popular FTP programs

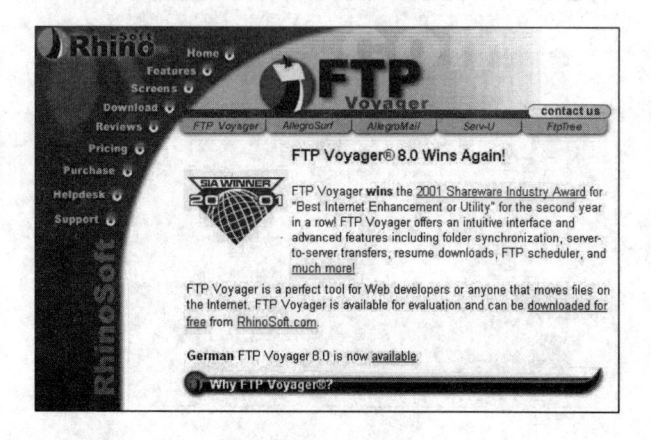

Let's recap: to gain access to an FTP site, you'll need to install an FTP program. FTP programs are available either as standalone separate software or a basic version may come built-in to your web browser. Internet Explorer and Netscape Navigator both include basic FTP components that will probably meet most needs. Whenever you visit a website that offers something to download, after you click the relevant download link, an FTP-compatible web browser automatically starts the download. However, some tasks – like uploading a website for example – are best left to web design software that includes a built-in FTP program, or use a separate dedicated FTP program.

Popular standalone free/shareware programs include:

- **CutFTP:** www.cuteftp.com/

- **FTP Explorer:** www.ftpx.com/

- **FTP Voyager:** www.ftpvoyager.com/

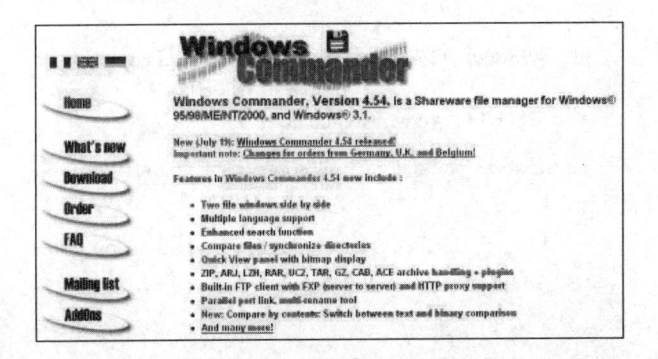

Downloading and uploading < 433

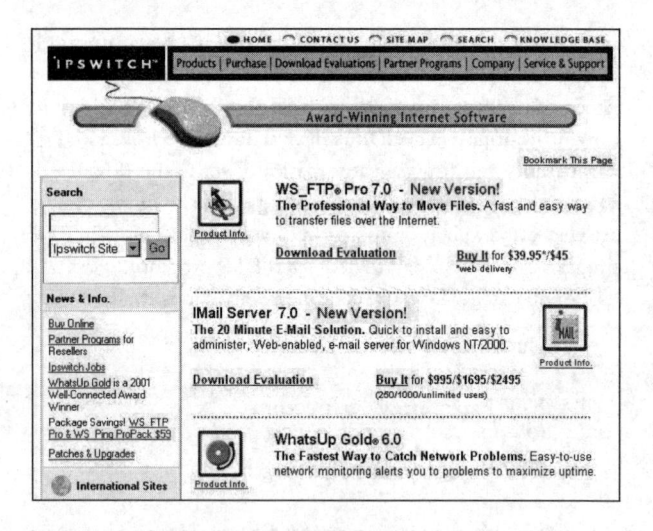

- **Windows Commander:** www.download.com/

- **WS-FTP:** www.ipswitch.com/

All the above standalone FTP software programs allow you to:

- Identify the files you want to copy to another computer on the Internet (upload).

- Find and choose those files you want to copy to your computer (download).

- Manage and find your way around FTP sites.

Retrieving broken downloads

While downloading files from an FTP site, sometimes your connection may break and you'll need to reconnect to the Internet and to the FTP site again. If the file you're downloading is large and perhaps you've already been online for several hours, you don't want to have to restart the download again: your patience and sanity will probably be stretched to the limit! The best FTP programs now allow you to resume the download from the position you were last at just before becoming disconnected, so all previous effort is not wasted, providing the FTP site to which you connected before the break also supports resume downloading.

If your chosen FTP program does not automatically support resumed downloading, my advice is get one installed as soon as possible: you can have more than one FTP program installed on your computer. WS_FTP is free, so is GoZilla, a relatively new kid on the block.

How to find FTP sites

So many files are available using FTP and a common question people ask is: "But how do I find the kinds of files I'm interested in?" Answer: like most other search problems on the Internet, use special search tools. Two popular ways to find FTP sites around the world is to use a tool called Archie and other websites that include FTP search tools. Archie is examined in more depth below.

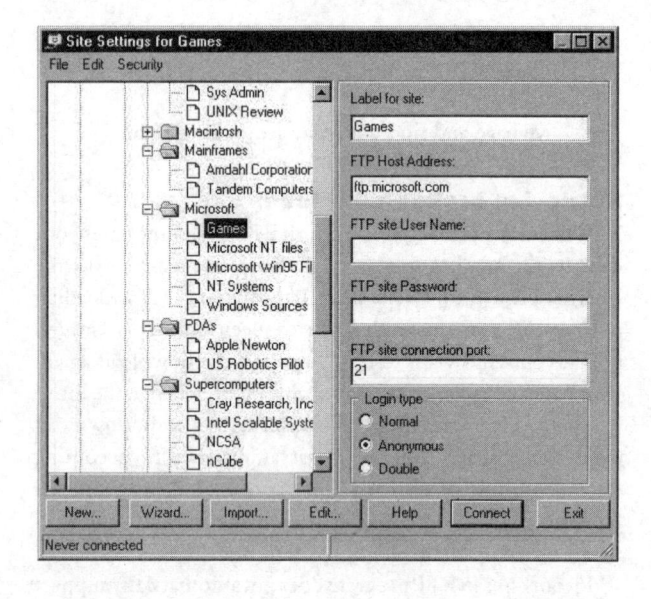

Popular FTP websites include: http://www.shareware.com Using Shareware.com, you can browse through FTP sites around the world or you can use their search engine to find specific files. To see a list containing most of the FTP sites

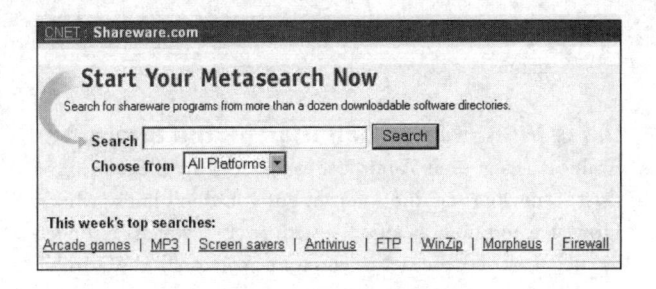

> **CNET : Shareware.com**
>
> ## Start Your Metasearch Now
> Search for shareware programs from more than a dozen downloadable software directories.
>
> Search [   ] [Search]
> Choose from [All Platforms ▼]
>
> **This week's top searches:**
> Arcade games | MP3 | Screen savers | Antivirus | FTP | WinZip | Morpheus | Firewall

available, try: http://hoohoo.ncsa.uiuc.edu/ftp-interface.html
Additional popular FTP sites include:

- ftp.lysator.liu.se (gardening).

- ftp.microsoft.com (wide range of software support products).

- ftp.dell.com (Dell computers: support software and files).

- ftp.mirrors.aol.com (AOL's music ftp site).

- ftp.mcp.com (an ebook site).

- ftp.apple.com (Apple Macintosh operating system support).

- ftp.zdnet.com (wide range of software products and games).

Using WSArchie to find files on the Internet

Archie is a great general-purpose tool to seek out files you know exist somewhere on the Internet but you don't know where. However, to find a specific file with Archie, you at least need to know part of the file name you want. You can find WSArchie and WSArchie services at:

- www.shareware.com/ (then enter WSArchie in the search box)

- www.lerc.nasa.gov/archieplex

- Rutgers University: archie.Rutgers.edu/archie.html

- http://archie.emnet.co.uk/services.html

- ftp://ftp.hkstar.com/.2/simtelnet/win95/inet/wsarch32.zip

- ftp://ftp.orst.edu/.1/simtelnet/win95/inet/wsarch32.zip

21

Creating your own website

The web allows anyone with the right tools and a little know-how to create their own web pages and publish these to the web for other people around the world to share and enjoy.

A web page is nothing more complex than a combination of various blocks of text, images, links to other pages and, optionally, other graphical, multimedia or animated special effects.

For businesses, however, a web page can be considered as an electronic brochure, so getting the right look and feel is particularly important. **Key point:** powerful software tools cannot substitute for the right skills.

Individuals like to create web pages about their favourite hobbies and interests or perhaps to share photos of special events, family gatherings, and so on. Business users can use the low cost yet long reach of the web to sell more goods and services and make new customers for a fraction of the normal offline cost.

Establishing what you need to create web pages

Essentially, four main components can help create a great website:

- A sound **plan of action** plus an understanding of why you want to create your web pages and whom they're intended to benefit (helps determine how).

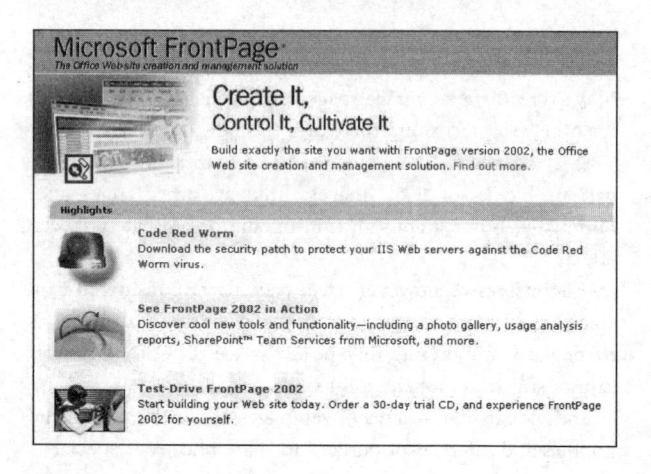

- **Software** to help you design and publish your web pages. Examples: Microsoft FrontPage, Macromedia Dreamweaver, NetObjects Fusion.

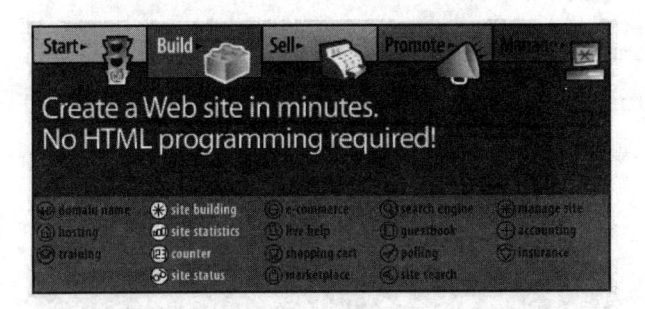

> Create a Web site in minutes.
> No HTML programming required!
>
> domain name · site building · e-commerce · search engine · manage site
> hosting · site statistics · live help · guestbook · accounting
> training · counter · shopping cart · polling · insurance
> site status · marketplace · site search

- **Ability** to use your preferred web design software and basic graphics editing software like Paint Shop Pro.

- **Web space** to hold and display your web pages.

Armed with the previous information, let's look at the two basic steps you'll need to perform to create a working website.

(1) Create your web pages using web design software.

(2) Then send copies of your web pages to a special location reserved for you on a computer permanently connected to the web called a web server.

You can gain access to a web server in three main ways:

- Through an **Internet Service Provider** – many provide some free web space with email accounts.

- You can **buy web space** from a web host – a company that rents web space by hosting websites for other people. Sometimes referred to as a virtual server.

- A third option is to **set up your own web server** with a permanent connection to the Internet! However,

have a big wad of money available. This option is often ideal for larger companies and organizations that have higher security needs and want total control. You'll probably need at least £15,000+ available annually and if you employ people to maintain and manage your website, multiply that rough cost many times. It's not hard to see why most people use free web space or the services of a web host, is it?

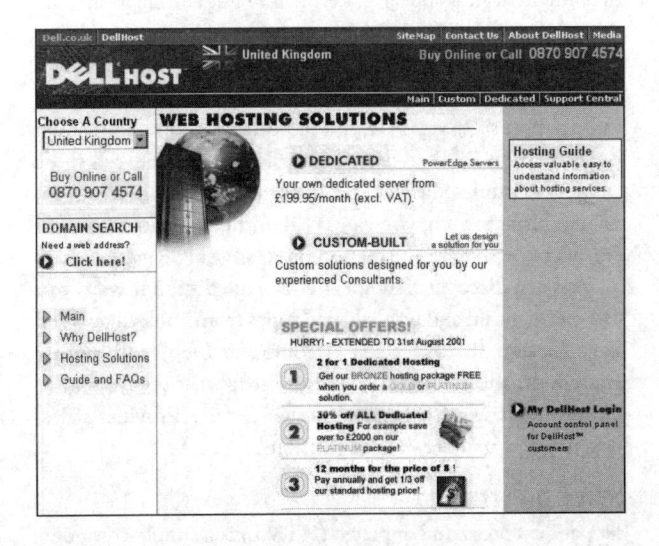

Planning and organising on paper

When you have some new web design software, you can spend as much time as you need trying out the commands and generally getting familiar with how to use it.

However, before starting to design your web pages or website, often you can save a lot of time later by roughly sketching on paper what you want to achieve and noting down any possible alternatives and various ideas – however wacky they might at first appear. Later, you might be able to include those "wacky" ideas to help create a better web page or website.

Generally, the main rule to consider – unless you have a compelling reason not to – is to divide up and organise your information so that you keep each different topic to its own page. A "page" in web design terms can be considered to be about 1 – 3 times the height of your display monitor screen. Using this approach, you can avoid putting what some might consider too much information on to any single page.

You can discover new ideas about the different ways you can create, build and publish web pages from books like "Web Page Design in easy steps" (Computer Step) and similar sources on the Internet. Make sure that what you intend to publish does not break any Internet Service Provider rules, decency and trade laws or regulations.

More on HTML

HyperText Markup Language (HTML) is a simple computer language used to create web pages. The more recently updated version – Dynamic HTML (DHTML) – can provide interactive components and lots of control over how a web page looks.

```
1  <html>
2
3  <head>
4  <title>Discover What's New at www.internettips.com</title>
5  <meta name="GENERATOR" content="Microsoft FrontPage 3.0">
6  </head>
7
8  <body background="../pix/bgd.GIF">
9
10 <table border="0" width="100%">
11   <tr>
12     <td width="24%"><a href="index.html"><img src="../pix/Home2.gif" a
13     <td width="76%"><p align="left"><img src="../pix/banner425.gif" al
14   </tr>
15   <tr>
16     <td width="24%"><img src="../pix/bannersub.GIF" alt="bannersub.GIF
17     <td width="76%"><img src="../pix/banner425bottom.GIF" alt="banner4
18   </tr>
19   <tr>
20     <td width="24%"></td>
21     <td width="76%"></td>
22   </tr>
23   <tr>
24     <td width="24%" valign="top" align="left"><form action="file:///to
25       <input type="hidden" name="back_url" value="/"><table width="140
26       <tr>
27         <td width="140"><table BORDER="0" CELLSPACING="0" CELLPADDIN
28           <tr>
29 <!-- subscribe dialog title -->
30             <td BGCOLOR="#ff0000"><table BORDER="0" CELLSPACING="0"
31               <tr>
32                 <td><font face="Tahoma, Arial, Helvetica" size="3" c
33                 </font><!-- /subscribe dialog title --> </td>
34               </tr>
```

Essentially, to create a web page, either directly or through using web design software, you write the HTML in plain text, include special text to make formatting tags, include the text to display images and create the text codes that form hyperlinks or links to other web pages.

You can create HyperText Markup Language (HTML) web pages using:

- Most basic **text editors** like Windows Notepad or word-processing software like Microsoft Word.

- A **HTML editor**: more user-friendly but you still face raw HTML.

- **Website design software**: here you can see how your web pages look as you create your layout and designs and the better packages can often help with the management of your website. Clearly, the best option.

Although HTML/DHTML is probably not one of your most exciting discoveries, it's useful and can provide some amazing special effects.

Most people nowadays prefer to use one of the dedicated WYSIWYG (What You See Is What You Get) web design software tools, like Microsoft FrontPage, NetObjects Fusion or Macromedia Dreamweaver. These tools can help you complete almost all web design tasks using a Desktop publishing approach, so you can see a page as you're building it and you don't need to have an in-depth knowledge about HTML commands to get the job done.

Nevertheless, if you're serious about web design, consider investing some time to learn about HTML and DHTML – you'll almost certainly need to know the details at some stage and sometimes even purpose-built web design software may not be able to create the precise effect you want easily.

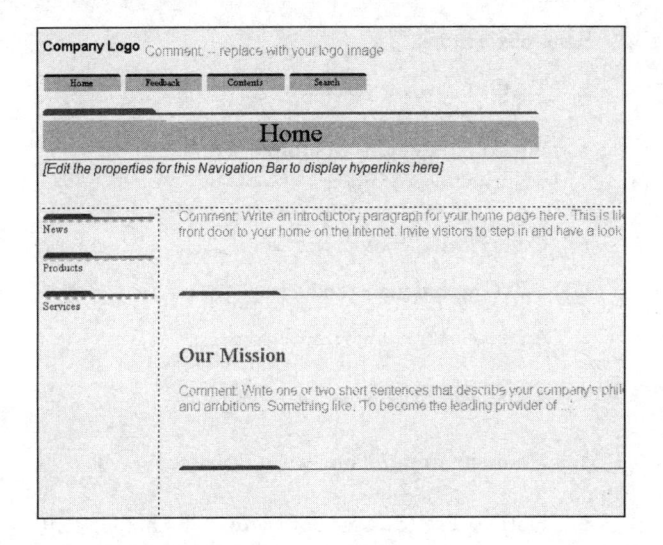

Web design software

A wide range of standalone web design software is available in the shops and on the Internet. Alternatively, some word-processing, DTP and graphics software – for example: Microsoft Word, Adobe InDesign, Corel WordPerfect and CorelDRAW! – let you save documents in web (HTML) format, so depending on your needs, you may not even need a more powerful and flexible web design package. The following list provides some options:

Basic text editors:

- **TextPad:** www.textpad.com/

- **Windows Notepad, Microsoft Word:** www.microsoft.com/

- **CuteHTML:** www.cuteftp.com/

WYSIWYG web design products:

- **Adobe GoLive:** www.adobe.com/

- **Adobe PageMill:** www.adobe.com/

- **Homesite from Allaire:** www.allaire.com/

- **HotDog Pro (Sausage Software):** www.hotdog.com/

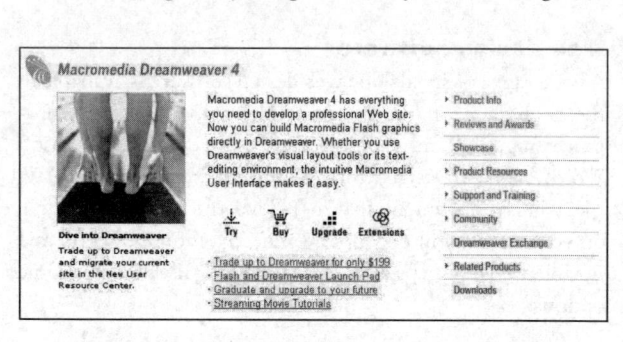

- **HotMetal Pro:** www.hotmetal.com/

- **Macromedia Dreamweaver:** www.macromedia.com/

- **Microsoft FrontPage:** www.microsoft.com/frontpage/

- **NetObjects Fusion:** www.netobjects.com/

- **WebExpress:** www.webexpress.com/

> Included with later versions of Microsoft Internet Explorer web browser, FrontPage Express is a free product ideal to help you learn some basics about how to create basic web pages and uploading (publishing) pages to the web.

Content management using only a web browser: the future today

A completely different approach involves using the services and tools of an online web design and hosting provider. Often, space for several web pages may be made available for free and the software tools you need are also provided, so if you choose this option you may not even need any web design software: usually, you'll only need a web browser and Internet access. For example, take a look at: www.SiteKit.net, www.ShopKit.net, or www.zy.com

Copyright and legal issues

Unless a website states that their text, graphics, designs and other components are free for anyone to use, they're probably not. If you want to 'borrow' some components from an existing website, always email the webmaster and ask. Even graphics that you can buy for use in web pages may have certain restrictions on how you can use them. Check the legal and copyright small print.

Introducing HTML tags

Here's an example web page showing the basic HTML:

```
<HTML>
<HEAD>
<TITLE>Welcome to my Home page!</TITLE>
</HEAD>
<BODY> BGCOLOR="BEIGE" TEXT="NAVY" (more
 here...)
(most of the page content goes here)
</BODY>
</HTML>
```

HTML tags are shown in capital letters enclosed between the (<) and (>) symbols. Often, these tags work together in pairs to form a command, with the ending tag having a forward slash (/) to signal the end of the tag command. You can learn about HTML in plain English from "HTML in easy steps" and

"Web Page Design in easy steps" (www.ineasysteps.com/), or from other similar books or check out sources on the Internet.

Establishing page size

You need to consider page width and length. Page width is affected by the resolution visitors use to view a web page and is measured in pixels (dots of light). For example, three popular

> **HOT TIP**
> Keep your page width to less than about 780 pixels to avoid forcing your visitors to have to scroll left to right – never popular. Or, you can create your design using percentages instead of pixels so that your page content "wraps" to fit the current window size.

resolutions include: 640 x 480, 800 x 600, 1200 x 740. Arguably, most computers now use 800 x 600 – 800 pixels wide by 600 high.

Page height: ideally, ensure your page content fits into a single browser window height or, if using lots of text, fewer than about 4 screen heights to avoid making a page too long. Use your own judgement to create your best presentation.

Web page background

Background options include: a solid colour, a variable or shaded colour, a watermark-type image, or even a full image.

> **HOT TIP**
> Make sure the overlying text has adequate contrast with the background, graphics and other overlying elements can be viewed clearly, and that the page background file size is not too large. Often, a "simple" background is best.

Also don't forget to consider using "white" (empty) space to frame your main page content and provide an uncluttered appearance. "Active" white space around an object actually helps the eye maintain focus on that object in a subtle way.

Working with colours on the web

Colour has a powerful pull on the eye. It creates mood and contrasting colours add vibrancy to a web page. Use colours that complement or work well together to create a superb finish.

Most computers today can produce 256 colours. However, 40 colours are reserved for use by the computer operating system and other functions. That leaves 216 "safe" colours. Although most web design software tools provide information about using safe web colours, most computers nowadays can display thousands (64 thousand) or millions (16 Million) of different colours and shades, so you may decide to have more flexibility in the colours you choose.

Inserting text onto a page

You can enter text much the same way as you would using word-processor software: add formatting like bold, italic or underline and use lists – both bullet point and numbered – and so on, to place special emphasis on specific text.

Adding links to a page

Links – or hyperlinks – are one of the most important components in a web page as links allow visitors to quickly move to the parts that interest them most. A link allows visitors to quickly move to:

- Somewhere else on the same page.

- A different page in the current website.

- Another website or new location on the Internet.

Web design software provides simple ways to create hyperlinks:

- Insert a text-based link onto a web page.

- Change the purpose of a normal image so that it becomes a graphical hyperlink – the object still looks the same except when a user moves the mouse pointer onto the image, the mouse pointer symbol changes to show that the image is also a link.

Traditionally, a text link is shown in underlined blue; however, you can use the later versions of HTML or DHTML to choose a different colour and to remove the underline when being viewed with the latest web browsers.

Things to consider when using images

Pictures and other graphical web objects can add interest, provide contrast, form the main component of a web page, or supplement the theme of the text, to create an interesting, engaging and compelling result.

Pure text in a web page displays quickly; images take longer to appear. Key point: the larger the physical size of an image, the longer it takes to fully display in a browser. Therefore, consider the following guidelines when working with web images:

- **Choose** images carefully: avoid poor quality images.

- Keep the **size** of an image as physically small as is acceptable to fulfil your goals for that image. Image size is given in pixels – each pixel is a dot of light. For example, a rectangular image of 100 pixels wide by 50 pixels high is described in HTML as HEIGHT=50 WIDTH=100.

- Images for use in a web page should be converted to the **correct format**. This ensures that an image downloads as quickly as possible to a visitor's browser. More on this important topic in the following paragraphs.

HistoricalPhotographic ArchiveCollections

House of Images - Free Interactive CD-ROM

Download your free Interactive House of Images CD-ROM.

[Download]

Please note you must have Windows 95/98/NT to view the application and Winzip to decompress the package.

t +44 (0) 1254 664464
f +44 (0) 1254 278646
sales@hoimages.co.uk

- HISTORICAL IMAGES
- HOUSE OF IMAGES
- PROTECT YOUR IMAGES
- INTERACTIVE CD
- NEWS
- INFO

- **Avoid having too many images** on a web page: the more images present, the longer a page takes to display in a visitor's web browser.

Finding images for your web pages

You can find the images you need using a variety of methods:

- **Create the images you want** to use on your computer using an image-drawing program or take your own live pictures using a digital camera.

- With the right permission (see copyright and legal issues earlier in this chapter) **modify an existing image** using image-editing software.

- **Copy (save) existing images** from the web or Internet. WARNING: get permission in writing from the copyright owners of the images you want to use before using them. Depending on how you want to use the images, copyright restrictions may apply, you may have to pay a fee, or permission may be refused.

- Using a **scanner**, you can copy existing images from printed pages. WARNING: the same legal implications apply as listed in the previous paragraph.

Image owners appreciate being asked and I suspect many will give permission with some reasonable conditions, especially for non-commercial uses.

Image formats and preparing images for the web

Images for use on web pages come in two main formats: **GIF** (pronounced "JIFF" or "GIFF") and **JPEG** (pronounced J-Peg). Other formats are available like Portable Network Graphics (PNG), but these have not yet gained widespread acceptance. GIF (.gif) is ideal for small images that contain only a few colours or shades like logos or simple geometric shapes.

JPEG (.jpeg or .jpe) is an ideal format to use for any image that contains many different colours and shades, like photographs.

However, all images for the web should be converted to use 256 or fewer colours – the fewer used, the smaller an image's file size, the faster it displays on a visitor's web browser. How: in your graphics program, reduce the number of colours to as few as possible without degrading the image quality. If you use too few colours, an image can look patchy. Usually, choose 256 or 16 colours or, for simple black and white images, even 2 colours may work fine.

Placing an image on a page

To include an image on a web page, you'll use the HTML <IMG> tag. For example: <IMG SRC="welcomelogo.gif">

If you're using web design software, you won't need to be concerned about the exact HTML format above, just place the image where you want it on the page. You can then choose from various image alignment options including: left, right, middle, text top and baseline.

Use the ALT image tag to include a brief text description for each image. Example: ALT="holiday in Venice, 2002". Why: ALT is necessary in case a visitor has turned off images in their web browser (to reduce download times) and to help search engines "index" (record) your page.

Creating a site navigation structure

When using websites that contain many pages, unless you design pages carefully, a visitor may soon become confused and lost. Remedy: create a clear page navigation structure using

> In **Site view**, add pages, name them, and arrange them by dragging and dropping page icons. NetObjects Fusion 5.0 updates links between your pages as quickly as you adjust their structure.
>
> When you want to add content to a page, double-click a page icon to see that page in Page view.

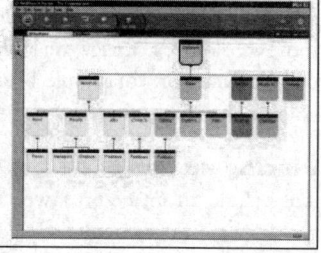

navigation bars and buttons where appropriate and always include a link on every page back to the Home/Index page and to the main categories of your website.

Saving a web page

Usually, you save your web pages using the .html or .htm filename extension (although more complex database-driven pages may use other filename extensions). Practice saving often – ideally every 15 minutes to protect your work and keep regular backup copies.

Previewing your web pages

You can see how your web page might look on the web by using the "Preview" command in your web design software if available. Then when you're happy with the finish, open the web page you want using your own installed web browser.

How: often, all you need do is double-click the web page filename you want in Windows Explorer or equivalent. However: not all browsers interpret the same web page in the same way. Remedy: ideally have at least the latest versions of Internet Explorer and Netscape Navigator installed on your computer (choose one as the default). Then check your web page using both web browsers to confirm the end result is what you expect. If not, make your changes and re-check the results.

Getting web space for individual and personal websites

Free web space often available from an Internet Service Provider is ideal for individual, hobby, or non-business-oriented websites. However, do remember that, usually, the final web address available from free Internet Service Providers may be longer than that of a true domain web address such as: www.ineasysteps.com

To illustrate, here's an imaginary web address dreamed up by my teenage daughter, that we might be able to use with the generous free web space available from the well-established British Internet Service Provider BT Internet: www.btintenet.com/~amanda.hugandkiss/index.html

Not the shortest web address you'll come across, and perhaps not the easiest to remember, but it may be perfectly acceptable for your needs. Just think twice before you consider trying to run a business using longer web addresses like these.

Spell-checking, proofreading, checking & testing

Before publishing your web page or website, use a spell checker to catch those errors that you miss visually. Also ideally, print out each page and check layout again and make any necessary changes. To get the best finish possible, you may have to repeat this checking / editing cycle several times, but hey, it's your baby right?

Publishing a "local" copy of your website

When you have finished your web page design you can publish. However, publish a "local" copy to your own computer first then open the web page using your web browser to view your page. If you have created a series of related web pages or an entire website, you can open the main Index or Home page – usually called something like: index.html – and then check all the other related pages by navigating around your website just like your visitors do when you publish to the web.

Double-check all pages and make sure all the links that you can check offline are working as they should. However, links that point to other web locations can only be properly checked once you publish your pages to the web.

Finally, view your web pages as described above using several different web browsers if possible. Certainly, check your pages with the latest versions of Microsoft Internet Explorer and Netscape Navigator/Communicator. Ideally, also use some earlier versions of each browser in the same way. Once you're happy that the local published copy of your website works perfectly, you're ready to make your website live and publish to the web.

Going live: publishing your website to the web

To publish your website, you'll need an FTP program. Often, web creation software may include this option. Alternatively, you can use a standalone product. See page 409 for more information about FTP software. You'll also need some web space to which you have permission to publish. Several options may be available.

If you use an Internet Service Provider (ISP) to gain access to the Internet and for email, they may make some free web space available to you. If you're in business, you'll probably want a "true" business domain name (example: www.yourname.com, rather than the longer format: www.ispname.com/yourname/index.htm).

Preferred business web hosting options

Serious business websites are usually published to the web using the facilities of a web hosting organisation, or to a dedicated web server that may be owned by the company publishing the website. Follow the instructions provided in your web software for publishing to the web. Your software may mention that you're publishing to a web server – remember, this is just another name for a powerful computer that will hold your website and make it available for anyone with Internet access to view on the web 24 hours a day.

Creating fancy websites

If you want to make an impression, create impact, provide more flexibility or make interactive web pages, you'll need to go beyond the simple. Lots of options are available so let's look at some of the more popular choices.

Using cool mouseover effects

A popular current trend is to set up a link, or some text or a graphic that changes in some way when you move the mouse pointer over it, or which changes some other component on the page – perhaps to display some alternative text. As soon as you move the mouse pointer away from the object, the page design re-displays its original look.

The currently popular mouseover technique – also known as rollover or hover – is often used to highlight website navigation buttons or other links and can provide an ideal way to display more information in the same physical space. The best web creation software packages like NetObjects Fusion and Microsoft FrontPage provide some predesigned mouseovers ready for you to use or you can create your own if you wish. See your web software guide for more information.

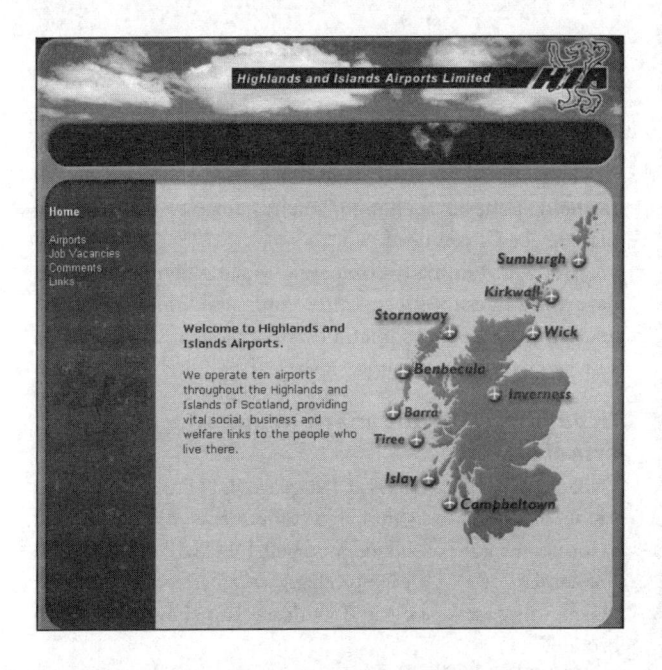

Getting noticed with animation

If you want to draw attention to one particular component on a web page, make that component move. Examples: animated buttons, scrolling text messages, advertisements and small self-running programs or presentations that when carefully designed can hold the viewer spellbound – at least for a few seconds – but that may be all you need.

However: too many competing moving components can have the opposite effect: cause confusion, slow down the loading of a page, can sometimes make too many demands on a browser and so cause it to crash.

Dynamic HTML and more about special effects

Dynamic HyperText Markup Language (DHTML) techniques can include their own animated components. As complicated as the name might sound, in a nutshell, DHTML simply allows the content of a web page to change even after the code that makes the page work has downloaded to the visitor's web browser.

DHTML mostly uses JavaScript – one of the easier computer languages to learn – to help provide all sorts of clever effects. Many JavaScript components are available on the Internet that you can use or add to your web page designs. Example: see what's available at: www.javascripts.com/

JavaScript should not be confused with the programming language called Java from Sun Microsystems which, is a completely different language. JavaScript uses little self-contained chunks of code which, when placed on a web page, could be interpreted by any computer no matter what operating system was used. You can find many sources for JavaScript on the Internet through your browser search engines.

Inserting META tags for maximum exposure

A web page can include more information about what you want to say than just what appears on the page. Extra information that is normally invisible can be added using HTML META tags, that can help the search engines index your website.

Example: you can include a brief description about your web page and include various keywords that you want your site to be associated with. Often, this information is used to help form what a visitor sees about your website displayed in the search listing of various search engines. See your web creation software guide for details or scan the Net using the exact search phrase: "HTML meta" to discover more information.

Inserting a website search box

If your website contains lots of information, one quick way to build in added value and make using the site easier and quicker for your visitors is to include a site search box.

Now, several non-specialist options are available. You can use predesigned JavaScript components that you just drop on to the page. Example: Coolmaps.com at **www.coolmaps.com/**

provide a superb range of "Components" for NetObjects Fusion users (www.netobjects.com/). Other software products like FrontPage provide similar predesigned modules that you can use. Or you can download predesigned JavaScript blocks of code from websites like: **www.javascripts.com/**

If your website has fewer than 500 pages, Atomz at www.atomz.com/ currently make the Atomz Search tool available free of charge.

Including Multimedia content

Multimedia refers to the combination of various types of media – text, still and moving pictures, animation, and sound. If you decide to include, say, video clips or large sound clips, remember that download times for your visitors will increase. Longer download times may be tolerated by your visitors providing they consider that the end result is worthwhile. Sound/video clips come in 2 main forms:

- **Discrete format:** here the entire clip has to be fully downloaded before it can be viewed or heard. Not ideal for anything that takes longer than a few minutes using a typical modem connection speed.

- **Streaming media:** content can start to play while it is downloading. Streaming media typically offers less delay so is usually a much better option for most purposes. However, your visitor will need the correct player software installed. RealPlayer from RealNetworks (www.realplayer.com/) and Microsoft NetShow (www.microsoft.com/netshow/) are two streaming multimedia players that are currently available free.

Currently free programs like Real Slideshow let you mix pictures with voice, music and other sound effects. Real Presenter – also free – converts Microsoft PowerPoint presentations into Internet video format.

Several of the free web hosting sites can now host your streaming media presentations at no charge: www.tripod.com, one of the pioneers in free websites, at the time of writing offers a program called ShowMotion. You can combine still photos with clips of video, scanned images, and backed with your narration. What's more, Tripod hosts it for free!

Adding sound to a web page

Sound information from a microphone is made up of lots of changing high and low notes or waves; electronically, we refer to this method as analogue. Computers however, use only two levels: 0 (zero) and 1 (one), or highs and lows to communicate and this effect is known as digital communication.

Background music: can add that extra something to a web page or can irritate your visitors. As you can't predict how a visitor is going to react to your taste in music, consider carefully whether to use background music. Always include a button or other mechanism that allows a visitor to turn off music. Also: as music and other sound components slow down the loading of a page, in an already graphically complex page, you might benefit by simply omitting music – unless of course you're in the music business.

To use sound on a web page, the sound information has to be converted to digital format. Fortunately, lots of digital sound clips, music and tunes have already been converted ready to use (check copyright issues though). Several varieties of sound file for web pages exist but all can be grouped as discrete or streaming audio.

If you include sound files that end in extensions like .wav and .au, these discrete files have to be completely downloaded to the web browser and have the correct player software installed before they can be heard. With audio streaming files however, a web page a user does not have to wait for the entire file to download before the sound can start to be heard. However, the correct audio player must be installed in the user's computer. Most players are available free of charge.

Rich Music Format (RMF) is a new interactive audio format that looks set to be "the" format for the web. Also, free or cheap programs are available on the Net to let you record audio as a simple WAV file, a RealAudio file or in the newer MP3 format. One easy to use program is Internet Audio Mix from www.aoustica.com/ which works with your sound card to record up to 4 digital tracks.

Another approach is use free programs like those available from www.GiveMeTalk.com/ that allow you to record your own talk show and then host it on their site ready for your customers to hear your masterpiece. Or you could record your information in MP3 format and upload articles to www.Live365.com/ where your talks can be made available continuously 24 hours a day and rotated regularly – and it's currently free of charge!

Using frames

Frames offer a way to keep one or more components in the same position while other parts of a web page can be scrolled through. An approach that is sometimes ideal for business websites that want to keep a logo, advertising banner, slogan, or navigation bar always visible in the same position.

How: using the <FRAMESET> </FRAMESET> tag pair in HTML, you can create the frame structure you want and apply it to all pages in your website. As you then don't need to repeat the exercise on every page, you can save many hours' work – plus updating is much easier. However: poorly designed frame web pages can cause more problems than they solve. See your HTML guide or web creation software Help files for more information about using framed page designs.

How about a WebCam on your website?

Also called NetCams, WebCams are digital cameras attached to a PC that can send live pictures/moving pictures at specific intervals on the Internet. A digital camera combined with WebCam software takes live, repeating, still photographs and transmits these at certain intervals; in this way, pictures might be transmitted at a rate of one frame each second. Images from a WebCam are sent to a video capture board that is typically installed in a spare slot in the main circuit board of the computer with the WebCam attached.

The video capture board changes the analogue information it receives from the WebCam that makes up each frame into a digital format that the computer can work with. As the make-up of each image is probably complex, the JPEG digital graphics format is usually used.

JPEG images are quick to load and are ideal for rendering images that contain a wide range of colours, tones and shades, like photographs. Each JPEG image is then associated with a specific web address (URL), so that whenever a visitor clicks the appropriate link on a web page, the most recent image from the WebCam is sent to the viewer. This cycle is repeated so that while a user is viewing, a continuous stream of photos provides the illusion of movement.

Although current generation WebCams are not pure continuous video quality, a WebCam can provide an ideal basic communication device today, and usage is probably set to increase as face-to-face video communication becomes more commonplace through the continuing development and ever closer ties of mobile phones, video phones, the Internet and television.

22
Jargon buster

Access provider: an organisation that provides individual access to the Internet. Also known as an Internet Access Provider (IAP) or Internet Service Provider (ISP).

ActiveX: self-running program components that can be downloaded and run in a web page. Also known as ActiveX Controls.

Active content: often refers to a web page containing components and self-running programs that can provide a variety of animated and interactive effects.

Active Desktop: a built in option within Microsoft Internet Explorer that enables a user to allow Internet Explorer and web channels to manage the entire appearance of the Microsoft Windows desktop.

Address book: a program used to store email addresses and key contact details.

ADSL (Asymmetrical Digital Subscriber Line): a system that allows fast data communications over traditional telephone lines. The speed at which data is sent from an ISP to a user (downstream) is much greater than sending data from a computer to an ISP (upstream). Typically, data comes to your computer at about 8 Mbps, while data goes away from your computer at 64 Kbps.

Anonymous FTP: an FTP site that accepts the user log-in name: "anonymous" (without the quotes) and the user's email address as the access password. Many FTP sites that provide software and other files for download free of charge allow anonymous FTP.

Applet: a small computer program that connects or is designed to work with a larger "partner" program.

Attachment: a computer file that is included with an email message.

Autoresponder: an email message that is sent automatically in response to an email message sent to another specific email address. Also known as Autobot or infobot.

Backbone: a main "highway" of the Internet that can carry a huge amount of Internet information or "traffic".

Bandwidth: essentially describes the amount and speed of an Internet connection and is measured in bits per second (bps). So when we talk about a high bandwidth connection to the Internet, we're saying that this connection can move more information each second compared to a low bandwidth connection. If more information is sent than can be processed, we experience delays and bottlenecks on the Internet. Internet Service Providers are always looking for better ways to provide more bandwidth and therefore provide faster, more reliable connections to the Net.

Banner advert: a small advertisement often placed on the top or bottom of a web page that when clicked links to the advertiser's website and which can provide income for the host website.

Baud rate: information transmitted from a modem continually changes between high and low levels. The baud rate is the number of these changes each second. Compare with bits per second (bps).

Bookmarks: a bookmark is a stored web address in Netscape Navigator so that you can return to a web page later without having to enter the web address you want. Microsoft Internet Explorer refers to bookmarks as Favorites.

Bounced email: an email message that is automatically returned to the sender – usually because the email address does not exist or is incorrect.

Bps (bits per second): in order to measure data, we have to chop it up into pieces. A "bit" is one piece of data. Bps measures the speed at which two modems communicate. Compare with baud rate.

Cache: temporary amount of space used to store popular web pages. Most web browsers have a cache to help provide quicker access to web pages that are visited regularly.

CGI (Common Gateway Interface): an interactive system installed on web servers to automatically process information entered into web page forms, guestbooks, and so on.

Channels: a method that can send a regularly updated stream of information from a website on a particular theme or topic to a "subscribed" browser. An interesting idea that to-date hasn't really taken off.

Client application: software that is designed to communicate with server software. For example, Outlook Express is an email client that 'talks' to a computer that handles email (mail server).

Cookie: a nice, tasty biscuit – no seriously, an Internet cookie is a small computer file that many websites send to your computer on your first visit to them, so that next time you visit, they can identify your web browser (you) and say "Hi." Usually, you can turn off cookies in your web browser, but then not all websites may work properly.

DHTML (Dynamic HyperText Markup Language): a language format based on HTML but which allows animated and interactive web pages to be created.

Domain name: identifies a website address. In "www.ineasysteps.com", for example, "ineasysteps.com" is the domain name.

E-commerce: performing business transactions on the Internet.

Email: electronic mail – messages sent on the Internet that may also include computer files as attachments.

Email address: a unique address to someone on the Internet. Typical example formats: "b.austin@mysite.com" and "info@mysite.com"

Favorites: a Favorite is a stored web address in Microsoft Internet Explorer, so that you can return to a web page later without having to enter the web address you want. Netscape Navigator refers to Favorites as bookmarks.

File Transfer Protocol (FTP): a standard way to send files around the Internet.

Firewall: security system for networked computers to control access into and out of the network.

Flame: an abusive email message or series of messages targeted at a single user.

Flash: a popular web technology often used to create fancy web presentations that can download to a web browser quickly.

A web browser requires the Flash Player plug-in – now provided free with Windows and Apple Mac operating systems.

Folder/directory: different names for the same thing – an area in your computer's memory to store a group of related files or documents.

GIF (Graphics Interchange Format): a popular web image format created by CompuServe and designed for quickly displaying simple images made up of a few colours or shades like basic logos for example. Contrast with JPEG images.

Guestbook: A web form in which visitors to a website can leave comments about their visit.

Home page: the main page from which you can navigate to all other pages in a website. Also known as Index page.

Host: a computer that makes available specified services to other computers on a network.

HTML (HyperText Markup Language): a language format used to create web pages.

HTTP (HyperText Transfer Protocol): a set of established rules for transmitting web pages on the Internet.

HTTPS (HyperText Transfer Protocol Secure): a more secure version of HTTP used for processing online credit card transactions or for handling sensitive information.

Hyperlink: an item on a web page that when clicked allows you to move to another location on the same web page or another location on the Internet.

Imagemap: a single web graphic in which different parts of the image, when clicked, link to various other web locations.

IMAP (Internet Message Access Protocol): an advanced system designed to process and store incoming email on a mail server. May eventually replace the current dominant alternative: POP3.

Internet Relay Chat (IRC): a system that allows Internet users to talk to each other live.

Internet Service Provider (Internet Access Provider): see Access provider.

Internet Telephony: making telephone calls using the Internet.

IP (Internet Protocol): Every computer connected to the Internet has a unique number: an IP address. Typically, an IP address is made up of four sets of numbers separated by full stops, for example: 123.107.59.45. As words make more sense to us, we use web addresses or URLs: "www.computerstep.com" is much easier to remember than 123.107.59.45.

IP address: a unique number given to every computer that accesses the Internet. *See also* IP.

ISDN (Integrated Services Digital Network): an agreed standard that allows information in digital format to be sent over the standard telephone lines. Typical connection speeds are 64 Kbps and 128 Kbps. *See also* ADSL.

Java: a compiled computer programming. Developed by Sun Microsystems.

JavaScript: an interpreted programming language that can provide a variety of special web page effects from your web browser when used as part of HTML.

JPEG (Joint Photographic Experts Group): a popular web image format designed for quickly displaying complex images made up of many colours or shades, like photographs for example. Contrast with GIF images.

Junk email: messages that are received but not asked for or usually wanted. Often, junk emailers send get-rich-quick offers or highly suspect proposals. Beware: sometimes various scams may be disguised as junk email. My advice is to treat junk email as you would any other junk.

Link: a shorthand name for a hyperlink.

Mail server: a computer that provides email services to a variety of users.

MIDI (Musical Instrument Digital Interface): a standard used for controlling sound cards, synthesizers etc. Rather than including the actual sound data, MIDI files contain key information on how to create the sounds required.

Mirror site: a copy of a website. Mirror sites are often set up so that users have alternative ways to get the same information more quickly.

MP3: highly compressed file format for music.

MUD (Multi-User Dungeon): Internet-based multi-user game.

Netiquette: responsible Internet behaviour based on consideration for others. Created from network etiquette

Newsreader: software that allows access to and use of newsgroups by providing a connection to a news server.

News server: a computer that makes newsgroup services available.

Operating system: the basic "housekeeping" software components that every computer needs to operate.

PDF (Portable Document Format): a well known highly compressed standard used for displaying and printing formatted documents especially popular on the Internet. Probably set to become the world standard for electronic documents.

Plug-ins: add-on software components that are necessary to work with specific types of files.

POP3 (Post Office Protocol 3): an established set of rules that ensures you can send and receive email from anywhere on the Internet.

Portal: a website that acts as a doorway or introduction to many other websites that are sometimes grouped into categories.

RealAudio: file format from Real Networks that allows sound information to download quickly on the web. Uses "streaming" technology – the RealAudio file can start playing while it is being downloaded to a visitor's browser.

RealMedia: a collective term to describe RealAudio and RealVideo files.

RealVideo: file format from Real Networks that allows video information to download quickly on the web. Uses "streaming" technology – the RealVideo file can start playing while it is being downloaded to a visitor's browser.

Search engine: a collection of information about a variety of different web pages including links to these pages.

Server: a computer that provides online access. Also sometimes called a host – example: web host. Server software runs a server and communicates with users of the server who use client software.

SMTP (Simple Mail Transfer Protocol): currently the most popular standard for sending email and for transferring it between mail servers.

Spam: the practice of sending the same email message to many Internet users at the same time and who did not ask for the usually commercially-oriented message, or of posting to multiple newsgroups in the same manner. Also known as Unsolicited Commercial Email (UCE)

Streaming: a fast Internet delivery technology that allows an audio and video file to be heard and viewed while it is downloading, rather than the user having to wait until the entire file has downloaded to their computer first.

TCP/IP (Transmission Control Protocol/Internet Protocol): the essential set of rules that govern how the Internet works.

The Net: the Internet.

Telnet: an agreed set of rules or protocol that allows you to connect to another computer anywhere in the world, in such a way that the remote computer thinks that you are using its own keyboard.

Trojan Horse (computer virus): a program containing another program hidden inside. Usually, the hidden program is the one designed to cause problems. Often sent within an email message, a Trojan Horse can't do any harm until you open the attachment and run it.

URL (Uniform Resource Locator): the system used for finding a web address on the Internet. A URL is also known as a web address.

Usenet: the most popular face of Internet newsgroups for swapping messages, in which topics are arranged into specific groups (alt., biz., comp., etc.)

V.92: agreed international standard for modems, governing speed and connection.

Web author: anyone who designs, creates and publishes web pages and websites.

Web browser: sometimes called a web client, allows a user to work with and move around the web and view web pages.

Currently the most popular web browsers are Microsoft Internet Explorer and Netscape Navigator.

Web host: an organisation with a permanent live connection to the Internet, that makes web space available for rent (usually).

Web page: a published document that is designed to be made available on the World Wide Web.

Web server: a computer that stores web pages and makes these available to users outside the organisation owning the web server.

Website: a collection of related web pages usually stored at the same location.

Winzipped files: computer files that have been compressed and converted into a single file using the popular file compression software WinZip.

Worm (computer virus): a program that attempts to make copies of itself. Can copy across hard drives, removable drives and email files.

WWW (World Wide Web): the most popular and visible branch of the Internet now more commonly known simply as the "web" and which contains billions of web pages.

WYSIWYG (What You See Is What You Get): describes modern computing methods like Microsoft Windows and Apple MacOS in which you see the effects of what you enter immediately.

Index

A

Abbreviations, email 323
Active Desktop 471
ActiveX 161, 471
Address book (email) 472
Adobe GoLive 448
Adobe PageMill 448
ADSL 85, 251, 472
Alta Vista search tool 192
Anonymous FTP 472
Antivirus software 182
Applet 161, 472
Archie (FTP search tool) 436
Attachments, email 332, 472
AutoComplete 155
Autoresponders 96, 280, 472

B

Backbone, Internet 472
Bandwidth 473
Banner ads 473
Baud 473
BCC field 319
Beta software, defined 419
Bits per second (bps) 474
Bookmarks 152, 473
Bounced mail 473
Broadband, defined 86
Broken downloads 435

C

Cable modems 254
Cache 154, 474
Call Waiting services 62
CGI 474
Channel (web) 474
Chargeable licence, defined 418

Chat. *See* Internet Relay Chat
Client 474
Commercial Online Service providers 87
Common Gateway Interface 474
Computer
  Choosing 236
  Display monitors 47
  DVD drive 51
  Hard drive 46
  Headsets 52
  Internet-ready specification 49
  Palmtop 76
  Speed 45
  Viruses 177
Cookies 166, 474
Copyright issues 29, 450
CPU 43
Cybercafés 82
Cyberspace 16

D

DHTML 130, 475
Dial-up Networking (DUN) 102
DNS, defined 37
Domain name 475
  Buying 4
  Defined 88
  Extensions 133
  Registrations (UK) 5
Downloading 20
DUN 102

E

E-commerce 475
Email 17, 475
  Adding emotion 322
  Address 475
  Address books 313
  Address, defined 277
  Address directory
    Bigfoot 206
    WhoWhere 206
    Yahoo PeopleSearch 207
  Address, finding 205
  Allocated storage space 286
  AOL addresses 283
  Attaching a file 332
  Autoresponders 96

Benefits and drawbacks 262
Blind Carbon Copy (BCC) field 314, 319
Bounced messages 339
Carbon Copy (CC) field 314, 319
Column width 310
Compressing an attachment 334
CompuServe addresses 283
Converting fax to email 343
Creating an email address 282
Creating messages (start) 317
Creating messages (style) 307
Creating new message folders 352
Digital ID 342
Finding an email address 316
Flames 356, 475
Forwarding a message 328
Free accounts 287
Getting an email account 283
Grouping messages 352
Header 302
How it works 275
HTML 276
IMAP 110
Incoming mail set-up 110, 293
ISP dial-up telephone number 292
Junk messages 345
Message file size 312
Message length 311
Netiquette 313
Newsgroups NNTP 110
Organizing messages 351
Outgoing mail set-up 110, 295
Paragraph size 311
Plain text 276
Plain text or HTML 308
POP3 110
Prohibited characters 280
Providers 286
Re-sending a message 331

Reading messages 305
Receiving in HTML format 340
Replying to a message 327
Requirements 273
Rerouting messages 355
Security 296, 340
Sending a message 324
Sending in HTML format 340
Sending to multiple recipients 330
Signature files 336
Smiley characters 265
SMTP 110, 480
Software
Installing and setting up 289
Sorting messages 352
SpeechMail 357
Subject box 321
Text alignment 310
Use of capitals 321
User name 292
Using abbreviations 323
vCard 339
Web-based 239, 288

Employment 5
Encyclopedias 234

F

Favorites 152, 475
Fax
Converting to email 343
Using 243
File Transfer Protocol (FTP) 136, 410, 475
Address 424
Anonymous 412
Archie (search tool) 436
Broken downloads 435
Compressed files 420
Copyright issues 417
Defined 412
Downloading stuff 424
Finding FTP sites 435
Popular FTP software 432
Private 412
Setting up 423
Single compressed file archives 421
Uploading stuff 428
Firewall software 189, 475
Flame (email) 356, 475

Flash technology 165, 475
Freeware, defined 418
FTP. *See* File Transfer Protocol (FTP)

G

Games
  Computer 359
  Downloading game software 362
  Finding what's available 366
  Getting started 363
  Multiplayer 5, 364
  Requirements 359
  WirePlay 366
Guestbook page 476
GUI, defined 40

H

Hackers, preventing 189
Helper applications 160
Hertz, defined 45
Home/Index page
  Changing 127
  Defined 126
Host 476
Hover buttons 462

HTML 130, 476
HTTP 476
HTTPS 216, 476
Hyperlink 476
HyperText Markup Language 130, 476

I

ICQ Instant messaging 407
Image formats
  GIF 476
  JPEG 478
Imagemap 477
IMAP 477
Income
  Earn online 9
Incoming mail setting 110
Information Superhighway 16
Instant messaging 405
Instant Messenger software 407
IntelliSense 151
Internet
  Access
    ADSL 245, 251
    Cybercafés 82
    ISDN 245

Low cost/free 76
Satellite 255
Trial offers 83
Using public libraries 83
Backbone 38, 472
Banking 220
Chat 398
Conferencing 397
Connecting first time 99
Connection problems 113, 241
Defined 16
Dial-up connection 74
Downloading files 162
Faxing documents 243
Finding specific information 199
Headsets 396
Instant messaging 405
Multimedia Chat 399
Radio 5, 8
Safe viewing 148, 230
Security 146, 189, 231
  Web browser 229
Service Provider
  Defined 84
  Evaluating 90
  Finding 89
Telephony 3
Traffic jams 249
Use, children 227
Internet Relay Chat 4, 17, 401
IP address 477
IRC 477
ISDN 245, 477
ISDN Terminal Adaptor 74
ISDN2 249
ISP. *See* Internet: Service Provider

J

Java 161, 478
JavaScript 130, 161, 478
Junk email 478

L

Leased lines 256

M

Macromedia Dreamweaver 449
Mail server 478
META tags 465

Microsoft
- FrontPage 449
- FrontPage Express 143
- IntelliSense 151
- Internet Explorer 144, 155
- NetMeeting 142, 397
- NetShow 140, 467
- Outlook 314
- Outlook Express 142, 261, 297
- Windows Media Player 143

MIDI, defined 478

Mobile phones 76, 242
- Sending email 357
- WAP 358

Modem
- Cable 254
- Defined 53
- Error correction 61
- External 69
- For networked PCs 57
- Handshaking 59
- Internal 65
- Sending/receiving faxes 64
- Types 54

Multimedia, streaming 139

N

Netiquette 29, 479

Netscape
- AOL Instant Messenger 148
- Composer 148
- Messenger 261
- Navigator 147
- NetWatch 148

Network (computer) 19
- Local Area Network (LAN) 20
- Wide Area Network (WAN) 20

News server 479

Newsgroups 17
- Blocking unwanted messages 392
- Combining file segments 390
- Dealing with flames 392
- Downloading files 390
- Downloading images 390
- Moderated 377
- Names 372
- Posting a message 386

Protecting an email
   address 375
Reading messages 385
Replying to a post 389
Spamming 388
Subscribing to 382
The FAQ document 385
Top-level categories 370
Unmoderated 377
Unsubscribing 382
Usenet 378
Virus warnings 367
Newsreader 479
   Configuring 373
   Software 372
NNTP setting 110
Nominet UK 5

O

Offline, defined 21
Online
   Defined 21
   Trading 220
Operating system 479
Outgoing mail settings 110

P

PC-Card modem 56
PCMCIA. See PC-Card
   modem
PDF 479
Pegasus email software
   261
PGP 341
PICS system 230
Ping software utility 246
Plug-ins 160
   Defined 479
POP3 479
Portable computers
   Battery life 238
   Connectors and adaptors
      238
Portable Document Format
   (PDF) 479
Portals 137, 479
Pretty Good Privacy (PGP)
   341
Printers 78
Proxy server, defined 248
Psion Organisers 76
Public domain, defined
   417

R

Radio online 5, 8
RAM, defined 43
RealAudio 163, 479
RealMedia 480
RealNetworks 140
RealPlayer 140, 148, 163
RealVideo 163, 480
Routers, defined 38
RSACi 231

S

Satellite Internet
    connections 255
Saving
  Parts of a web page 156
  Web page 155
Search engine 192, 480
Search results
  Making sense of 201
Search tools (web) 192
  How they work 197
Secure Sockets Layer
    (SSL), defined 213
Server, defined 480
Shareware, defined 418
Shockwave 165

Shopping online 5
  Benefits 211
  Flowers 13
  Gifts 14
  Import duty 214
  Precautions 213
  Secure web pages 216
  Supermarket (Tesco) 15
  VAT queries 214
Signature files 336
Smiley characters 265
SMTP 110, 480
Software
  Stuffit Expander 420
  WinZip 420, 482
Spam 345, 480
SpeechMail 357
Streaming multimedia
    139, 466, 480
Stuffit Expander 420

T

TCP/IP 35, 481
Telnet 481
Trace Route software utility
    247
Trojan Horse (computer
    virus) 481

U

Unsolicited Commercial Email (UCE). *See* Email: Junk messages
Uploading 20
URL 131, 481
Usenet 378, 481

V

Viruses 20, 177
  Bubbleboy 181
  Dealing with infection 186
  Email 179
  Happy99.exe 180
  Preventing infection 185
  VBS/LoveLetter.A 181

W

W3C 27, 125
WAN. *See* Network (computer): Wide Area Network
WAP mobile phones 358
Web (World Wide Web) 16
  Channels 145
  Defined 21
  Directories 192
  Fun things to do 122
  Portals 137
  Search tools 192
  Site filtering 148, 230, 231
Web browser 124
  Address box 151
  AutoComplete 155
  Bookmarks 152
  Build numbers (IE) 144
  Cache 154
  Changing default settings 157
  Cookies 166
  Favorites 152
  Forward/Back buttons 150
  Go To box 151
  Helper applications 160
  Hiding images 158
  History list 153
  Home button 150
  Key tips on using 170
  Menu bar 149
  Plug-ins 160
  Popular types 120, 144, 147
  Printing web pages 157

Refresh button 150
Right mouse button short-cuts 151
Saving a web page 155
Stop button 150
Toolbars 149
Viewing source code 168
Web design 15
  Adding hyperlinks 453
  Adding sound 467
  Adobe GoLive 448
  Animation 464
  Basic page structure 450
  Basic text editors 448
  Cookies 166
  DHTML effects 464
  DTP-like approach 448
  Establishing page height 451
  Establishing page width 451
  Flash components 165
  Frames 469
  Image formats 456
  Inserting text 452
  META tags 465
  Mouseover effects 462
  Multimedia content 466
  Page background 451
  Page navigation structure 458
  Planning 444
  Previewing a page 459
  Publishing local copy 460
  Publishing to the web 461
  Search box 465
  Software 447
  Streaming multimedia 466
  Working with colour 452
  WYSIWYG software 448
Web email 239, 288
Web page animation 464
Web pages
  Defined 124
  Viewing offline 169
Web server, defined 482
Website
  Filtering undesirable content 230
  Home/Index page 126
  Hosting
    CGI-bin, defined 96
    Evaluating 95
  Video clips 139

WebTV 18, 76, 79
WinZip 420, 482
WirePlay (games) 366
World Wide Web
    Consortium 27, 125
Worm (computer virus)
    482
WSArchie 438
WYSIWYG 40, 482

Z

ZoneAlarm firewall software
    190